W9-BLN-722

More than Class

SUNY Series in the Anthropology of Work
June C. Nash, Editor

More than Class

Studying Power in U.S. Workplaces

Ann E. Kingsolver, Editor

State University of New York Press

Author photo on back cover by Jon Kersey. © 1996 U. C. Regents.

Published by
State University of New York Press, Albany

For information, address State University of New York
Press, State University Plaza, Albany, N.Y., 12246

Production by E. Moore
Marketing by Anne M. Valentine

Library of Congress Cataloging-in-Publication Data

More than class : studying power in U.S. workplaces / Ann E.
    Kingsolver, editor.
        p.   cm. — (SUNY series in the anthropology of work)
        Includes bibliographical references and index.
        ISBN 0-7914-3719-1. — ISBN 0-7914-3720-5 (pbk.)
        1. Industrial sociology—United States. 2. Business anthropology-
    -United States. 3. Minorities—Employment—United States—Case
    studies. 4. Social classes—United States. 5. Power (Social
    sciences)—United States. I. Kingsolver, Ann E., 1960–
    II. Series.
    HD6957.U6M674 1998
    306.3′0973—dc21   97-19762
                                                                            CIP

10 9 8 7 6 5 4 3 2 1

Dedicated to
Sylvia Helen Forman, Anthropologist

Contents

Acknowledgments

I thank the authors for their patience through the course of this publication project; as also June Nash, Don Brenneis, and an anonymous reviewer for their very helpful comments; Ulrika Dahl, Paulla Ebron, Sara Palmer, and Mark Whitaker for their encouragement and help in various ways; and, especially, Michelle Rosenthal for her excellent eye and good humor as an editorial assistant. Janet M. Fitchen was an inspiration with her energetic interest in U.S. ethnography. Also, I appreciate the support for this collection provided by the University of California–Santa Cruz and the University of South Carolina.

Chapter 1

Introduction

Ann E. Kingsolver

Definitions of work, workers, work roles, and workplaces are contested frequently in the U.S., as elsewhere. In our efforts to describe the experiences, identities, and ideologies of workers, researchers of labor and power in the U.S. sometimes confront the limits of class analysis. Centralized and decentralized technologies, the changing organization of production and consumption, the competing loci of control over worksites (as, for example, at the intersections of multinational corporate ownership and local management), and workplaces that in no way resemble shop floors all contribute to the need for forms of analysis that take into account complex power relations and the confusing hat-swapping between labor and management invoked by "shared" management models. In these times of blurred boundaries, in which livelihoods are not always housed within the walls of a single, traditional workplace and opportunities for labor organization are decreasing, we need to look for the complex ways in which workers defy anonymity and actively define work and work relations. Approaches for studying the changing texture of power and work in the U.S. are the focal concern of the authors in this volume.

All of the authors collected here have been trained in political economic approaches, and remain friendly to class analysis as a powerful tool for engaging inequalities at the core of U.S. social and economic organization. The authors see class-related inequalities manifested in a variety of worksites—with permutations in other forms of unequal access to resources by gender; "racial," ethnic or national identity; and age. However useful we may find dichotomous models (e.g., the owners of the means of production and the laborers, or the dominant and subordinate) for actively organizing for social change, we find that recent theories in which power is seen as multidimensional can be used to enhance class analysis in ways allowing us to see more subtle forms of workplace discrimination. Drawing on the work of Foucault and others who have focused on the workings of institutional power relations, while still attending to Marx, the authors have studied power in a range of U.S. work settings. While the work sites (given the machinations of capital these days) could also be defined as transnational in many cases, we focus specifically on a variety of workplaces in the U.S., for those interested in studying the production and reproduction of inequalities in "home" sites of U.S. capital.

Anthropologists and sociologists of work, along with scholars in other disciplines and also outside the academy, have used many approaches to studying power in workplaces—ranging from an emphasis on identity and experiences of workers to an emphasis on the restructuring of global capital.

RELATED STUDIES OF WORK AND POWER

Labor and Identity

The powerful valorization of identities through work, and manipulation of service tendencies or class allegiance, has been one area of study. Beynon and Blackburn (1972), for example, studied perceptions of work and the importance of employment for self-worth in industrial societies. Sacks (1979) provides a historical overview of the valorization of men's work over women's work through the lens of social Darwinism in those societies with dominant European ideologies. She demonstrates just how culturally bound that system of valorization is. The authors collected in Wallman (1979) offer insights on the culturally based valorization and definitions of work in a number of settings. Ronco and Peattie (1988) discuss the importance of the *meaning* of work in the U.S. in the 1980s. They observed people drawing significant boundaries between work and nonwork ("making work," if necessary) as part of the construction of self-respect.

Close to home, for those of us whose workplaces are academic, those writing in Sharff and Saunders (1994) detail the interactional effects between notions of professional identity and increasing segmentation of the academic workforce into low-paying, low-security, low-status jobs and fewer higher-paying, secure, higher-status jobs. Rueschemeyer's (1986) discussion of power and the division of labor would indicate that the power constellation secure in the latter will be likely to push for the replication of such segmentation.

Historical materialist and interpretive approaches have converged in approaches focusing on labor and identity. Willis (1977), and Foley (1990) in his duplication of Willis's study in a U.S. site, for example, focus on school-based training to see how class (and, in Foley's case, ethnic and gender) identity is learned, valorized, and reproduced by young people in institutional (quasi-industrial) settings. Kondo (1990), using a Foucauldian analysis of power as reproduced through direct social interaction, studied the powerful formation of social identity through workplace relations in Japan. Like these researchers, the authors in this volume are interested in the intersections of workplace identity and the reproduction of power relations in other areas of social life.

Rethinking Class and Capital

Innovative approaches to studying class itself, in the U.S. and elsewhere, have also been articulated across the social sciences in the late twentieth century. Building on the work begun by sociologist C. Wright Mills (1956) on the power elite, anthropologists in the 1960s (e.g., many of those writing in Hymes 1969) pivoted the dialectic used to study colonizers and the colonized to also study workers—in all their diversity—and those holding structural power in the U.S. Subjugation not only through the division of labor, but also through colonial and postcolonial regimes of power (often defined in terms of race or ethnicity), has produced in the U.S. what Gilbert and Kahl (1982) see as a range of economic and social class positions with differential access to resources and sites of power. Further, in the U.S., class must be considered in the social matrix of "age, race, sex, and class" (Lorde 1988). This realization should shape discussions of the future of ethnic and class relations in U.S. policy (Franklin 1988). Omi and Winant (1994) document usefully the history of *racial formation* in the U.S.—the process through which inequalities in the distribution of power and resources have been linked with changing "racial" definitions of bodies through time. Sacks (1996) argues that race, class, and gender-based systems of subordination are mutually defined and exploited by employers in capitalist relations of power.

This point is particularly salient in the mid-1990s as Affirmative Action legislation is being dismantled in such actions as California's passage of Proposition 209 in the 1996 elections (with governors and legislators in other states looking to that proposition as a model). As Colson (1977:382) states, "control over resources is evidence of power rather than the source of power." Thus, any consideration of the power mobilized through control of the means of production and distribution, in a Marxist analysis, needs to also consider the other social means through which that power is legitimized. The intersections of gender inequality, racialized models of power distribution, and class inequities are examined excellently, for example, by Zavella (1991). Earlier, these intersections were also examined, along with contemporary iterations of theories of class and class formation, by those collected in Giddens and Held (1982).

There continues to be a lively debate about what constitutes class and class formation among Marxist scholars, ranging from a classical reading of Marx as viewing the ruling and subordinate classes as being pitted in a dualistic struggle against each other (Giddens and Held 1982:4), to Giddens's revised version of class "structuration," in which he takes into account the other social factors—for example, education (as others mentioned above have documented)—that limit class mobility and access to power through space and time (see Giddens 1979).

Of course, there is always the possibility, put so well by the authors in Williams and Chrisman (1994), that any theorization of class-based and other inequalities coming from Euro-centered cultural contexts overlooks alternative conceptualizations of power that could critically contribute to addressing inequalities anywhere. Bearing in mind the interconnectedness of forms of oppression, the authors in this volume, interested in methods to be used in U.S. worksites, find that the dialectical traditions of class analysis remain powerful tools.

As Varenne (1986:8) has noted, there are marked ideological themes in U.S. culture—"individualism, choice, progress through machines, the state and the corporation"—that often contradict one another. It is through examining the contradictions between the logic of capitalism and other logics of valorization (e.g., of particular identities) that students of work and power in the U.S. can better understand the perpetuation, and points for possible redress, of inequalities in the workplace. However, workers and workplaces in the U.S. need to be considered in a global context, especially as transnational production, distribution, and consumption soar, and the power of capital often outweighs political power.

Influenced by Marxian models of the development and organization of international capitalism (e.g., Gunder Frank 1969, on dependency theory; Wallerstein 1979, on world systems theory; and Mandel 1978, on late capitalism), as well as by Gramsci's articulation of state hegemony (Hoare and Smith 1971), anthropologists and sociologists have been studying the relationship between workplaces in many localities, state regulation (or nonregulation), and changing control of global production, consumption, and distribution patterns. Ong (1987), for example, describes the potential for cultural miscommunication between labor and management in transnational industry as resistance, in her study of spirit possession of Malaysian microelectronics workers on shop floors controlled by U.S. managers.

Nash (1989) did an ethnography of corporate irresponsibility to community in documenting the restructuring of the General Electric plant in Pittsfield, Massachusetts, and the very powerful local effects that deindustrialization (as a global capitalist policy) had in the community of workers who were devastated by job losses. Ward's (1990) edited volume focuses on women as workers on the global assembly line (whether a formal or a metaphorical one). She argues that it was the exploitation of women's labor that fueled the boom in global restructuring, especially in the electronics, pharmaceutical, service, and garment industries (Ward 1990:1–2), and the case studies demonstrate the centrality of women's labor—mostly unacknowledged and unfairly compensated—in those transnationally owned industries, often encouraged in their exploitation of women's labor by national governments. Rothstein and Blim's (1992) collection advocates the use of anthropological approaches to study the global factory:

> An anthropology focusing on the global factory can investigate the ways in which local peoples mobilize culturally distinctive capacities to shape their unfolding economic destinies as well as documenting their struggles to resist the world capitalist logic in whole or in part. (Blim 1992:26)

The authors collected in Rothstein and Blim (1992) work to link their studies of specific workplaces, and the communities in which they are situated, with working models of the global factory. As Rothstein (1992:240) points out, an ethnographic approach to studying the global factory complicates the picture of producers and consumers through illustrating that "we are women or men, young or old, and we are also family members and members of racial-ethnic groups, with religious, regional, and national identities." By combining an analysis of the changing structure of global capitalism with ethnographic approaches, the authors in this collection hope also to be able to describe the subtle (and not so subtle) ways in which inequalities are played out in and around the workplace (viewed here as a nexus between local social relations and global capital relations).

Recent Studies of Power and U.S. Worksites

In 1990, when three of us with chapters in this volume and several others presented our work in the session "It Takes More than Class: Approaches to the Study of Power in U.S. Workplaces" at the American Anthropological Association meetings in New Orleans, we were influenced by the work already being done by anthropologists of the global factory. In our work, we were exploring the possibilities of late–twentieth-century understandings of power (whether asserted on the basis of gender, ethnicity, age, regional identity, or ownership of capital) for articulating the very specific ways in which power is claimed and contested in U.S. work settings. Before I move on to discuss the various theories and ethnographies of power that have informed, and can inform, the study of work, I want to mention research which has been done in the intervening six years that also draws together class analysis and other theoretical frameworks for understanding workplace inequalities.

Grint (1991:145) notes that corporations provide a particularly effective medium for comparing modernist and postmodern theories. Viewed by modernists, according to Grint, organizations are stable, rational, and perpetuate themselves through computer-aided decision-making. But through the lens of postmodern theories, Grint describes organizations as unstable, often without a unified intent, and as definitely out of "control"—yet not without the power to discipline individuals. That control is communicated and experienced through language, according to postmodernists. This counters the modernist view of language as "the neutral carrier of information—a transparent mechanism for carrying the meaning of an organization" (Grint 1991:146).

One theorist who has paid particular attention to the powerful implications of language for studying class is Bourdieu. He points out that while members of the same social and economic classes "on paper" are not actually and completely in contact as a group of people, mobilized for struggle, they occupy a similar space of relations, motivating them to respond to situations similarly, and their alliance is provoked perceptually as well as materially (Bourdieu 1991:231–33)—and it is that categorical construction of class, through the use of language, on which he focuses. In the 1990s, whether or not there can be a chronological charting of a "postmodern era," there has been much attention to communicative interactions in U.S. workplaces. The authors in this volume join that intellectual project, drawing on the possibilities of linguistic analysis (and other means of studying the subtle workings of power) with activist aims.

There are three recent edited volumes, in particular, that are closely related to the project in this book. McNall, Levine, and Fantasia's 1991 collection, *Bringing Class Back In: Contemporary and Historical Perspectives*, is the first. The editors contrast Weberian perspectives on class, which they characterize as the multidimensional "summation or some weighted combination of a variety of position effects, e.g., property, income, occupation, authority, education, or prestige" (McNall, Levine, and Fantasia 1991:2) with Marxist class analyses, which they characterize as always focusing on dualistic class struggle over exploitation of the working class's labor. Current theories of power are not so much the focus of their collection as are theories of class structure.

It is useful for those of us engaged in the project of studying power in U.S. workplaces, however, to be reminded by McNall, Levine, and Fantasia that multidimensional theorization of class is largely derived from the work of Weber and that there are historical examples to examine in the U.S. They note, for instance, that industrialization and segmented, migrant labor forces, along with transclass parties and organizations (blurring class boundaries and potential conflict) have shaped U.S. class relations for the nation's entire history, unlike many other contexts in which class inequalities have been studied (McNall, Levine, and Fantasia 1991:5). In this volume, then, we see the U.S., with its ingrained workplace inequalities and cultural ambivalence toward, or obfuscation of, inequality as all the more appropriate a setting for applying subtle analyses of power in combination with class approaches.

Three articles from *Bringing Class Back In* are directly relevant to the project of this collection. Jerry Lembcke, in his chapter "Class Analysis and Studies of the U.S. Working Class: Theoretical, Conceptual, and Methodological Issues" (1991), argues for attending to the lately ignored question of whether the working class can be an agent for the transformation of capitalist exploitation in the U.S. To that end, he suggests focusing on the potential for collective agency among workers—in other words, a working class—rather than on the individual worker as the unit of analysis. By focusing in this volume on different webs of power through which workers redefine their work and workplaces, we can contribute to just such a research project. I would argue that Foucauldian theories of power, which focus on the subjugation of the individual through institutions, do not prevent—but instead facilitate—our seeing the potential for collective agency (perhaps, in fact, allowing us to see an even broader field of options than some other approaches).

Further, Lembke raises interesting methodological questions about how researchers can "see" collectivities as more than aggregate individuals, and argues for cultural analysis over, say, survey methods alone. He believes that a comparison between geographically distinct social sites, rather than participant observation in only one site, would lead to a better understanding of collective working-class agency and the potential for agency. Multilocal ethnography is in fact a growing area in social science methods, particularly for studying transnational capitalism, and in the future perhaps there will not be drawn such a strong dichotomy between ethnographic research as illustrative of the "local" and statistical research as affording global comparison in studies of class.

An example of the kind of linguistic organizational analysis advocated by Bourdieu is found in Orr and McNall's (1991) chapter in *Bringing Class Back In*. They studied historical fraternal orders in Kansas, and argue that "the pledge of brotherhood mute[d] class conflict and limit[ed] the workers' ability to articulate their grievances and form autonomous organizations" (Orr and McNall 1991:102). As Anglin does in this volume, they studied the overlap of discursive domains in shaping workers' empowerment or disempowerment. Orr and McNall use discursive analysis to better understand class relations in a historical context (where participant observation is impossible, of course, and reading the spaces between the written lines is what is left for the researcher to do):

It is through discourse, then, that humans become conscious subjects
before they become class subjects; different discourse streams flow
together to produce subjects and classes. As we will see, the nineteenth-
century U.S. worker stood at the confluence of streams of religious
rhetoric, republican ideology, German socialist ideology, and social
Darwinism, to name but a few. These different streams produced, in
varying locales and moments, different subjects. (Orr and McNall
1991:104)

Such an analysis can be done not only historically but through participant
observation, as several of the authors contributing to this volume demonstrate.

Steinberg, also writing in McNall, Levine, and Fantasia (1991), would
counter my easy elision between that volume and this one, perhaps, by saying
that poststructuralist theory and methods and structuralist ones ought not to be
joined in any analysis. Steinberg charges that "for the poststructuralists, discourse is the only avenue for social change" (1991:263). And he argues:

The paramount problem in poststructuralist accounts is that discourse
acts upon people, rather than people acting through discourse. By sub-
suming the social within the discursive, these theories cast into serious
doubt people's agency and autonomy for collective action. (Steinberg
1991:264)

The poststructuralists seem to be straw theorists for Steinberg, and his
reminder that "people actuate meaning—not the other way around"
(1991:277) is perhaps redundant for some ethnographers who draw on poststructuralist methods while remaining dedicated to more structuralist (e.g.
Marxist) analyses. The feasibility of drawing from both poststructuralist and
structuralist theories in studies of work and power is a productive area of current debate.

Nash (1992) articulates the reluctance that many Marxists may feel in
using discourse analysis in her article about a political conflict in Bolivia. Yet
she demonstrates how helpful interpretive methods could be in understanding
the role of symbolic power in a face-off between activists and soldiers at a
moment when the activists laid down a national flag to block the military's
way. The soldiers were caught between their ideological relatedness to the
women as citizens and their trained alienation from the women as members of
the political opposition (Nash 1992).

A better understanding of such ambiguities of power and relatedness
can be helpful in finding avenues for change. To those who would argue that
one must take a position as either a poststructuralist theorist of power or a
Marxist theorist of class struggle, I would argue along with Isaac (1987) that

the two bodies of theory illuminate one another's limits. It is not impossible to have elements of both approaches in one's toolbox.

A recent collection that demonstrates this point well is Calagione, Francis, and Nugent's (1992) *Workers' Expressions: Beyond Accommodation and Resistance*. The articles in that book expand the analytic workplace to include cultural processes, without shifting the focus from labor processes. In their introduction, Calagione and Nugent argue:

> Intersections of work and everyday life are not simply confined to the rankings of occupations or careers in society. Understanding the meanings of work entails the position that it is at all points creative and—not merely productive—human activity. (Calagione and Nugent 1992:7)

By looking at the multiplicity of ways in which workers, as creative cultural agents rather than simply objects of class relations, create cultural understandings of work and power, the authors in Calagione, Francis, and Nugent's collection follow through on their promise to extend the anthropology of work beyond the dualistic framing of shop floor time and leisure time, or of accommodation and resistance.

A third contemporary volume relevant to the shared project of the authors in this book, especially as it also concerns changing worksites in the U.S., is Lamphere, Stepick, and Grenier's (1994) *Newcomers in the Workplace: Immigrants and the Restructuring of the U.S. Economy*. Focusing on sites in Kansas, Florida, and Pennsylvania, the authors document the kinds of work available—in work sectors that are being rapidly restructured—to recent immigrants to the U.S., and how those workers are involved in reshaping workplace and community relationships. In addition to immigration issues (relevant to Ibarra and Cogan's chapters in this volume), Lamphere, Stepick, and Grenier attend to gender and ethnicity as dimensions of workers' experience in and out of the workplace. Their collection demonstrates the importance of challenging oversimplifying narratives about labor and power relations, since the authors heard varied interpretations of the way new immigrant workers structured, and were structured by, their U.S. workplaces and communities.

WHY STUDY POWER?

Power is not, for the authors in this book, an end for study in itself. As a concept, it is meaningful to us only in the context of relationships that define workers as "different" from one another. Furthermore, we are interested in the ways in which the power of difference—either by job title (and resulting class compensation, monetary or not) or by some other aspect of identity—is invoked to legitimize inequality in the workplace and in relationships beyond the workplace. Stamm and Ryff (1984:3) view power usefully as:

> An element of *all* social relationships and activities. As such, it can be defined as the ability of an individual to influence or exert control over resources, actions, or social relationships which are valued by the community or group in which she/he participates.

They see people as having either "positional power," formally assigned and ideologically sanctioned (e.g., Mills's "power elite," supported institutionally in ways that range from tax codes to dress codes), or "personal power," which is exerted informally through an individual's acknowledged ability to make decisions (Stamm and Ryff 1984:3).

Sacks (1988:79–80) argues (related to Stamm and Ryff's view of "personal power") that "centerpeople" have significant roles in influencing decision-making within various networks, even though (and perhaps, at times, because) they do not hold officially "legitimate" authority. One can look at a worker in terms of identity and discourses of authority, or one can invoke the worker's "power over" or "power to" (Pred 1981) or another of many models of collective agency. But whether one focuses on the individual or the group, power is expressed relationally.

Foucault's approach to studying power, by situating individuals within institutional contexts, is effective for making sense of everyday experiences (as well as historical patterns) of inequality in that the student of power need not choose between the individual and the collective as an exclusive unit of analysis. Foucault sees power as being produced and reproduced through constant social interaction, from many different directions.

While not entirely sidestepping dynamic conflict theory himself, Foucault counters arguments that power is embodied in constitutive dualisms (such as between management and labor) with questions about what propels those dualisms in social life. In particular, he sees acts of resistance in shifting venues so that the same individuals might not always be in the same roles in a web of power. He describes power as being problematic, contested, and requiring constant, disciplined persuasion to convince those construed as powerless of their powerlessness and those construed as powerful of their powerfulness.

My interpretation of Foucault's writing is, perhaps, more hopefully Marxist than his own; in Foucault's own words, power is at least:

> Not an institution, and not a structure; neither is it a certain strength we are endowed with; it is the name that one attributes to a complex strategical situation in a particular society. (Foucault 1990:93)

Similarly, Kondo (1990:307) views power as "creative, coercive, and coextensive with meaning." Through attention to the language used in constituting as well as contesting power relations, ethnographers of work and of other domains of social life have been able to understand more specifically how inequalities are both individually experienced and socially enforced. Admittedly, Foucauldian methods for studying power are not universally appropriate, since he wrote about disciplinary power in institutions historically and culturally situated in European (and related U.S.) industrial settings. But since that is precisely the milieu with which we are concerned in this volume, they are useful.

Our aim in studying power, drawing on many approaches to do so, is to work on challenging those inequalities that are (thoughtfully or not) produced and reproduced in work settings. This book's title is "more than class" because, while we believe that inequalities framed by capitalist logic are central in the U.S., class labels do not always fully describe the dynamics of unequal access to resources—whether those resources are economic or social (e.g., a sense of worth). What follows is an example of the need for approaches other than class analysis for studying power.

An Example of Class Complications

How can we study relationships of inequality when workers cannot be labeled as the exploited class and the exploiting class, but instead shift between those roles? Beyond explaining the relationship between conflicting class positions, how can we understand the meaning those positions have for those endlessly creating them? Are people as unaware of inequalities and their role in producing them as some iterations of "false consciousness" would represent them to be? I argue that new approaches to studying work and power can help us make sense of situations like the following one, which I documented in the late 1980s in east central Kentucky.

Imagine a place where livelihoods, family networks, and industries (agriculture and textiles, for example) overlap. There is a more complicated tale to tell, of course, but many workers in what I will call "Cedar," Kentucky—in a county with small, hilly farms and seven thousand residents—work in both textiles and tobacco. In the (now) multinationally owned textile plant, men make and dye cloth, and women sew it into garments, in adjacent buildings. The burley tobacco is produced in allotments attached to property deeds through the Agricultural Adjustment Act of 1933, in a labor-intensive cycle that I would also call part of a multinational industry, since each cigarette is a product of labor in several countries—each labor force contributing a variety of tobacco with a different quality necessary for that one cigarette. (Burley tobacco is responsible for holding artificial flavorings.) Despite the

1997 acknowledgment of responsibility for health problems by some multi-national tobacco companies, international product promotion and Kentucky tobacco production continue.

Until the late 1980s, the textile plant was still locally owned and under strong patron management (the white patron drawing labor into the plant through his own tobacco production networks), and work in tobacco was mostly done as exchange (noncash) labor through extended kin and fictive kin networks. Especially intensive points in the burley tobacco production cycle are "setting," when the plants are hand-set out in the field from beds where they are grown from seed; "cutting," when the mature plants are chopped off by hand with a tobacco knife and run through with a stake; "hanging," when those stakes are hung up on tiers in a ventilated barn; and "stripping," when the dried leaves are stripped off the plant stalks and prepared for sale in a regional warehouse. Labor parties for those seasonal, heavy jobs in tobacco have traditionally been assembled (with male workers, mostly) after hours from factory jobs. But the global capitalist regime of requiring flexible over-time (with resulting uncertainty about the end of any workday) took its toll in Cedar's textile plant and other plants in the region (e.g., the new Toyota assembly plant) in the late 1980s. The factory-working farmers, no longer able to predictably organize their own after-hours labor, began to employ Mexican migrant workers through the regional tobacco warehouses.

Here is, then, a low-wage employment scenario for Cedar residents and migrant workers. Those women and men from the area who *are* employed often work in more than one industry. Workers in the agricultural industry, including the recent migrant workforce, are not unionized either because (1) as farm owners, they define themselves as independent producers (albeit for the multinational tobacco industry) or because (2) their isolation and the con-ditions of their migration into an area and a type of work not traditionally organized through migrant labor networks discourage unionization. Workers in the textile industry, on the other hand, are not unionized because (1) they were often recruited originally, by the patron manager, through tobacco labor networks and tended to see themselves (through the ideology of agrarian inde-pendence) as independent farmers (whether men or, increasingly, women) who happened also to work in a factory; and (2) there have been, both under patron and multinational management, intense preventive measures taken against labor organizing at the plant—including a symbolic funeral for the idea of a union (in which workers were forced to bury a coffin in the front yard of the plant) and threats to move the plant to Jamaica.

Under patron management, textile plant labor relations were glossed as familial, and as such, often outside the regulatory framework of U.S. labor law. Even though the new multinational managers of the textile plant dis-placed their legal responsibility for the labor force by rerouting hiring through a regional employment agency (after losing a hiring discrimination suit brought by an African-American woman), there remains a blurring of boundaries between management and labor (and ensuing "class allegiance") among Cedar workers, since some managers in the multinationally-owned factory are also workers in other community members' tobacco fields, when they are off shift.

How do workers in one exploited labor force justify exploiting new sources of *lower*-wage labor? How do various markers of identity affect those rationalizations of inequality? I argue that notions of equality have been used to explain labor practices in each setting. Instead of labeling this "false consciousness"—in which the workers would not recognize exploitive conditions—we need methods for understanding the specific ways in which explanations are employed by individuals who are momentarily situated as worker or as manager to promote, resist, or obscure labor relations.

The first use of the term "false consciousness" was by Lukàcs (1967:50), when he referred to the double bind of not an individual but a class in being unable to both subjectively and objectively assess its aims in relation to the society as a whole. While Lembcke (1991) has worked seriously on the problem of analyzing the experiences of an entire social class, in many studies of work there is a slippage between the individual and the class that leaves one grasping for methods. This is where I think it is useful to frame questions about power in terms of class relations, yet to use methods that allow us to understand workers as agents of explanation situated in various social sites.

When I wanted to try to understand the shifting power relations in different Cedar work settings, I found class analysis to be limited in that workers were simultaneously in contradictory positions vis-à-vis the production and reproduction of inequality. Methods of discursive analysis were useful to me in sorting out the kinds of explanation of inequality (or equality) that were voiced by workers who were related to one another in complicated ways (Kingsolver 1991).

As Wolff and Resnick (1987:218) suggest in their class process approach, individual workers can be seen as participating in numerous *sites* of social processes. Labor relations are produced and reproduced—and explained—in households, other workplaces, and state venues, for example. Interpretive methods of analysis can be employed to understand, rather than to avoid or silence in analyses of work, the various voices that create labor relations at any moment, whether in a barn, on a shop floor, or in an academic workplace. Nash (1992) and Hossfeld (1990) have demonstrated well ways in which ideologies can be manipulated as a form of resistance.

I have suggested (Kingsolver 1992) that in Cedar, workers in textiles and tobacco understand their constraints quite clearly, and they manipulate workplace "equality" explanations in a number of ways that cannot be classified generically as in their best interests—or not—as a class, but which allow them to resist being exploited by a single industry. Yet our analyses of exploitation do not always translate into action in addressing workplace inequalities. Attention to fields of power in addition to class exploitation can help us understand the practices of inequality that indeed perpetuate those very divisions.

Without losing sight of class exploitation, I argue, then, that it is useful to focus on the active, ongoing, decentralized process of interwoven explanations of power and work that go beyond dualistic, binding analytical claims on power by the "active" over the "resistant." The authors in this volume use a variety of methods in studying power to show (in Foucauldian terms) the capillarylike ways in which power is created through ongoing relationships.

PROJECTS IN THIS COLLECTION

By paying very close attention to the language, technologies, and processes of interaction between individuals at work, the authors in this collection demonstrate methods for watching *power* at work, and for understanding its social implications. We hope these approaches will be useful to readers working to challenge inequalities in many other venues as well.

Monica Schoch-Spana uses a Foucauldian approach to power most directly in her study of the disciplining of worker, work, and workplace boundaries in a nuclear plant that is in transition to nonactivity (in many senses).

Worker discourses (spoken, unspoken, and acted) reproduce relations of social inequality in different ways. In analyzing discourses of which the workers are very much aware—and which they manipulate—Mary Anglin uses the blurring of boundaries between worksites and religious sites (and talk) to explore how power in the workplace can be shaped by religious discourse, and vice versa.

Tressa Berman, in her analysis of Native American women's artistic labor, crosses traditional boundaries in studies of work. She focuses on the community as worksite to challenge binary constructions of public/private, wage/nonwage, and kin/nonkin labor. Her method for studying power in that context is to reconceptualize very usefully the valorization of "ceremonial relations of production."

Anita Puckett's close attention to the words used by those training others in specific work tasks shows how power is communicated and reproduced. Her study is related to Willis's (1977) and Foley's (1990) analyses of how class is learned, but provides new insight into the uses of linguistic techniques in investigating power.

Taking gender into account in work relations, Suzanne Tallichet discusses nonparticipant observation as a method for understanding—through women's tales from the mines—the ways in which sexual harassment has been used to isolate workers and prevent their active organization or promotion. Her analysis demonstrates the continuing usefulness of dualistic categories for differential power (e.g., male and female) in analyses of work.

María de la Luz Ibarra makes the important point that domestic labor in the U.S. has been naturalized as a single work category, without adequate attention to the diversity of work experiences and life experiences in that labor sector. She combines life history with other interview approaches to provide a more textured understanding of what tasks are glossed as domestic labor, and of the multiple lenses through which work identities and life experiences of domestic workers can be discussed, including transnational migration.

Daniel Cogan also discusses immigration and workplace isolation, using videography methods to show the spatial aspects of labor force segregation in a college cafeteria. Visual approaches to studying power enable one to study the nonverbal forms power takes in workplaces.

Mary Hoyer contributes a community activist's perspective to this volume, discussing current inequalities in work opportunities in the U.S.—drawing on the city of Hartford, Connecticut, as an example. She explains the differences between numerous strategies for popular analyses of power and working conditions. She also discusses methods for, and case examples of, participatory economic reorganization. I see this chapter as a fitting conclusion to our discussion in this volume, since it provides the transition from analysis to action.

REFERENCES CITED

Beynon, H., and R.M. Blackburn
   1972 *Perceptions of Work: Variations within a Factory.* Cambridge: Cambridge University Press.

Blim, Michael L.
   1992 Introduction: The emerging global factory and anthropology. In *Anthropology and the Global Factory: Studies of the New Industrialization in the Late Twentieth Century.* Frances Abrahamer Rothstein and Michael L. Blim, eds. Pp. 1–30. New York: Bergin & Garvey.

Bourdieu, Pierre
   1991 *Language and Symbolic Power.* Cambridge, MA: Harvard University Press.

Calagione, John, and Daniel Nugent
   1992 Workers' expressions: Beyond accommodation and resistance on the margins of capitalism. In *Workers' Expressions: Beyond Accommodation and Resistance.* John Calagione, Doris Francis, and Daniel Nugent, eds. Pp. 1–11. Albany: State University of New York Press.

Calagione, John, Doris Francis, and Daniel Nugent, eds.
   1992 *Workers' Expressions: Beyond Accommodation and Resistance.* Albany: State
      University of New York Press.

Colson, Elizabeth
   1977 Power at large: Meditation on "the symposium of power." In *The Anthropol-
      ogy of Power: Ethnographic Studies from Asia, Oceania, and the New
      World.* Raymond D. Fogelson and Richard N. Adams, eds. Pp. 375–86. New
      York: Academic Press.

Foley, Douglas E.
   1990 *Learning Capitalist Culture: Deep in the Heart of Tejas.* Philadelphia: Uni-
      versity of Pennsylvania Press.

Foucault, Michel
   1990[1978] *The History of Sexuality. Volume 1: An Introduction.* Robert Hurley,
      trans. New York: Vintage Books.

Franklin, Raymond S.
   1988 Race, class, and gender beyond the welfare state. In *Racism and Sexism: An
      Integrated Study.* Paula S. Rothenberg, ed. Pp. 391–401. New York: St. Mar-
      tin's Press.

Giddens, Anthony
   1979 *Central Problems in Social Theory: Action, Structure and Contradiction in
      Social Analysis.* Berkeley: University of California Press.

Giddens, Anthony, and David Held
   1982 Introduction. In *Classes, Power, and Conflict: Classical and Contemporary
      Debates.* Anthony Giddens and David Held, eds. Pp. 3–11. Berkeley: Uni-
      versity of California Press.

Giddens, Anthony, and David Held, eds.
   1982 *Classes, Power, and Conflict: Classical and Contemporary Debates.* Berke-
      ley: University of California Press.

Gilbert, Dennis L., and Joseph A. Kahl
   1982 *The American Class Structure: A New Synthesis.* Homewood, IL: Dorsey
      Press.

Grint, Keith
   1991 *The Sociology of Work: An Introduction.* Cambridge, U.K.: Polity Press.

Gunder Frank, André
   1969 *Capitalism and Underdevelopment in Latin America.* New York: Monthly
      Review Press.

Hoare, Quintin, and Geoffrey Nowell Smith, eds.
   1971 *Selections from the Prison Notebooks of Antonio Gramsci.* London: Lawrence
      & Wishart.

Hossfeld, Karen J.
1990 'Their logic against them': contradictions in sex, race, and class in Silicon
Valley. In *Women Workers and Global Restructuring*. Kathryn Ward, ed. Pp.
149–78. Ithaca, NY: ILR Press, Cornell University.

Hymes, Dell, ed.
1969 *Reinventing Anthropology*. New York: Vintage Books.

Isaac, Jeffrey C.
1987 *Power and Marxist Theory: A Realist View*. Ithaca, NY: Cornell University
Press.

Kingsolver, Ann E.
1992 Tobacco, textiles, and Toyota: Working for multinational corporations in rural
Kentucky. In *Anthropology and the Global Factory: Studies of the New
Industrialization in the Late Twentieth Century*. Frances Abrahamer Rothstein and Michael L. Blim, eds. Pp. 191–205. New York: Bergin & Garvey.
1991 *Tobacco, Toyota, and Subaltern Development Discourses: Constructing
Livelihoods and Community in Rural Kentucky*. Dissertation. Amherst: University of Massachusetts.

Kondo, Dorinne K.
1990 *Crafting Selves: Power, Gender, and Discourses of Identity in a Japanese
Workplace*. Chicago: University of Chicago Press.

Lamphere, Louise, Alex Stepick, and Guillermo Grenier, eds.
1994 *Newcomers in the Workplace: Immigrants and the Restructuring of the U.S.
Economy*. Philadelphia: Temple University Press.

Lembcke, Jerry
1991 Class analysis and studies of the U.S. working class: Theoretical, conceptual,
and methodological issues. In *Bringing Class Back In: Contemporary and
Historical Perspectives*. Scott G. McNall, Rhonda F. Levine, and Rick Fantasia, eds. Pp. 83–97. Boulder, CO: Westview Press.

Lorde, Audre
1988 Age, race, class, and sex: Women redefining difference. In *Racism and Sexism: An Integrated Study*. Paula S. Rothenberg, ed. Pp. 352–59. New York:
St. Martin's Press.

Lukàcs, Georg
1967 *History and Class Consciousness: Studies in Marxist Dialectics*. Rodney Liv-
ingstone, trans. Cambridge, MA: MIT Press.

Mandel, Ernest
1978 *Late Capitalism*. London: Verso.

McNall, Scott G., Rhonda F. Levine, and Rick Fantasia
1991 Introduction. In *Bringing Class Back In: Contemporary and Historical Perspectives*. Scott G. McNall, Rhonda F. Levine, and Rick Fantasia, eds. Pp.
1–14. Boulder, CO: Westview Press.

McNall, Scott G., Rhonda F. Levine, and Rick Fantasia, eds.
1991 *Bringing Class Back In: Contemporary and Historical Perspectives*. Boulder, CO: Westview Press.

Mills, C. Wright
1956 *The Power Elite*. New York: Oxford University Press.

Nash, June C.
1992 Interpreting social movements: Bolivian resistance to economic conditions imposed by the International Monetary Fund. *American Ethnologist* 19(2):275–93.
1989 *From Tank Town to High Tech: The Clash of Community and Industrial Cycles*. Albany: State University of New York Press.

Omi, Michael, and Howard Winant
1994 *Racial Formation in the United States from the 1960s to the 1990s*. New York: Routledge.

Ong, Aihwa
1987 *Spirits of Resistance and Capitalist Discipline: Factory Women in Malaysia*. Albany: State University of New York Press.

Orr, James R., and Scott G. McNall
1991 Fraternal orders and working-class formation in nineteenth-century Kansas. In *Bringing Class Back In: Contemporary and Historical Perspectives*. Scott G. McNall, Rhonda F. Levine, and Rick Fantasia, eds. Pp. 101–17. Boulder, CO: Westview Press.

Pred, Allan
1981 *Power, everyday practice, and the discipline of human geography*. Lund, Sweden: Lund Studies in Geography (48):30–56.

Ronco, William, and Lisa Peattie
1988 Making work: A perspective from social science. In *On Work: Historical, Comparative and Theoretical Approaches*. R.E. Paul, ed. Pp. 709–21. New York: Basil Blackwell.

Rothstein, Frances Abrahamer
1992 Conclusion: New waves and old—industrialization, labor, and the struggle for a new world order. In *Anthropology and the Global Factory: Studies of the New Industrialization in the Late Twentieth Century*. Frances Abrahamer Rothstein and Michael L. Blim, eds. Pp. 238–46. New York: Bergin & Garvey.

Rothstein, Frances Abrahamer, and Michael L. Blim, eds.
1992 *Anthropology and the Global Factory: Studies of the New Industrialization in the Late Twentieth Century*. New York: Bergin & Garvey.

Rueschemeyer, Dietrich
1986 *Power and the Division of Labour*. Stanford: Stanford University Press.

Sacks, Karen Brodkin
  1996 The metaorganization of American capitalism: Scissors, paper, rock. Paper presented at the meetings of the American Ethnological Society, San Juan, Puerto Rico, April.
  1988 Gender and grassroots leadership. In *Women and the Politics of Empowerment*. Ann Bookman and Sandra Morgen, eds. Pp. 77–96. Philadelphia: Temple University Press.
  1979 *Sisters and Wives: The Past and Future of Sexual Equality*. Urbana: University of Illinois Press.

Sharff, Jagna, and Lucie Wood Saunders, contributing eds.
  1994 Demystifying the Changing Structure of Academic Work. *Anthropology of Work Review* (XV)1: Spring.

Stamm, Liesa, and Carol D. Ryff
  1984 Introduction: An interdisciplinary perspective on women's power and influence. In *Social Power and Influence of Women*. Liesa Stamm and Carol D. Ryff, eds. Pp. 1–11. Boulder, CO: Westview Press.

Steinberg, Marc W.
  1991 Talkin' class: Discourse, ideology, and their roles in class conflict. In *Bringing Class Back In: Contemporary and Historical Perspectives*. Scott G. McNall, Rhonda F. Levine, and Rick Fantasia, eds. Pp. 261–84. Boulder, CO: Westview Press.

Varenne, Hervé
  1986 Introduction. In *Symbolizing America*. Hervé Varenne, ed. Pp. 1–9. Lincoln: University of Nebraska Press.

Wallerstein, Immanuel
  1979 *The Capitalist World-Economy*. Cambridge: Cambridge University Press.

Wallman, Sandra, ed.
  1979 *Social Anthropology of Work*. London: Academic Press.

Ward, Kathryn, ed.
  1990 *Women Workers and Global Restructuring*. Ithaca, NY: ILR Press, Cornell University.

Williams, Patrick, and Laura Chrisman, eds.
  1994 *Colonial Discourse and Post-colonial Theory: A Reader*. New York: Columbia University Press.

Willis, Paul
  1977 *Learning to Labour: How Working Class Kids Get Working Class Jobs*. Farnborough: Saxon House.

Wolff, Richard D., and Stephen A. Resnick
  1987 *Economics: Marxian versus Neoclassical*. Baltimore: Johns Hopkins University Press.

Zavella, Patricia
  1991 Mujeres in factories: Race and class perspectives on women, work, and family. In *Gender at the Crossroads of Knowledge: Feminist Anthropology in the Postmodern Era*. Micaela di Leonardo, ed. Pp. 312–36. Berkeley: University of California Press.

Chapter 2

National Security and Radiological Control: Worker Discipline in the Nuclear Weapons Complex

Monica Schoch-Spana

Conceptualizing power in a state endeavor that turned "the whole country into a factory," as physicist and Nobel laureate Niels Bohr once put it (quoted in Rhodes 1986:500), is a daunting task. This discussion of work discipline comprises part of a larger study, an ethnographic history of work at one installation in the nuclear weapons complex now undergoing a tumultuous reorganization of priorities. Focusing on worker experiences during and after the Cold War, I consider how the cultural symbols of production, reproduction, nature, and nation have evolved within American society and in relation to state policies regarding defense and the environment. My fundamental question is how the work of making nuclear materials and bombs compares, both conceptually and materially, to that of cleaning up the mess left behind. I follow a nuclear materials production facility from its construction in the early 1950s, through its production heyday, and finally to its current reorientation to managing waste and remedying environmental pollution.

For my purposes I treat all research subjects as "workers" whose day-to-day activities, feelings, and relationships need interpretation in order to construct some understanding of the workplace as a whole, an institution of power mediating the lives of a tremendous workforce, their families and communities. I frame my inquiries into power within this social arena by drawing on various perspectives offered by studies in labor history, the social production of "objective" knowledge, and the culture and history of nuclear weaponry. I incorporate insights from these literatures along with Foucault's (1979) discussion regarding discipline. Attentive to the ways in which some members of the workforce exercise greater control over their destinies than others, I am most interested in answering the artless question of how the embodied experience of work (managerial, technical, manual, and service) at the nuclear materials production facility has evolved in conjunction with large-scale political, economic, and social processes.

In assessing the work of one class of employees, the technical experts, I am inspired by critical studies of science that suggest culture shapes the very categories by which scientists discover the natural world and through which they convey their discoveries (Martin 1991:485; see Haraway 1989; Martin 1994). Analysts of nuclear discourse in particular have drawn attention to the unexpected and counterintuitive sexual, procreative, and religious metaphors that color the language of experts who design and deploy a potentially destructive technology (Cohn 1987; Easlea 1983; Keller 1990; Traweek 1988).

As a contributor to this literature, I am interested in discovering what cultural notions seem to shape the burgeoning fields of waste management and environmental restoration. I also want to evaluate the discourse and experience of "nonexperts," generally ignored by cultural studies focusing on the work and ideas of nuclear experts (e.g., Arney 1991; Reynolds 1991). Labor history, in accounting for the differential authority and skill accorded to managers, engineers, and laborers (e.g., Montgomery 1979; Noble 1984, 1977), makes clear the necessity of focusing on "experts" and "nonexperts." Combining science and labor studies, I can inquire if the domestication of destructive technology (in expert discourse) plays some role in the unequal relations between those who conceive and organize production and those who execute it.

Integrating a research agenda derived from labor studies and critical studies of science, I am keen on avoiding a reliance on linguistic data alone with which to understand work at the production facility. Cultural analyses of nuclear technologies have been limited in their exclusive focus on expert discourse. Labor histories, while inclusive of experts and nonexperts, have often assumed from the start relations of empowerment and disempowerment. I am concerned with how these relationships are created, perpetuated, and undermined in the routine operations of the facility. Accounts of labor control processes nonetheless overcome a linguistic focus by describing a worker's experience in terms of the calculated organization of space and time as well as bodily habits (e.g., Van Onselen 1976; Thompson 1967; Rabinbach 1986).

Foucault's concepts of *disciplinary power* and the *techniques of surveillance* through which it operates attend to some of the deficits in the above literature by focusing on embodied experience and by characterizing power as a "continuous field" implicating the "supervisors" as well as the "perpetually supervised" (Foucault 1979:177). His historical and philosophical treatment of the "practice of imprisonment" (1991:75) also delves into details—architectural, administrative, and bodily—that make his account hauntingly relevant to a discussion of two comprehensive programs at the nuclear materials facility: *security* and *radiological control*.[1] These two systems of body postures, space arrangements, symbols, and social classifications are common denominators of experience for a highly stratified workforce.

In this paper, I rely upon Foucault's notion of power in describing workers' experiences with *security* and *radiological control*. At the same time, my analysis provides an ethnographic corrective to his depiction of modern social life and discipline in the workplace. This local portrait undermines in part a Foucauldian rendering of society as a "network of omnipresent relations of subjugating power" (Gordon 1991:5) by reasserting a component missing from his image of regimented life in the factory, school, prison, and hospital—the face-to-face relationships that people create among themselves. Employees at the facility, rather than subordinates to a seamless process of surveillance, realize the *security program* in personally meaningful ways. Relatedly, the case study inquires into the specific cultural forms or idioms through which techniques of surveillance operate. The security program has incorporated the image of "home" in depicting the importance of workplace controls.

Research subjects also discuss the *security program* in terms of relations of intimacy, dependency, and trust. Lacking in Foucault's analysis is perhaps the most important feature for understanding labor control in this case— the creation of feelings of familiarity and suspicion. These sentiments, as the following case reflects, are often embedded within social processes of differentiation including gender, age, sexual orientation, ethnic and racial identity, and national identity.

By attending to the ways people make sense of *security*, this ethnographic account elucidates Foucault's project in understanding contemporary state power, the "government of all and of each" (Gordon 1991:3; Foucault 1988). Working at a facility in the nuclear weapons complex, I argue, is a potent, localized incidence of a more generalized, recursive process by which individuals come to recognize themselves as part of a totality, "the nation" (see Handler 1988:11,27).[2] Their work is certainly not the only activity by which these "citizens" develop their sense of being Americans, nor of the existence of an American nation that needs defending by means of nuclear weapons. Workers in this manufacturing environment, however, stand in a particularly unique relationship to the "imagined community" of the nation (Anderson 1983).

Producing nuclear materials for national defense, rather than providing goods or services for consumer markets, is the primary objective of this industry. Through their unusual product, workers can and do identify closely with the nation. More importantly for a discussion of discipline, *national security* and the need to protect nuclear materials and knowledge from *foreign entities* are the institutional (i.e., state) rationales for orchestrating individual and collective work activities in calculated, restricted ways, and for certifying some persons over others as morally eligible for this particular kind of work.

I analyze work at the nuclear materials facility in terms of the material and social ways in which people become conscious of a national entity of which they are a part. Nationalist rhetoric abounds in this work environment and certainly plays an important role in cultivating nationalist sentiment. I plan to emphasize in the following account the more corporeal means by which nation-making as a cultural process takes place. A worker's habitual movements and postures contribute to the self-evident, taken-for-granted nature of the nation (Bourdieu 1977; Jackson 1983; see Connerton 1989). The very acts of working and following the prescriptions of the *security program* are an embodied civics lesson regarding "the nation as a bounded, sovereign, and essentially distinctive community" (Foster 1991:249).

The *radiological control program* of which I can give only cursory treatment in this paper also reinforces this lesson. The individual human body, as much ethnography has demonstrated, is a powerful symbol with which people imagine social collectivities or polities (Scheper-Hughes and Lock 1987). I stress in the following rendering of the *rad control program* those surveillance practices regarding an employee's own bodily boundaries. The case of *rad control* also underlines how expert discourse (in this case, atomic properties and health threats) translates into material consequences for all members of the workforce.

As Anderson (1983:15) poignantly states, a nation is an imagined community "because the members of even the smallest nation will never know most of their fellow-members, meet them, or even hear of them, yet in the minds of each lives the image of their communion." Crucial to this imagined fellowship is a sense of boundedness—a boundedness interpreted and represented as an enclosed territory, a shared history, and a primordial connectedness or relatedness (Alonso 1994). Each of these attributes, as Anderson and others have demonstrated, has historical roots. The distinctiveness of a nation is, in principle, a "homogeneity which encompasses diversity" (Handler 1988:6). Nation-building therefore relies upon a classificatory process, a sorting of "true" members of the polity from those who are not (Williams 1989:407,429). Outsiders can be either the members of other nations or the morally questionable or socially peripheral within the nation itself.

Through a program of *security*, employees experience the workplace as a territorialized, moral community, one with direct significance for a greater territorialized and moralized community—the nation. Grounding a sense of unity and fraternity within the abstracted national community are those relationships and experiences more locally realized (Herzfeld 1995). Governing the daily existence of the nuclear material worker is a preponderance of boundaries to be respected and upheld—borders that are materialized in fences, concrete barricades, and electronic surveillance equipment, borders that one may traverse only with the social and moral authority to do so, as rationed by the *security system* but also as interpreted individually and contextually.

"WORK" IN THE POST–COLD WAR NUCLEAR WEAPONS COMPLEX

The Department of Energy (DOE), the federal agency entrusted with the design, development, manufacture, testing, and maintenance of nuclear weapons, faces a formidable slate of alterations to its objectives and organizational structures. As a result of arms reduction agreements, the DOE confronts a dramatic increase in the scale and pace of weapons dismantlement as well as the challenge of managing the nuclear materials recovered. Its manufacturing duties curtailed, the agency must now deal with a five-decade legacy of hazardous waste and environmental pollution. Citizen action groups and regulatory agencies, citing compromises in public health, worker safety, and the environment, have also demanded that the DOE reconsider its self-regulating stance and its obligations to local communities.

Promoting institutional reform, former Secretary of Energy Admiral James Watkins in 1989 acknowledged a longstanding assumption among DOE and its contractors that "adequate production of defense nuclear materials and a healthy, safe environment were not compatible objectives." Watkins promised to cultivate a new *culture* within the DOE—that is, agency accountability for safety, health, and the environment, and a departure from *secrecy*, an agenda augmented under his successor, Secretary Hazel O'Leary.

The political and social climate are not, however, the only source of dramatic change for the government-owned and contractor-operated facilities that comprise the weapons complex. In a time of heightened concern regarding deficit spending, government waste, and contractor fraud, the Energy Department has faced significant budget cuts. Confronting an injunction to purchase more for its money and reductions in production requirements in the post–Cold War era, the DOE has *downsized* its contractor and federal employee workforces across the nuclear weapons complex.

The Savannah River Site (SRS), the field site for this study, is a microcosm of the complex and its objectives. Construction of this materials production facility in South Carolina began in 1951. This particular expansion of the weapons complex was instigated by a presumed Soviet nuclear threat, as evidenced by the testing of their first atomic weapon in 1949, and the American government's commitment to maintain nuclear superiority by developing the hydrogen bomb. Fabricating key ingredients for thermonuclear weapons for almost four decades, the facility was a cornerstone of the complex during the Cold War. The SRS is now experiencing, however, those contemporary changes rippling throughout the entire complex: *downsizing*,[3] curtailed production, and increased activities in managing waste and remedying environmental pollution.

Formerly under the control and budget of the DOE's defense programs, the SRS, as of January 1995, resides in the Department's Environmental Management Program. The transition in *mission* from *production* to *clean-up*, as they are known locally, also follows upon a relatively recent (1989) changeover in the contractor who manages and operates the facility. This transition in management, the first in the history of the SRS, and the dramatic shift in international nuclear politics, have created an air of anxiety about the site's future. Many members of the workforce and residents of nearby communities do not view the new *mission* as evocative or as cohesive as the former one of *production*. Moreover, some workers interpret their expanded responsibilities in *clean-up* as a moral judgment of their past environmental practices and a denigration of their commitment to *production*. A striking feature of the workforce is the lengthy tenure that many employees hold at the facility.

During 1993 to 1995, I resided in a town near the SRS that was home to many of its employees. Over the course of eighteen months, I developed a network of contacts among former and current employees (contractor and federal) and their families. Moving across occupational strata and different generations of the workforce, I collected personal work histories, commentary on current changes at the site, comparisons between production and environmental work, and, from area or issue experts, detailed knowledge on specific programs and technologies. I also interviewed spouses, gathering information on divisions of labor at home, relationships between **family** and work life, and those between the community and the SRS. To complement interview data, I was a participant-observer of worker experiences in and out of the workplace as professionals, family members, friends, industry watchers, and community members. I attended worker training sessions, periodic professional society meetings, industry workshops, and employee social functions, and had access to a number of facilities at the SRS.

Security had very tangible, personal consequences for me as an ethnographer. Through the cooperation of local DOE managers who are striving toward *openness*, I acquired the necessary authority to move somewhat freely on the site (how freely becomes apparent below). By receiving an identification *badge* and traversing work spaces, I learned and practiced the *security* system myself. Employees follow the rules in part to keep their jobs; similarly, I followed the rules to protect access to my field site.

Disciplined as much as an employee while conducting research, I take a liberty here that some subjects might themselves find awkward—that is, discussing *security* details. With respect to the organizing principles and rules of *security*, I draw from my interviews with managers designated to speak with me about the program as well as orientation materials (both video and print) for new employees. I rely also upon my own experiences and those conveyed to me by subjects to depict *security* routines and the meanings people attribute them. Recognizing *security* as a sensitive issue, I asked two contacts to review this paper to identify any personal anecdotes or details best left out. In preparing this analysis, I recognize the intersection between *security* as a form of discipline and the ethics of ethnographic practice in protecting the well-being of informants.

DISCIPLINE IN THE NUCLEAR MATERIALS WORKPLACE: THE CASE OF SECURITY

"Security," one learns in the mandatory video briefing prior to receiving a site identification *badge*, "is more than guards and fences. It is the system in which we all take part to protect facilities, property, personnel, information, and special nuclear materials." The script writers anticipate the predilection for potential employees to conceive of *security* as a coercive force outside themselves, embodied in physical barriers and armed sentries. "Gates, guns, and guards" is how one man sums up the repressive features of the program. The narrator, too, acknowledges these militaristic qualities, but turns the attention of nascent members of the workforce instead to their own agency within the program: *security* is a system "in which we all take part." So begins one's initial orientation and inclusion within a system that lends itself readily to characterization as a form of discipline—"a subtle, calculated technology of subjection" (Foucault 1979:221). Consenting to *security* measures is a condition of employment, and for nonemployees, a condition for access to SRS facilities.

When I asked people to describe their experiences in an industry with extreme controls over personal movement and information exchange, a number of them replied that they "never really thought about it." *Security*, their remarks suggest, organizes their experiences so thoroughly as to reach the level of the mundane and unremarkable. Weighing whether their work lives are unusual or ordinary in comparison to people not in the same business, they often conclude that security regardless is "all part of the job." One recently retired employee relates: "Most of us felt that it was necessary. All of us dislike it, of course, because it made our jobs much more difficult, much more inefficient, . . . [it gave] much more aggravation, but . . . most of us . . . accepted the fact that there are a lot of bad guys out there. . . . It was really sort of a philosophical point of view. We just sort of lived with it."

Access: Boundary Making

There is a strong military quality to this industrial workplace, even if the original antiaircraft guns that once guarded the airspace are now gone. The *security* program demonstrates considerable investment in architecture and artifact: fences, barricades, check points, identification *badges*, entry technologies, and controlled traffic patterns. Comprised of over three hundred square miles of land, the SRS hosts a collection of facilities that constitute a complete manufacturing cycle: from the fabrication of raw materials to be used in reactors, the production of weapons grade materials, to the separation of fission products, and finally, to the processing, storage, and disposal of radioactive and other industrial waste.

The basic rule of thumb, a manager explains, is that *security* becomes tighter the more one moves to the center of the site where the production facilities are. A series of physical barriers nest one within another: fences mark off the perimeter and enclose specialty areas. Moats, dugout waterless channels, are strategically placed. Members of the *security forces* man posts that control general road access toward the center (*perimeter barricades*) and to specific production areas (*internal barricades*). SRS design reflects the principle of "hierarchized surveillance," a rationalized use of space with which to observe and to control the comings and goings of people, as well as their behaviors in between (Foucault 1979:171–72).

A rule of "graded security" divides the SRS into various "layers," explains a manager. From least to most controlled are areas designated as *general site, controlled areas, security areas (limited and protected), material access areas,* and *exclusion areas.* People, signs, and technologies in varying combinations create barriers to these spaces. Arriving at the perimeter fenceline before entering the *general site,* a driver reads that he or she should enter only on "official business." *Security police officers* scrutinize the identification *badges* of all those entering either by vehicle or foot into an area with limited access.[4] *Access control devices* also serve as a further barrier for *protected areas* and *materials access areas.* In use are coded locks as well as *biometric* technologies that "recognize" authorized personnel by unique physical attributes such as hand print geometry. Scattered through the site are myriad secured spaces, including locked cabinets and vaults.

Passing through barriers, as the discussion on the *badging* system describes below, is an invocation of identity, one's insider status or statuses depending on what level of secured space one accesses. It is an embodied experience and a spatial pedagogy: "spatial contexts— . . . and . . . the processes that are played out within them—are themselves major media of socialization invisibly tuning the minds and bodies of those who people them to their inner logic" (Comaroff 1985:54). The overdetermined experience of

SRS space is one of boundaries, of distinctions between an inside and an outside. Workers and community members speak of the SRS as if it were a distinctive and bounded entity. At least one of the ways in which they acquire this sense is through their experiences of the many and varied *security* lines drawn in the sand.

During my fieldwork, I considered this carnal experience of boundaries consciously. Driving through a *perimeter* barrier one afternoon and capturing the experience of a boundary was most in my mind. Leaving the site, I slowed down from 55 mph to 45 mph, and then close, but not down, to the posted 15 mph near the barrier. I decelerated near the guard shack. Not stopped for inspection, I then accelerated toward home. After I did this, I dissected the sensation of passing through the *security* checkpoint, a motion of constriction, of squeezing, tightening, and freeing. Having driven through the barrier many times, I had gotten used to the feeling of slowing down and speeding up again.

Driving into the site, one is subject to random inspection, the object of the entry search being *contraband*. Leaving the site, the object of search tends to be government property.[5] The lesson is one of boundary maintenance, of self-revelation, and of identifying things of compromise such as *contraband*. When selected for inspection, a person pulls his or her vehicle to the side and follows the instructions of the officer. After noting down information such as the vehicle's tag numbers and personal information from the *badge*, the officer inspects the multiple interiors of the vehicle: trunk, glove compartment, truck bed, boxes, and any other object capable of enclosing another. Non-government owned vehicles (e.g., those of outside contractors) entering the *internal barricades*, not the *perimeter* ones, are subject to greater scrutiny as officers open up the hood and use a long-handled mirror (which looks like a gigantic dental instrument) to look at the underside of the car or truck.

I discovered this attention to interiors going through inspection myself. The principle was especially clear in one particular incident. After pulling over, I was already anticipating the officer's need to inspect my vehicle inside. I opened up the voids of my truck for scrutiny: the glove compartment, the cap over my truck bed, even a large storage container in the back. The officer soon instructed me to open the toolbox stashed behind my seat, a "closed" object I had forgotten altogether.

Horror was the experience of one employee as she was once stopped going to work. Just as she was pulling the car off to the side as she was directed, she remembered that she was carrying alcohol left over from a shopping trip for cheap liquor. She had loaded the bottles in her trunk and had forgotten about them until that moment. This transgression was a substantial one: *security infractions* weigh against one's continued employment. Through the benevolence of the officer who intercepted her and that of his supervisor, she received the option of not entering the site until her trunk was emptied of the *contraband*. She drove to a nearby convenience and gas store, and pleaded with them to hold her belongings until she came back. She was already late for a meeting. They laughed because this was a favor they had provided others.

Identity: The Badging System

Physical structures, technologies, and trained *security personnel* aid the controlled movements of people in and out of variably secured areas at the SRS. Identification is, however, the cornerstone of the *security* system. Every employee and every visitor to controlled areas acquires a *badge*. An employee wears his or her *badge* in a location most easily read by others: "in the chest area, not clipped around the belt, on a sleeve, or on a hat," as employee orientation instructs. Having a *badge* is the first symbolic cut between "self" and "other" in the SRS community.[6]

Employees learned the authority of the *badge* system in a 1953 plant newspaper in the following manner:

> If Uncle Joe Stalin had a badge for this plant, our guards would be required to pass him through the gate. Chances of this happening are highly improbable. However, the badge is a means of personal identification and checking badges is the official method of giving clearance to authorized employees. (*Savannah River Plant News*, March 6, page 2)

Because having a *badge* marks one's affiliation with the facility, employees are under instructions to secrete their *badges* when not on site, thereby obscuring their social status as workers in this industry. World events have changed, the narrator of the *security* video explains, but personnel must still attend to the need to protect *national security*. One must never wear his or her *badge* in public, as this may make him or her vulnerable to *foreign entities*. When off site, *one should BIP IT*—that is, put the badge in a pocket or purse. Furthermore, employees should avoid shop talk in public places as this may also make one vulnerable as a target to *foreign entities*. If approached by any outsider regarding the site, workers are instructed to immediately report the incident. *Security* rules such as *BIP IT* are reproduced on posters distributed throughout the site. Through practices such as *BIP IT*, an imagined global community of potentially belligerent nations becomes a localized fear: a concern with a personal threat, the approach of a *foreign entity*—namely, another person. As often as they try to follow the *BIP IT* rule, however, some employees use their site badges as simply one of a multitude of identification pieces that govern contemporary life.

One woman says that she once had to break the rule in order to cash a check, since her site *badge* was the only form of ID she had on her. Getting a government rate at a hotel by showing his site *badge*, says another employee, is how he once transgressed the system. Risking the chance encounter with a *foreign entity*, some employees flash their badges to get through other circumstances in which proving one's identity has been necessary or helpful. The site's badging system is really quite an ordinary thing, suggests one employee, referring to the fact you have to have identification to do many things these days like have "a pass in order to go on the causeway or the ferry."

Badged, a person is incorporated in a classificatory system called *clearances*. The degree of *clearance* determines the magnitude of access one has to controlled spaces, information, and materials. *Higher* levels of *clearance* allow one greater mobility within SRS spaces. The *badging* and *clearance* system is based on the principle of *need to know*, an inheritance from World War II's Manhattan Project.[7] When a person is first employed, a manager explains, *security* authorities ask themselves the questions, "What will this person be doing?" and "Where will he or she be doing it?" to determine the necessary *clearance*. *Badges* contain a picture of the employee with which *security officers*, and all members of the *security system* (i.e., other workers) can identify the employee. Additionally, they can confirm the person with the person's *clearance*. The picture must be a "true" representation of the person's ordinary appearance. Should an individual change his appearance, by growing a beard, for example, he is responsible for obtaining a new *badge* to reflect the change.

Color coded, *badges* indicate *clearance* level, and therefore, what areas (and their contents) one can access.[8] At the bottom of this hierarchy is the *uncleared* status identified by a *red badge* and permitting access to the *general site, controlled areas*, and *property protection areas*. A *red badge* (note that just as patients become the disease with which they are diagnosed, so too do workers become the *badge* and *clearance* level to which they are assigned) can, however, enter some *security areas* if under the supervision or *escort* of an individual holding the appropriate *clearance*. Yellow indicates that one is *L cleared. Unescorted*, a person with a *yellow badge* can move through *limited areas*, and if *escorted* by someone with the higher *Q clearance*, can also access *protected areas* and *exclusion areas*. To enter a *limited area*, a person must pass through a barrier manned by *security police officers* who review the *badge* for appropriate *clearance* and match picture to face.

In the past, every individual entering a *limited area* surrendered his or her belongings (e.g., purse, briefcase) for inspection by the guard who searched for contraband. Now, however, workers are subject to random inspections. Entering or exiting the *security* barrier of an area, one passes his or her hand over a machine that beeps and lights up either a green or red light indicating selection for inspection. People with *Q clearances*, marked by a *blue badge*, can access *protected areas* unescorted. A *Q clearance* is also required for access to *material access areas* and *exclusion areas*. *Clearance* is the basis for access to particular areas, but not the only entry criterion. One must also have the authority, defined by the scope of one's work, to enter particular facilities. *Badges*, therefore, also contain information, coded by alphabetical letters, regarding which facilities one can enter.

Moral Regulation: The Clearance Process

The higher *clearance* an employee needs to obtain, the more information he must reveal about himself. By disclosing name, address, affiliation, and social security number, showing a picture ID, and claiming U.S. citizenship, nonemployee guests of the site (e.g., members of the public, potential contractors, visiting dignitaries) can obtain an *uncleared visitor's badge*. At the end of the visit, they return their temporary *badge* and any claim of membership within the SRS community. Employees, however, obtain more durable coded *badges*. An *uncleared red badge* employee discloses information similar to that of the visitor. In contrast, *L* and *Q cleared* employees undergo a closer examination of character through a *background check* process. As a manager explains, an *L clearance background check* entails "an extensive network check through phone calls and letters" while a *Q clearance* involves personal interviews with the applicant's current and former associates. Averaging about twenty thousand dollars, a *Q clearance* is a considerable investment in an employee.

Security, predicated on the protection of valuables within the industry such as information, nuclear materials, and property, also functions as an arbiter of personal behavior. The earliest generation of workers whose consciousness regarding *national security* was formed during World War II tend to consider *background checks* and most aspects of the *security program* a reasonable practice.[9] A few of the younger workers, perhaps expressing greater cynicism toward government in general, bristle somewhat at the invasion of privacy. In addition to appraising one's trustworthiness, honesty, and psychological balance, the *background check* serves to identify those aspects of an individual's personal life that might render him or her *vulnerable* to blackmail, and therefore in a position to compromise *security*. To someone blackmailed, the reasoning goes, controlled information could become a valuable commodity with which to extricate oneself. One employee recounts the basic principle she sees at work in screening for *clearances*: "Security people are paranoid, of course. They have to be. That's what their job is. They don't give credit for somebody being loyal and trustworthy and so forth. They automatically assume that everybody can be bought."

Background checks, the ritualized process of investigating a worker's character, associations, and activities, are an instance of "moral regulation"—that is, the process by which "state activity makes and symbolizes the permissible, the sole imaginable, parameters of individual identity" (Foster 1991:247). In determining and enforcing standards as to who is a *security risk*, state functionaries re-create a particular vision of who is an appropriate member of the nation as a moral community. Workers with a long history in the industry note that the behaviors and social mores against which one is judged a *security risk* have changed. In earlier decades, homosexuality, infidelity, and public drunkenness were counterindications to *security*. Lately, these employees suggest, substance abuse figures most prominently in *security* checks although attention to various signs of undesirability continue (e.g., serious marital problems, a criminal record).

Sexuality has been a significant domain for processes of moral regulation at the facility. One man jokingly complains at how details about one's sexual life were once assiduously pursued:

> This was the McCarthy era where people were really uptight about security, and they felt very, very strongly that your personal life could have a direct influence on compromising security. At that time, if somebody was, for example, homosexual, they were not hired because the feeling was that since everyone was in the closet at that time, that you could threaten them with taking them out of the closet and then you could therefore compromise their position. So, they pursued that kind of thing very, very diligently, and for us . . . heterosexuals, that was sort of annoying to say the least.

Homosexuality does not automatically disqualify a person for a *high-level security clearance* as it did in the past. Nonetheless, the equation of homosexuality with a *security risk* is still a well-entrenched assumption among some members of the workforce as one example instructs. Contractor management recently implemented a *diversity* awareness program to promote mutual respect among employees. A few people, while receiving an orientation to this program, found the suggestion that homosexuality also constituted a form of *diversity* as cause for alarm. The *security* office received a number of phone calls for clarification: Was *diversity* undermining a tenet of *security*?

Many subjects consider the *security* features of their workplace, however elaborate or excessive, as ultimately sensible. It is, as one young woman puts it, "a matter of national security." *Security* "keeps the baddies out!" proclaims the wife of a retired worker whom she first met while working in *security* herself during the wartime Manhattan Project. The "baddies" are not distant foreign bodies threatening the nation. *Security*, as some people interpret it, has a personal immediacy, and this lends practices such as the *background check* their poignancy. One long-time engineer explains: "We found no real problem with people's characters getting scrutinized in terms of were they going to be reliable people to be working with. . . . Their personal morals may be no good, but from the standpoint of whether they are going to help you protect yourself and you protect them and that sort of thing, that's another thing."

One woman who sat through FBI interviews about her neighbors acquiring *clearances* and who saw her own husband go through such a process defends the investigation in equally familiar terms:

> I felt really good that they were being that careful. I didn't really want any weak links out there. . . . I didn't know whether it could blow to kingdom come and I really didn't want anybody who was a threat. So I felt kind of good that they were doing their job and making sure that everybody was okay . . . Having experienced the war...your life depended on other people and, you know, if they weren't the kind of people that you'd want to *depend* on, it was kind of a scary thing.

The institutional process for creating dependable and reliable associates in the workplace and the nation relies upon inquiries among a worker's other intimates. For one young employee acquiring a *Q clearance*, this was the source of her aggravation over the *background check*, the feeling of encroachment by a program she otherwise sees necessary. She explains: "People were prying into my business. People were calling my neighbors . . . going to see my step-father, asking questions about me. I had to list who my real father was, that I had not had contact with since I was [very young], and little did I know that they could have gone out and showed up on his doorstep and asked about his relationship with me. Did I want that to happen? No!"

Responding to how she felt about having her "character and behavior subject to scrutiny" to acquire a clearance, a recently retired employee laughingly replies, "I came from a small community and that was done all the time. It was not a problem. I never thought about it in those terms." She adds: "I've tried to live my life so I wouldn't care if anyone eavesdropped or anything else."

Having a *higher clearance* permits greater mobility within SRS borders and access to valuable information and materials. This "freedom" of mobility hinges on an intense evaluation of character. A research subject describes her experience of holding a *clearance* as both a matter of burden and privilege. Working with *classified* documents, she jumped at the offer to transfer to another position that did not involve handling such information. She has a *blue badge* but "does not like the responsibilities that come with it." A young engineer feels honored with the charge of *classified* documents: "Being that my first job in was in classification, I learned a lot of classified stuff. Not that I would remember much of it now, but I saw a lot of neat stuff and heard a lot of neat stuff. . . . At that time, I thought it was cool to have a clearance and be trusted with stuff that the government considered classified and no one outside my little cubby hole should know about."

Like the young engineer, other employees readily incorporate their *clearance* with their sense of self. A chemical engineer now retired but occasionally still working as a consultant to the SRS, complains about the lack of recognition he experiences when going through *security* at other DOE facilities: "I've been a consultant that had a weapons data clearance all my life—the highest level clearance—yet they treat you as if you had nothing." The *security clearance* system comes to operate as a common currency for personal integrity: one man explains he has "no problem" undergoing a *background check* because he has "nothing to hide."

Because *security checks* and their periodic renewal are expensive, some employees have had their *clearances downgraded* as a cost-saving measure at the facility. Some people have taken their reclassification as a "personal affront," notes one woman. Those around them, explains a colleague, occasionally speculate as to what these individuals "did" to "lose" their *clearance*. The *badge* does not simply serve as a purveyor of *clearance* social statuses, but also as a record of local history. A *low number badge* (*badge*s are issued sequentially in numeric order for payroll purposes) indicates that the wearer is one of the earliest workers at the plant, a venerable status in the eyes of some.

Shared Surveillance: Escorts and the Challenge System

Employees stand equally in relationship to the *security program*, a manager explains, because *infractions* are leveled at individuals. Workers must comply with *security* rules and regulations, policing themselves effectively. They also take on the obligation of scrutinizing peers and anyone else entering the controlled space(s) of the SRS. During *general employee training*, workers learn their duties within *the challenge system*, the process to:

> . . . prevent unauthorized personnel from obtaining access to *classified* information, *classified* work, or areas not officially required in the performance of their assigned duties. This ensures that all persons onsite are properly identified. A challenge is made by politely asking the individual if they [sic] need assistance or help. "May I help you?"

Posters and road signs throughout the SRS serve as reminders to practice *the challenge system*. One such poster depicts an individual addressing a person entering a room marked "authorized personnel only" with the words, "May I help you?" The cartoon simultaneously conveys the *thoughts* of the person invoking *the challenge system*: "Who is this person? Where is he going? Where is his *escort*?"

The challenge system, a *security* measure to ensure "that all persons onsite are properly identified," in effect deputizes all workers as *security* enforcement personnel in arbitrating who goes where. It is a system of "calculated gazes," a form of power that operates in a ubiquitous fashion:

> It is the apparatus as a whole that produces "power" and distributes individuals in this permanent and continuous field. This enables the disciplinary power to be both absolutely indiscreet, since it is everywhere and always alert, since by its very principle it leaves no zone of shade and constantly supervises the very individuals who are entrusted with the task of supervising; and absolutely "discreet," for it functions permanently and largely in silence. (Foucault 1979:177)

Early on, the *security* program deployed the image of "home" to infuse with personal meaning the practice of judging person-to-place-to-clearance. *Security* is a state that the "official" program and employees attribute to variably scaled entities—the workplace, the home, and the nation:

> "If you found a stranger in your living room, you'd quickly find out what he was doing there and who he was. Here at the plant, it's even more important that you react the same way." . . . Emphasizing the need for alertness on the part of everyone, the security supervisor called on all employees to challenge strangers noticed on the job (*Savannah River Plant News*, March 6, 1953, page 1)

Home is also how the wife of one long-time employee interprets the current political situation in which the United States finds itself after the end of the Cold War. "We should be smart about the way we deal with nuclear weapons," she says referring to disarmament. "It is kind of like how it is at home. You don't want to have to put bars on your windows and doors, but at the same time, you should be smart enough to latch your door and lock your windows."

I often found myself caught up in *the challenge system*, the very first time being when I acquired my own *security badge*. The woman at the *badging office* who was processing my paperwork instructed me to "go to the final hallway on the right and ask the first person I saw there to show me the *security* orientation film." I went down the hallway as she instructed, but the first few offices were empty. Everyone was congregated at the end of the hall and clustered around a room that had a big sign over it stating, "STOP! Authorized

Personnel Only." Walking slowly down the hall and debating how best to resolve the woman's instructions to me with the sign's warning, I eventually caught the eye of a young man who abruptly asked "if he could help me." Not having to feign naivety, I explained that I had been told to come here and ask to view the orientation film. He quickly *escorted* me to the viewing room.

Another instance presented itself when I was well into my fieldwork. Sitting within view of a secretary across the hall, I waited in one manager's office while he went off to retrieve information for me. A second manager with whom I had interacted on several occasions asked me where my *escort* was. Because I was in a controlled area and seemingly on my own, I knew *why* he was asking the question. I still felt personally offended (weren't our prior meetings enough for him to know I was trustworthy?) as well as protective of the other manager who had acted responsibly in instructing the secretary to keep an eye on me. I felt disdain for the question also because I had sat within the purview of the secretary consciously to make her involuntary *escort* duty less troublesome.

The responsibility of obliging and importuning others to follow *security* regulations extends into the role of the *escort*. *Escorting* permits the movement of people with *lower clearances* through secured areas. An *uncleared* person's responsibilities as the *escorted* include, as the employee training manual instructs, cooperating with your *escort*, trying not to become separated, and if separated, finding a *cleared* person for assistance. An *escort's* responsibilities amount to maintaining "constant voice, line-of-sight control," discussing only authorized information, and not deviating from specified routes. *Escort*s are personally responsible for their charge's compliance with *security* regulations, and *infractions* can be leveled against the *escort* for another's transgressions.

In executing their duties, *escorts* import their own standards of trust and distrust into this "official" social relationship. They carry out their *escort* and other responsibilities in the *security* system in accordance with their position of authority, their self-identity, and those with whom they are interacting. One woman, for instance, who accompanied me and a group of outside contractors surveying historical documents, explained that she did not feel the need to keep the researchers in her immediate line of vision because she had, over time, struck up a rapport with them and "trusted" them to act appropriately. I, on the other hand, was someone whom she had just met, and was, therefore, someone she would have to watch more closely.

In another case, two contacts of mine at an off site facility exercised varying degrees of supervision. One was particularly heavyhanded in her oversight of me, keeping me in view at all times, as I looked over the materials she provided and viewed a video regarding her program. She even *escorted* me out the front door. In this building, however, my *red badge* was indeed enough authority for me to walk around freely. In contrast, my other contact left me unattended to review the information she provided me and then wished me good-bye from her desk as I walked away, out of her sight, and toward the exit.

The overinterpretation of *escorting* by the first contact makes more sense in light of her remarks to me about how grateful she is to have her job, particularly at a bad time in the economy. Her income is doubly important now that she is newly divorced and supporting children on her own. Judging my presence and my requests for information as possible sources of jeopardy, she may have exercised extreme caution in her dealings with me.

Escorting creates a relationship of dependency, and workers use parental metaphors when describing the experience of *escorting* and being *escorted*. One man said that having only a *red badge* while waiting for his *higher clearance* to come through was oftentimes a humiliating experience for him. Being *escorted* made him "feel like a child." When I asked one of my *escorts* what she considered her task to be in keeping an eye on me and other cohorts in a controlled documents area, she unhesitatingly said one word, "baby-sitting." Assaults to one's sense of personal autonomy and adulthood when being *escorted* are most clear when a trip to the bathroom becomes a necessity.

Joking is one way in which workers resolve the dilemma of *security* requirements and the social absurdity of one adult taking another to the bathroom. One gentleman remarked that if his *escort* was coming with him, then perhaps his companion could "hold it for him, too." Another man recounted the time he was responsible for waiting outside the bathroom door for his charge. When a manager he knew and did not particularly like came along, he asked if the manager would kindly cover his escort duties for him. His prank amounted to inconveniencing the manager by leaving him waiting at the bathroom door. His joke, however, also points to another facet of the *escort's* social role.

Being *escorted* is experienced as a disempowered or submissive role. On the other hand, *escorting* sometimes takes on a lesser social status as one is tied to another person. *Escorting* can be a hassle and an inconvenience. The burden may fall, therefore, on someone lower in the occupational hierarchy: *cleared* secretaries sometimes *escort* people in for appointments.

Having only a *red badge* myself, I was constantly in the role of the person being *escorted*. Numerous times, I received instructions from informants to call them from the *guard shack* so that they could come out and get me. After putting in the call, I would wait for their arrival. The wait was occasionally boring, but sometimes unnerving depending on how long it took for my companion to arrive. During one wait of twenty minutes at a guard checkpoint near the laboratory, for instance, I had the profound feeling of being out of place, of not having anywhere to go. Watching the other workers with the appropriate *clearance* routinely, swiftly, and unthinkingly pass their hands over the random search scanner, walk past the guards, and enter their workplace, I felt as if I did not belong there. If I did, I would have as "easily" entered the facility as they had.

Waiting at the gate, I often felt like an object of others' curiosity as some people passed by, looking at my face and *badge* as they moved through the checkpoint. Infrequently someone would inquire for whom I was waiting or where I needed to go, trying to decide if perhaps he could *escort* me in. Once when I was waiting at the gate to join environmental sampling staff in the field, a member of the group driving out recognized me and called out that "someone is coming to get you."

A Speech Community: Controlling Information Flows

Security contributes to the creation of social relations through controls over space: incorporation into the social body of the SRS is experienced as incorporation into controlled spaces. By organizing people in space, *security* creates sensibilities regarding self and other with respect to the site. It also, I argue, creates the basis for notions of self and other at the level of nation-state. Moreover, *security* creates these relations of inclusion and exclusion through controls over communication. Apart from measures to protect the facility from "industrial espionage and sabotage," a one-time *security* manager explains, the program is also "a matter of controlling information or putting barriers to the flow of information. That is, having procedures to control discussions or putting controls on modems in computers." He considers himself as holding a distinct notion of *security*. His former colleagues thought they should "prevent information from flowing." In contrast, he wanted "to prevent the wrong information from flowing." Hence he did not always agree with their measures to "create barriers between people and between types of information."

Discussions at the workplace stand in stark contrast to discussions outside the workplace, although this situation is undergoing change. Until quite recently workers were not allowed to discuss details about the SRS or their jobs outside the workplace. A man formerly in construction management recounts his instructions to people receiving their initial orientation: "Just don't say anything about what you do. . . . You just tell people, 'I'm a carpenter.' Well, carpenters do the same thing everywhere and that's all you talk about. You don't say exactly what you do." Even within the workplace, employees faced the injunction not to discuss the details of their particular facility with employees from another area unless it was directly pertinent to their job, and then, only if they had the appropriate *clearance*.

As an indication of how *secret* workers were about their jobs and the SRS, many people cite the case that employees historically could not even tell their spouses about their work. The extent to which this scenario held true is debated by some, but it is telling that people seize on one of the most intimate relationships to convey the magnitude of restrictions placed on off site conversations. One wife relates: "What was it forty years . . . ? And I had never been to his office. I had never seen—I put it jokingly—whose picture he had on his desk. And everytime he came home, I'd say, 'How was your day?,' and I heard one word, 'Busy.' That's all he could discuss about his work."

A working husband from this same generation explains his position: "You can talk an awful lot about what you do without revealing anything— not because you suspect your wife, your spouse, but because you wanted to be sure somehow it didn't leak out." For couples who did engage in conversations about site-related work, the dividing line usually fell between "unspoken" technical or process details and "spoken" personal or social details.

Identified with a *red badge* (and perhaps for other outsider identity reasons—my age, my gender) my presence seemed to temper conversations in classes I attended with *cleared* employees. I enrolled in a nuclear reactor physics course organized through the local technical college, held on site, attended by SRS employees, and taught by a nuclear engineer employed at the facility. During one class discussion, a student asked the instructor why his examples always centered on commercial power reactors rather than production reactors (such as the ones used to make bomb grade materials). The instructor replied that the course's focus was on commercial reactors but he would try to include some details about production reactors gathered from his own experience with the ones at the SRS. Furthermore, the instructor went on to explain while also looking at me, "Some of us are red badges." "Some" was one, me.

In another class on plutonium and tritium technology, attended by *cleared* personnel and me, the content of material to be covered was debated in *security* terms. At the beginning of class, a student asked the instructor, "Will there be any discussion of classified information?" The instructor explained that the office of training had reviewed the course materials and determined that they did not contain any *classified* information. If someone should happen to ask a question that elicited a *classified* answer, he continued, he would have to say, "I don't know." True to his word, the instructor did on occasion say, "I don't know." Later in the course, the instructor confronted a student who provided an anecdote with nuclear details by inquiring, "Can you be telling us that?" Just as *security clearances* facilitate different congregations of people in privileged spaces, so too do *security* injunctions on discussing *classified* information facilitate different speech communities.

WORKER DISCIPLINE THROUGH
RADIOLOGICAL CONTROL

Work in a radiological environment reinforces practices and assumptions regarding the creation, maintenance, and hypervigilance of boundaries, the key element of *security*. With respect to radiological contamination, one protects points of vulnerability, keeping things at skin's distance (variably constructed) and out of the body. Work with nuclear materials at the SRS requires its own detailed discussion. Although cursory here, a consideration of *radiological control* complements discussions of *security* discipline because the *rad control* program also socializes employees into a conceptual and experiential order emphasizing boundaries. This program, focusing on individual human bodies, provides perhaps the most visceral lesson in boundary control. Paradoxically, the substance (nuclear material) scrutinized in this program exhibits varying degrees of power to traverse (*penetrate*) borders.

Just as the *graded security system* divides SRS space into variably restricted zones, so too does a system of *radiological control* portion areas into different levels of exposure (and health risk) with concomitant regulation of access. Each classification has its own requirements (e.g., level of training, paperwork, authorization from authorities, form of dress, devices worn by employees to record exposure, a set of monitoring practices) for entry to, work in, and exit from the area. The first order of control is defined as a *radiologically controlled area*, an area to which access is restricted due to the presence or potential presence of radioactive materials or elevated radiation levels. This designated area serves as a buffer zone between *clean* (i.e., nonradiological) and radiological areas. The remaining designations, marked by variable levels of exposure or contamination, include *radiation area, high radiation area, very high radiation area, contamination area*, and *airborne activity areas*, and a few other gradations. An extensive system of postings, signs, and labels announce the radiological qualities of a particular work environment, such that employees "know" that they are crossing over from one distinct place to another.

All employees receive an orientation to basic atomic and radiological concepts, the biological effects of radiation, facility policies regarding controlled areas, the system of radiological signs and symbols, the equipment and devices used to measure and detect radiation and contamination, the behaviors to *monitor* themselves for contamination, and the responsibilities of each employee to observe and obey *radiological controls*. What knowledge they obtain in the classroom setting is reinforced by the physical manifestations they encounter throughout the SRS—the signs, the fences, the ropes, the postings, the *monitoring* devices, and so forth. Workers who carry out their jobs in radiological environments are more deeply inculcated with the requirements for conducting oneself in a controlled area. As an example of the type of knowledge and experience that employees obtain as radiological workers, I consider some of the content of the *radiological worker training* course I attended that had both classroom and practical components to instruction.

Consciousness about "insides" and "outsides," as well as barriers between the two, pervades radiological knowledge and work. When reviewing the different types of ionizing radiation, worker students learn not only atomic properties but also those aspects related to obviating its negative health consequences—for instance, the type of *shielding* necessary to stop the radiation in its tracks and the type of hazard posed by each form. *Shielding*, our materials instruct us, takes the form of various barriers: a sheet of paper or the outer layer of skin is sufficient enough, one learns, to "stop" alpha particles. In contrast, most beta particles with a "limited penetrating ability" are shielded by plastic, glass, metal foil, and safety glasses. Gamma rays, with "very high penetrating power" are "best shielded by very dense materials, such as concrete, lead or steel."

Hazards of different ionizing radiation are defined in spatial terms, whether external or internal relative to the body: "Alpha particles are not considered an external radiation hazard . . . because they are easily stopped by the dead layer of skin. Should an alpha emitter be inhaled or ingested, it becomes a source of internal exposure." A beta emitter, if ingested or inhaled, "can be an internal hazard due to its short range. Externally, beta particles are potentially hazardous to the skin and eyes."

Workers learn the requirements for moving in and out of *radiologically controlled areas*, the lesson being a vigilance regarding one's radiation exposure as well as the potential for one to track contamination outside an area, posing an exposure threat to others. Just as workers' movements in and out of controlled areas are monitored, so too is the potential for the movement of contamination on and in their bodies. One activity required upon exiting a *radiologically controlled area* is monitoring for personal contamination by devices that detect the presence of radioactive material: a hand held *count rate meter* (using this is known as *frisking*) followed by stepping into a *personnel contamination monitor* that conducts a *whole body frisk*. Workers pass the probe of the *count rate meter* over the whole of their body surface areas, pausing at vulnerable points such as the mouth and nose (checking for the possibility of internal contamination) and the knees and elbows, which may have made contact with contaminated surfaces.

Rad worker training students learn by instruction, observation, and then by practice themselves the correct method of *dressing out*—that is, the *donning of personal protective clothing* one wears in a contaminated work area. To explain how *protective clothing* (PCs) helps one prevent the spread of nuclear materials from one area to the next, our instructor drew on a very domestic metaphor:

The way I get people to understand how PC's work is I tell them that *this* area has a quarter inch of coal dust on it, and *this* area over here is that white rug you've been saving all that money for and that you've just put in. You really want to keep it clean. The PC's provide a barrier between you and the coal dust, and it gives you a way of keeping the coal dust in the dirty area so you're not tracking it onto your white rug. When you take off that PC, you're going to be real careful to keep the coal dust on that so you're not taking it over on the clean area. . . . There is a line drawn at the step off pad [i.e., a mat where one steps after removing the PC and just before entering the non-radiological area] which tells you that there is a barrier between the coal dust area and the white rug.

Dressing out is a repeated, everyday occurrence for workers in radiological areas, such that the prescribed procedure becomes second nature as the following case suggests. During our training, one student remarked that he was having some difficulty learning the demonstrated *donning* procedure because it was different from the one he habitually performed for many years. Each facility had its own method of *dressing out* in the past, but now the SRS has one standardized procedure, that demonstrated in our class.

Before *dressing out*, a person first checks his or her cotton coveralls for any damage and then begins a series of preordained steps. When putting on the following clothing, one must be concerned with creating a seamless exterior, a boundary to oneself vis-à-vis outside contamination: (1) Cloth shoe covers or booties over one's own shoes. (2) Coveralls. One folds his or her coverall pant legs inward and then tapes them down around the ankle and directly to the shoe covers. (3) Rubber overshoes. (4) Cotton glove liners. (5) Rubber gloves with the cuffs of the overalls tucked underneath and then taped over. One first checks the rubber gloves for holes by blowing up them up like balloons, holding them, and looking for leaks. (6) Hood.

Removing one's clothing after a job and before exiting requires one to have a heightened sense of inside and outside. Inside is *clean* while outside is dirty. These two distinctions are hard to maintain as one peels off outer clothing. For instance, the rubber overshoes are pulled from the heel, neither from the inside (which is clean) nor the bottom (likely to be the most contaminated area on the body). Gloves are removed by pinching the outside and pulling the cuff down, so that it is pulled off inside out.

When the instructor demonstrated how to put on and then take off a double set of coveralls (a *dress out* procedure for some radiological areas), our dichotomous world was put to a severe test. The middle coverall between the inner body and the outer coverall did not fit our binary model very well, as evidenced by a debate between the instructor and a seasoned radiological worker. The worker "corrected" the instructor when he was removing the inner coverall because he did one action (reaching across his chest to pull off a sleeve) that could possibly *crosscontaminate*. The instructor defended his own method, arguing that the inner coverall was *clean* so he did not have to worry about reaching across.

THE COUNTERINTUITIVENESS OF
RECENT "OPENNESS" INITIATIVES

Secretary O'Leary directed the Department of Energy to implement a number of *openness initiatives* in response to the agency's critics who argued that it historically abused its authority in the name of *national security*. A management principle of *secrecy* contributed, the critics claim, to compromises in environmental protection, public health, and worker safety. As redress for its past isolationist behavior and to recover the public's faith in the agency, the Secretary took a number of steps to demonstrate that the Department is now more *open*. At a December 7, 1993, press conference, she released previously *classified* information of a significant nature including unannounced nuclear weapons tests and the location and quantity of plutonium in the complex. She also called for an in-depth review of the DOE's information policies with the goals of reducing the amount of *classified* material produced and speeding up the *declassification* of existing documents for public consumption. Her administration advocated for the inclusion of local community and public interest groups in the Department's decision- and priority-making processes.

One local DOE initiative that has had consequences for work routines is an effort to make the SRS itself more accessible to the public. In describing the development of DOE *openness* policy, a manager re-creates the association between a house and the SRS: "Prior to the current move toward openness, we had opened the window a little. Back at Rocky Flats [where I used to work] the decision was 'Okay, we'll open the gate but the fence will stay up,' and this early move toward openness was part of an effort to educate the public, create greater peace of mind about the competency of the site, and act like a good neighbor. With openness in the last two years, the window has flown open."

"How can we protect but still allow public access?" is how he describes recent alterations to *security* mechanisms to accommodate *openness*. "By consolidating what we need to protect and putting it in one corner, it will be possible to open some areas to the public," he explains. As of December 1993, guards at the barrier to the controlled front office area (for both the primary contractor and DOE management) no longer wear blue military officer uniforms and black combat boots. Manning the entrance by which the majority of the "public" (i.e., nonemployee visitors) pass, these guards now sport slacks, sweater vests, ties, and jackets as part of an effort to remove "the armed camp appearance of the site" as one employee puts it. *Security officers* at the numerous barriers, guard shacks, and checkpoints scattered across the site and through which the majority of the workforce pass, however, remain in uniform.

The newly demilitarized appearance of the front office guards draws mixed reactions from the workforce, both laughter and concern. One woman jokes that the guards now look like "airline ticket staff." In contrast, another employee notes that many people in the administrative offices feel more vulnerable than they did before the *security officers* altered their dress code and the SRS opened up in limited ways to the public. Not only is the presence of "outsiders" likely to increase in particular areas on site, but, at the same time, the highly visible military means for securing borders is disappearing.

These contradictory developments go against a *security* common sense created under different circumstances. Some workers feel less protected by the men clad in more benevolent clothing. At the same time, the guards themselves also feel less capable of protecting. A manager explains that the new appearance of the *security* officers indeed raised, as he put it, "perceptual issues." Some of the guards remarked that they "look different from everyone else [in the security forces]." In reply to their concerns, the manager argued that they were in a better position to provide protection by their ability to blend in, rather than by looking like everyone else "with combat boots, uniform, and jingling keys." The dress change in the front office *security officers* has had a further effect, the manager continues, in that they are "more friendly," a beneficial contribution to a campaign to make the public not feel "intimidated."

This dressing down of officers is not the only change among the *security* forces evoking a new sense of vulnerability among people used to an "armed camp" atmosphere. One informant who works in an area storing controlled documents thinks that it is "crazy" that the *security officers* are not allowed to carry guns there anymore. She does not feel "as safe." As she sees it, "what's to keep somebody from coming in here and bringing a bomb? Especially with all those 'diaperheads' running around [on site]." "Diaperheads," she explains, are people such as "Iranians [that is], everyone running around with turbans on their heads. Half of [the company's construction workforce] are those kind of people and *they're* the ones rebuilding Iraq."

This woman is concerned about the apparent contradiction between the decreasing (in her view) *security* measures and the increasing ethnic diversification of the workforce. Measures in place to keep "others" out, her reasoning reveals, are dissolving at the same time that "others" are increasingly con-

stituting the ranks of the workforce. Here her own definitions of *security* and
the American nation conflict with those administered by *security* authorities
in granting *clearances* to American workers from diverse ethnic and racial
backgrounds. This woman's remarks reveal the classificatory process within
nation-building whereby "the ethnic identity of the dominant group [in this
case, Caucasian Americans] is privileged as the core of imagined community"
(Alonso 1994:390).

The *security* officers' new behavior and the presence of the public, or
"outsiders," on-site evoke liberating and debilitating feelings among the
workforce. Some employees feel a very real, personal threat as *security* measures with which they are familiar disappear. One employee worries about
increased public access at a time of lowered *security* barriers. He points to the
case of the World Trade Center bombing: "What's to keep a terrorist from
coming into the [front office area] with something explosive, blowing out the
front of that building?"

In contrast, some of his peers breathe a sigh of relief as aspects of military force depart from the SRS, their fear being tied more to the immediate
threat of guards "taking their jobs too seriously," as one employee describes
it. "Have you been to any of the areas where the guys are walking around with
M-16s?" was an instructive question from a number of contacts.

Recent alterations in *security* measures have affected, for some, a sense
of their physical selves. Such alterations have also had consequences for people's social identities and their sense of worth. Representatives from government, industry, and academia attended a SRS-sponsored robotics demonstration. One attendee, while waiting for the remainder of our group to be *badged*,
spoke excitedly about the prospects of sharing technical knowledge originally
developed in this defense industion. During the time he had worked for the
Navy, he had wanted to share information about some of his projects, but
faced restrictions on communication. For us, he described in great detail the
design and use of a remote vehicle that could go over any obstacle. At this
time and throughout the day, he readily opened up his briefcase, pulled out a
brochure, and launched into a proud description of this and other projects he
was involved in. Similarly, a local chemical engineer anticipates that the
recent *openness initiative* provides him the opportunity to acquire a larger
readership for some of his research. Technical papers to which he had contributed for limited circulation could now be made available to his larger pro-
fession, perhaps allowing for greater peer recognition.

The joy of now being able to talk about one's work is not just tied to
recognition for one's technical achievements, but for other informants, to
more localized relationships. One informant points to the possibility for more
camaraderie and intimacy among workers when they encounter each other
outside of work: "Previously, everything was kept in-house. Let's say I met

someone out in the community one day, working on our cars. We got to talking and come to find out we both work at the site. That's where the conversation stopped—knowing that we worked there. We didn't go into any more detail about what exactly we did. The chance to talk about what we do is a dramatic change." This man spoke positively about the loosening of the *need to know* rule in terms of a chance to reveal more information about himself. In contrast, another man appraises *openness* and its accompanying *declassification* agenda in more negative personal terms. A few older workers question aloud the intelligence and political savvy of Secretary O'Leary, seen as threatening "to give all our secrets away" and jeopardizing the military strength of the country. In contrast, this peer of theirs admits that the current revelation of formerly *classified* information makes him feel "stupid." The historic effort of him and his companions to keep information *secret* seems to hold no value currently. He wonders whether or not he might have been a dupe for being true to the rule of silence over the years.

CONCLUSION

Foucauldian notions of power and discipline have proven useful in appreciating worker experiences within *security*, *radiological control*, and *openness* programs. *Security*, with a feature such as *the challenge system*, reflects power that operates in a "continuous field," controlling workers at the same time that it presumes *their* capacity to act as agents of control. In this respect, power is indeed generative rather than oppressive (Foucault 1979:194). Ethnographic materials have also demonstrated the importance of inquiring into the culturally specific ways in which work discipline is accomplished. Trust, dependability, and familiarity are some of the sentiments of surveillance in this workplace. Security at the workplace, for many employees, makes sense in light of the value of protecting the home, an intimate and sacred place. Similarly, national defense is meaningful in terms of domestic security.

By attending to the face-to-face relationships that people create among themselves, I do see some deficits within Foucault's concepts, for better or for worse. Surveillance is not omnipresent, as Foucault's (1979) rendering might suggest. Rather than generic subjects, workers are sociable people who enact *security* within particular contexts. They interpret and recreate the *security program* in ways meaningful to themselves. At the same time, their actions and interpretations often reproduce social processes of differentiation including class, gender, age, ethnicity, national identity, and sexual orientation.

One woman, for instance, expresses an inchoate fear about the increasing numbers of people of Middle Eastern origin in the workplace at the same time that security measures relax. Analyses that draw upon Foucault's model of power, therefore, must conceptualize power in terms of the agents through which it acts, agents subject to different social groupings and identities.

Workers in this industry experience profound regulation, spatially and morally. Throughout a working day, they encounter a panoply of reminders that personal conduct has a direct bearing on the well-being of another greater entity, the nation. Workers, to varying degrees, are entrusted with the *security* of the nation on a daily basis. They carry out this charge by attending to the minutiae of their behavior, conversations, and form of dress. Those with the most intimate of ties to the nation, it would seem, are also those who experience an acute form of discipline. The self-evidence of a "nation" in need of *security* is both a necessary condition for and result of this work.

This ethnography suggests that employees experience their workplace in terms of Niels Bohr's image, only inverted: a factory turned into a country. Employees have, however, begun to experience the newly emerging program of *openness*. The deep feeling of personal vulnerability with *openness* suggests the deep levels to which *security* as an embodied sensibility exists for some members of the workforce. *Security* and *openness* are programs envisioned by state functionaries in specific political circumstances to foster an ordering of people—spatially, socially, morally.

ACKNOWLEDGMENTS

I wish to thank my friends in the field and Kamran Ali, Donald Carter, Gillian Feeley-Harnik, Paul Marvy, Erik Mueggler, and Felicity Northcott for their insightful comments on earlier versions of this paper. Field research for this paper and the overall study of which it is a part was made possible by a fellowship from the Department of Anthropology at the Johns Hopkins University, and a joint grant from the National Science Foundation's Programs in Anthropology and Science and Technology Studies.

NOTES

1. Throughout this paper, I highlight in italics those terms used by subjects in the field.

2. Here, I offset the word "nation" in quotations as an indication to the reader that a "nation" is, contrary to its standing as a self-evident social grouping, not a primordial entity but an ideological formation tied to state power. For the remainder of the article, however, I refrain from using quotation marks for the ease of reading.

3. Beginning in June 1995, the SRS began a RIF, a "reduction in force," eventually to total 20% of former employment levels for both federal and contractor

employees. During my fieldwork (October 1993 to March 1995), the workforce totalled over 20,000. Following the latest RIF, employment levels are at approximately 16,000.

4. The number of personnel devoted exclusively to security support services is substantial. In 1993, the security contractor had 215 support staff members (e.g., maintenance, armor assistance, administration) and 850 *protective force* members. *Protective forces* include unarmed officers and *security police officers* who carry a sidearm and carry out law enforcement duties (e.g., traffic control, theft and criminal conduct). In addition, there is a select group of personnel who make up the *special response team* (comparable to a SWAT team) and a canine division responsible for locating narcotics and explosives, and capable of tracking and locating intruders.

5. *Contraband* within the confines of the *general site* include weapons, ammunition, explosives, narcotics and illegal drugs, and alcoholic beverages. In addition to these, *contraband* within *security areas* include copying or recording devices, cameras or undeveloped film, radio transmitters and cellular phones, and knives with blades longer than three inches.

6. To further illustrate the point of wearing a *badge* as an insider status is the case of an activist whose organization has monitored SRS activity for a number of years. Although visiting the Site on numerous occasions, he only recently acquired a semipermanent *badge* as a member of a community advisory group. Having a semipermanent *badge* would have made his prior trips more convenient in that he could have avoided the time and paperwork necessary to acquire a temporary *visitor's badge*. He resisted for a long time, however, inclusion in the badging system, and therefore, in the community of the SRS.

7. General Leslie R. Groves who oversaw the Army project that produced the atomic bomb during World War II explained his conceptualization of security in the following terms: "Compartmentalization of knowledge . . . was the very heart of security. My rule was simple and not capable of misinterpretation—each man should know everything he needed to know to do his job and nothing else. [This] not only provided an adequate measure of security, but . . . it made quite clear to all concerned that the project existed to produce a specific end product" (quoted in Gosling and Fehner 1994:1–2).

8. A number of other *badges* and *passes* are in use at the SRS. A person may obtain a *pass* to exempt him or her from the *contraband* rule should one or some of these items be necessary for his or her job. Furthermore, a *materials and package pass* allows either the removal of SRS property in order for him or her to conduct a job or the entry of "personal owned electronic equipment" in areas other than security ones. A newly emerging badge system is *accountability*. By passing through one's barcoded *badge* into an electronic system (not yet in place in all facilities) upon entry, one's presence is recorded, the rationale being if an emergency evacuation occurred, all people in or out of a facility could be accounted for.

9. A retired engineer explains his historical perspective on clearances: "The clearance had several limitations. One of them was, in a sense, a responsibility, very

much responsibility. The reason our work was being done was, if you will, national defense kind of work, and it's just a continuation of all those things from way back during the war. You may have heard some of those old sayings, 'Loose Lips Sink Ships' and things like that. Well, it was defense work."

REFERENCES CITED

Alonso, Ana María
    1994 The politics of space, time and substance: State formation, nationalism, and ethnicity. *Annual Review of Anthropology* 23:379–405.

Anderson, Benedict
    1983 *Imagined Communities: Reflections on the Origins and Spread of Nationalism*. London: Verso.

Arney, William Ray
    1991 *Experts in the Age of Systems*. Albuquerque: University of New Mexico Press.

Bourdieu, Pierre
    1977 *Outline of a Theory of Practice*. Translated by R. Nice. Cambridge, U.K.: Cambridge University Press.

Cohn, Carol
    1987 Sex and death in the rational world of defense intellectuals. *Signs: Journal of Women in Culture and Society* 12(4):687–718.

Comaroff, Jean
    1985 *Body of Power, Spirit of Resistance: The Culture and History of a South African People*. Chicago: University of Chicago Press.

Connerton, P.
    1989 *How Societies Remember*. Cambridge, U.K.: Cambridge University Press.

Easlea, Brian
    1983 *Fathering the Unthinkable: Masculinity, Scientists and the Nuclear Arms Race*. London: Pluto Press.

Foster, Robert J.
    1991 Making national cultures in the global ecumene. *Annual Review of Anthropology* 20:235–60.

Foucault, Michel
    1991 Questions of method. In *The Foucault Effect: Studies in Governmentality*. Graham Burchell, Colin Gordon, and Peter Miller, eds. Pp. 73–86. Chicago: University of Chicago Press.
    1988 The political technology of individuals. In *Technologies of the Self: A Seminar with Michel Foucault*. Luther Martin, Huck Gutman, and Patrick Hutton, eds. Pp. 145–62. Amherst: University of Massachusetts Press.
    1979 [1975] *Discipline and Punish: The Birth of the Prison*. New York: Vintage.

Gordon, Colin
1991 Governmental rationality: An introduction. In *The Foucault Effect: Studies in Governmentality*. Graham Burchell, Colin Gordon, and Peter Miller, eds. Pp. 1–51. Chicago: University of Chicago Press.

Gosling, F.G., and Terrence R. Fehner
1994 Closing the Circle: The Department of Energy and Environmental Management 1942–1994 [Draft]. History Division, Executive Secretariat, Department of Energy, March.

Handler, Richard
1988 *Nationalism and the Politics of Culture in Quebec*. Madison: University of Wisconsin Press.

Haraway, Donna
1989 *Primate Visions: Gender, Race, and Nature in the World of Modern Science*. New York: Routledge.

Herzfeld, Michael
1995 Cultural intimacy: The social poetics of the nation state. Seminar in the Department of Anthropology, Baltimore: Johns Hopkins University, October 12.

Jackson, Michael
1983 Knowledge of the body. *Man* 18:327–45.

Keller, Evelyn Fox
1990 From secrets of life to secrets of death. In *Body/Politics: Women and the Discourses of Science*. Mary Jacobus, Evelyn Fox Keller, and Sally Shuttleworth, eds. Pp. 177–91. New York: Routledge.

Martin, Emily
1994 *Flexible Bodies: Tracking Immunity in American Culture From the Days of Polio to the Age of AIDS*. Boston: Beacon Press.
1991 The egg and the sperm: How science has constructed a romance based on stereotypical male-female roles. *Signs: Journal of Women in Culture and Society* 16(3):485–501.

Montgomery, David
1979 *Workers' Control in America: Studies in the History of Work, Technology and Labor Struggles*. Cambridge, U.K.: Cambridge University Press.

Noble, David
1984 *The Forces of Production: A Social History*. New York: Knopf.
1977 *America by Design: Science, Technology and the Rise of Corporate Capitalism*. New York: Oxford University Press.

Rabinbach, Anson
1986 The European science of work: The economy of the body at the end of the nineteenth century. In *Work in France: Representations, Meaning, Organization, and Practice*. S.L. Kaplan and C.J. Koepp, eds. Pp. 475–513. Ithaca, NY: Cornell University Press.

Reynolds, Peter C.
    1991 *Stealing Fire: The Atomic Bomb as Symbolic Body*. Palo Alto, CA: Iconic
        Anthropology Press.

Rhodes, Richard
    1986 *The Making of the Atomic Bomb*. New York: Simon and Schuster.

Scheper-Hughes, Nancy, and Margaret Lock
    1987 The mindful body: A prolegomenon to future work in medical anthropology.
        Medical Anthropology Quarterly 1(1):1–41.

Thompson, E.P.
    1967 Time, work-discipline and industrial capitalism. *Past and Present* 38:56–97.

Traweek, Sharon
    1988 *Beamtimes and Lifetimes: The World of High Energy Physicists*. Cambridge,
        MA: Harvard University Press.

Van Onselen, C.
    1976 *Chibaro: African Mine Labour in Southern Rhodesia, 1900–1933*. London:
        Pluto.

Williams, Brackette F.
    1989 A class act: Anthropology and the race to nation across ethnic terrain. *Annual
        Review of Anthropology* 18:401–44.

Chapter 3

Looking Beyond the Factory:
Regional Culture and Practices of Dissent

Mary K. Anglin

This essay draws upon field research with mica workers in southern Appalachia to offer a reading of factory life that extends beyond the notion of "work cultures" or a narrowly construed politics of production.[1] Research in a mica factory showed me that what happened on the shop floor was as much a reflection of local histories, community/kin relations, and regional tradition as it was a response to particular working conditions.

To describe that factory setting, in other words, required an expanded reading of culture that neither restricted culture to the interactions that occurred around production nor presented regional tradition as ahistorical and depoliticized. Instead, what is called for is an examination of power in the context of the community traditions that infused work relations and life outside the factory, in addition to looking at power through the lens of productive processes and company policy. These two dimensions of power, as I will argue, were neither separate nor static but together informed workers' and owners' understandings of waged labor.

The analysis of religion, more specifically evangelical Protestantism, offers a way to examine the intersection of these two sites of power. Near the mica factory were a number of Protestant churches, whose presence bespoke a calculus of status and power within the community. This essay focuses on one church in particular, Long Hill Baptist Church, which was attended by mica workers and other factory workers.

Activities at Long Hill serve to illustrate power relations within the church and the ways that recourse to religious belief was used as a means of dissent or "back-talk," both in relation to church hierarchy and factory work. However, as indicated by the story of a young man suddenly disabled by cancer, the church also represented a vital means of material, social, and emotional support to the working class community in which it was located.

The experiences of two women on the "Upper End," a department in the mica factory, offer examples of the ways workers negotiated factory work in conjunction with their intense involvement in the church. One of the women was a member of Long Hill; the other was an older woman whose mica work spanned several generations and whose religious involvement reflected the early history of evangelical Protestantism in this region. An important dimension of both women's stories is that they portray solitary, as well as social, dimensions of religious belief and dissent. Moreover, their stories help illustrate the limits of dissent from the vantage point of two women as co-workers from different generations.

I did not start this research with the intention of exploring the interconnection of churches, kin/community ties, and work in the mica factory. This emphasis developed as a result of conversations and participant observation in the factory, and the insistence of factory workers about what mattered to *them*. In other words, what happened within the context of that particular field situation was not so much an effort to abandon Marxist feminist analyses as recognition of the need to recover what was valuable from that literature in a setting that did not present itself as I had expected.

FACTORY LIFE AT MOTH HILL

I first met Hazel Roberts and Zona Watson when I began my fieldwork at Moth Hill Mica Company, a small (approximately fifty workers) factory that processed mica, a mineral found in abundance in the mountains of western North Carolina. Much could be said about mica as a mineral and an industry of economic importance to the region. Suffice it to say that mica has been used as a form of insulation in various military and "high tech" applications, but has been largely replaced by synthetic materials. Thus, the mica industry was in decline, and Moth Hill carried on in a scaled-down version of its former operations.

Moth Hill relied upon a skeleton crew of workers, as well as upon the principles of deskilling and speeding up productive processes well known in the textile industry and other factory settings. However, due to the irregularities of naturally occurring materials such as mica, mica processing cannot be fully mechanized. For this reason of technology—and for historical reasons—workers have retained some small degree of control over their labor processes. This dimension of productive relations must, of course, be measured against the generally negative forecast for the mica industry in general, and the specter of declining production at Moth Hill.

I met Zona and Hazel because they were part of the department in the factory with which I became allied, the Upper End. My initial reason for meeting Zona was that, as a woman in her mid-seventies, she was one of the older workers in the factory and someone who could tell me about the history of the place. Hazel befriended me as someone who was roughly her age and, perhaps more significant, quite obviously out of place. On my visits to the factory, I began to spend a large part of my time with Hazel, and Zona on the days when she was working.

What I found, and this is my awakening story, was that they—like other women at Moth Hill—were not so much interested in talking about factory life as in telling me about their families, their experiences growing up in the mountains, their churches. And while I struggled to keep Zona and Hazel "on track," my "track," they persisted in telling me about their lives.

At Moth Hill, Hazel and Zona worked with three other women in the Upper End, where sheets of laminated mica, or mica plate, were produced.[2] The women worked collaboratively when factory orders called for the production of a particular kind of plate, once the specialty of the company, but ordered and produced only sporadically during my tenure. This was a production process at which Zona was particularly skilled and for which she would be called in to work. In this way, Zona was able to maintain her health insurance, a critical issue for her as with many of the factory workers. Moth Hill was able to capitalize on an experienced worker who accepted erratic work assignments at minimum wage.[3]

At other times, the group of women would break into smaller teams and work separately at different processes and equipment. When orders for particular kinds of mica plate were "down," Hazel and her steady work partner, Frances Stokes, would be temporarily "laid off" along with Zona Watson. Gertie Russell and Annie Burleson, sisters in their mid- to late sixties, would then be left to keep production going on a much reduced scale. When all five women were at work, even if on different machinery, they would trade labor and assist each other in various ways. Moreover, they would come together at lunch time, and odd moments throughout the day, to talk or share food or exchange information about the status of orders and changes in departmental operations.

As Lamphere, Sacks, and others have termed it, the women of the Upper End could be said to form a work culture.[4] As is characteristic of the work cultures described by Zavella, Westwood, and others, the work culture of the Upper End was organized around the specifics of production, the alliances established between workers in that department, and the relationship of the Upper End to other departments within the factory vis-à-vis productive processes and worker networks.

Women on the Upper End shared the exigencies of production, albeit with differential vulnerability to the possibility of layoff, and "their under-standings and values about work and workplace social relations."[5] In other words, participation in work cultures made possible the sharing of resources, material and otherwise, and the creation of solidarity. However, as Lamphere has noted, it was a solidarity that could serve to foster complicity insofar as work cultures humanized the routines of factory life, or to foster dissent by means of contestatory notions of workplace relations articulated through such networks. In either event, through work cultures, workers created and engaged in their own variants of activism, grounded in the specifics of fac-tory/work life and the politics of gender and ethnicity. This is the contribution of the work culture literature: that it broadens the lens through which we examine the workplace and renders more complex and more *subtle* the ques-tion of dissent.

What I wish to consider here is the need to extend the analysis still fur-ther, in directions inspired by the proponents of the work cultures approach[6] as well as their critics.[7] What I propose is an investigation of the ways that constructions of ethnicity and regional culture inform the productive sphere, locating workers in networks that extended beyond factory walls and inscrib-ing traditions of understanding that spoke to the politics of production *and* to community life.

This is not to suggest that everyone in the factory participated in an overarching set of traditions,[8] nor in the same community-based networks, for workers at Moth Hill and on the Upper End disaggregated into different rural settlements, kin groups, class fractions, and patterns of daily living. Workers at Moth Hill articulated selective renderings of kinship, in part based on the political and economic location of constituent members of the kin group. Thus, I heard numerous references to people "who were kin but wouldn't claim it": articulations of difference inside the factory and beyond it.[9]

Indeed, workers at Moth Hill brought their settlements and kin ties *into* Moth Hill as a means of looking out for each other and framing activities on the shop floor. Thus, Annie Burleson interceded with management and was able to secure a job for her sister, once a Moth Hill employee and now retired from other work, so that Gertie could be her co-worker on the Upper End. No one in the factory doubted the importance of kin and community ties, although some workers—notably those without such connections—criticized some of the ends to which they were put. For their part, the owners at Moth Hill relied on kin and community ties in order to recruit new workers and dis-cipline current workers. Likewise, factory workers used familiarity with the managers and factory owners as Annie had in finding her sister a job, and also to make complaints about working conditions. As women on the Upper End noted repeatedly, one of the most positive aspects of working at Moth Hill was that it was "close home" (Anglin 1993a,b).

In working "close home," women brought not only kin but local church networks and various renderings of Protestant Christianity to Moth Hill. What Zona Watson, Hazel Roberts, and their colleagues on the Upper End taught me was that I could not understand their place within the mica company without first examining their participation in the traditions of evangelical Protestantism. If women on the Upper End engaged in their own forms of activism, it was an activism grounded in the language of their faith.[10] Moreover, the importance of religious belief served, in general terms, to counterbalance the claims of the workplace.

WORKING FOR GOD

I encountered the importance of Protestant Christianity directly upon my arrival at the factory. Having gained my entry through the factory owners, the Paynes, and on being introduced to women in the factory, I was asked two questions. The first was where did "my people" live? The second was what church did I belong to? Thus from the beginning, I had to deconstruct myself as a Virginian and a lapsed Episcopalian, further indication of the gulf that separated me from those I hoped would be my informants. However, the conversation did not end there. The women who asked me those questions went on to talk about their own experiences of being saved and to invite me to their churches.

I politely declined their invitations, as I have done with neighbors in western Carolina, for such invitations are both symbolic requests and the first step in inscribing oneself in a new network of obligations: becoming a member of the church. We talked about religion, about their churches and mine when I was growing up.

When I finally allied myself with one department, the Upper End, I started regularly attending Long Hill Baptist Church with Hazel Roberts and I visited the churches of Zona Watson and Frances Stokes.[11] A devout Christian, Gertie Russell engaged in her own private worship at home, as did Annie Burleson and, indeed, many women in western North Carolina.

All five women talked regularly with each other and with me about what their faith meant to them. All this I treated as part of the business of becoming part of the factory network: making myself more approachable, as well as learning about the background and traditions of the women on the Upper End. We talked about religious doctrine, moving delicately around the differences between the Pentecostalism of Frances's church and the Missionary Baptist churches with which Zona and Hazel identified. With greater directness, we discussed the class location of other churches: the Methodist church referred to as "the Payne Family religion," since it was established by the founder of Moth Hill, and the Presbyterian church attended by doctors, lawyers, and the other elite family in the area.[12]

Two months into my fieldwork at the mica factory, I started accompanying Hazel to Long Hill Baptist Church. Established right after the Civil War, Long Hill was the oldest church in the settlement. It had housed the local grade school in Zona's day. The community cemetery was still maintained by Long Hill Baptist Church, and was located next to the church buildings.

In the first several months of my attendance at Long Hill, I was invariably singled out by the deacons and the preacher in their morning greetings to the congregation. Welcoming the visitors there that morning, they invited us to "be at home" in the church. As Deacon Lonnie put it, *making* oneself "sounds like work" but *being at home* meant knowing you were where you belonged.

After the morning greetings, we went to the Sunday School class for "older women," all of whom were a good two decades older than Hazel but were closer to her spiritually than her own cohort of women in their twenties and thirties. Each week, Etta led the Sunday School class, with Hazel as assistant Sunday School teacher. Etta followed a printed Sunday School guide, which outlined passages from the Bible and the lesson for each week, but invariably the lessons broached issues closer to the particular group assembled.

Thus, we heard Etta's commentary on preachers like Jimmy Swaggart and Jim Bakker who overstepped the limits of their authority. In a barely veiled critique of Long Hill's pastor, to which members of the class assented, Etta challenged the claims of such men of "having been called by God." Without the backing of the church, preachers would have nowhere to proclaim God's word, but "the church would still go on" without a preacher.

Etta also disagreed with the notion that women should submit to the authority of their husbands. As she figured it, women might be physically weaker than men but they were equally deserving of respect. In a setting where they were accorded respect, women talked about their daily lives: the jobs they held and the shifts they were forced to work, their families, and the importance of the Lord.

The theme for many Sunday School conversations was that, regardless of what others might think, God was in control. To quote Sister Louise, an elder in the class, "There's the righteous and the rest of the world running wild with sin." The subtext to this statement, discussed at length on at least one occasion, was that not only was God a comfort to the righteous but God would avenge the wrongs done to them. What the righteous were to do was testify to their faith—to co-workers, friends, and family. They might not eradicate the sins of the world, but they could make a stand.[13]

These themes were echoed in the daily regimens of the Upper End.

Hazel kept religious memorabilia near the plate-making machine she frequently tended with Frances. These, along with signs of unknown authorship declaring "on strike" and "this machine runs at a hundred miles an hour," were there for passersby to see. In addition to discussing religious belief and church events with her colleagues, Hazel sought out those in the factory she knew were not saved. To these she spoke about the power of God, and encouraged them to go to church. As Hazel had noted in one Sunday School conversation:

> The Devil knows that when you're at home, you're just around your family. But when you're on a job you have the chance to witness to a lot of people so he makes it hard for you. [The Devil] gives you all sorts of excuses about being tired, having too much to do, because he knows you're working for God.

In this spirit, Hazel and Frances took it upon themselves to educate me about evangelical Protestantism. For Valentine's Day, they gave me a King James version of the Bible to take to church—a symbol of their efforts at conversion and my ignorance of Baptist traditions.

Hazel also sought the advice of Zona, whom she referred to as her "second mama," and the advice of Gertie, whom Hazel likened to her mother as well as herself for having old-fashioned ways and deep-seated religious convictions. Because they were kin in ways that mattered, Hazel could go to Zona and Gertie for counsel on family matters, problems with male co-workers, or concerns about getting laid off. By the same token, she helped them all she could since, as Hazel stated in the prayer she gave one morning in Sunday school, "the stuff we do for others is part of our faith."

While Hazel helped me better understand the activist traditions of fundamentalist Christianity, it was Zona who taught me about spirituality through stories about her mother and her own life. Raised in the tradition of circuit-riding ministers, Zona and her siblings would be hauled off by their zealous father to the Presbyterian Church for Sunday school and then "to whichever church was having the preaching." Her mother—a Baptist—would stay behind to tend the farm and cook "a good Sunday dinner" for her children and the friends they invariably brought home with them. Although she might have been churning butter while her family was listening to the preacher, Zona's mother was a devout woman who read the Bible daily and taught her children her religious beliefs.

Zona, once married, joined the Baptist Church in her settlement because it was a little church and "she felt needed" there. As with Hazel, she had held an office in the church and taught Sunday school for many years. Now widowed and in frail health, Zona went to church on those infrequent occasions when she could get a ride with her children but, like her mother, always read her Bible and made a big Sunday dinner.

When she first started talking to me, I heard Zona's stories as background, as biographical context for the information I sought from her. I wanted to know more about how Zona saw things in the factory and the history of her involvement in mica work. Zona was happy to talk with me about how she got started at Moth Hill and the other work she and her husband had done, but she quietly persisted in talking to me about her faith. That was the bedrock of her life, come what may.

It took me a long time, but I finally heard Zona's point. She was not trying to convert me or to witness; she was telling me about her life. Once I really thought about what Zona had said, it made me reconsider the discussions we had had at Moth Hill. Some of the conversations were avowedly political in trying to size up the loyalties of various constituencies within the factory, including myself. Other times, Zona and Gertie, in particular, would simply talk about what mattered to them and bring that broader context into the atmosphere of the Upper End.

THE TRIBULATIONS OF PARNELL

Participating in the life of the church had important consequences in the lives of working class men and women, however, as illustrated by the experience of Parnell Hayes. A contemporary of Hazel Roberts, Parnell was also deacon of Long Hill Baptist Church. He sat on the pew with Hazel, her brother, myself, and two other Moth Hill employees. One Sunday, Parnell failed to come to church and we later heard that he had had ten seizures over the course of the day.

Parnell had been taken to the hospital, where he was diagnosed with lung cancer, which had already spread to his brain. The doctors removed the brain tumor and told him that his chances for survival were poor. On hearing this news the following Sunday, the congregation responded by voting to help pay his hospital bills and ongoing medical treatment, and by visiting Parnell and praying for him.

No one expected it when Parnell returned to church just two weeks after his initial hospitalization. Parnell had changed dramatically. He walked unsteadily, aided by a cane, and he was completely bald due to surgery and subsequent radiation treatments. While Parnell had always been a slender man, now he was almost skeletal. He had become an old man, almost overnight.

Weakened physical condition notwithstanding, Parnell moved with great determination. He stood beside the preacher and his fellow deacons to welcome the churchgoers. When it came time for the service, Parnell sat alone in the very front, instead of in his customary place in the back pew with us.

Parnell asked for the opportunity to come before the church to explain what had happened. He spoke with great emotion. He interpreted his life-threatening illness in theological terms, lamenting his condition as a disabled worker while affirming his connection with the church. Parnell thanked everyone for their prayers and the money they had voted him. He said that he did not want to hurt the financial standing of the church, however. He asked to take over the responsibilities of janitor and ground keeper for the church since he could not hold a job any longer. It was this last which had hurt him the most, he told us, because he was used to working fourteen- and sixteen-hour days. It had been his life. (To this, the congregation assented while acknowledging, through murmured conversations and pained expressions, the futility of the request.)

Parnell planned to use the days left him to *testify* to visitors at home and in the hospital. He understood his illness to be a punishment from God for the sins of his kin, who would not attend church even after he had been made deacon. Rather than anger, Parnell witnessed to the power of his faith as he told us he was ready to die "if that be the Lord's will." "You-uns are my brothers and sisters," he told the church. This was his family; this was where he had come home.

Once Parnell had finished, he sat down. The preacher came forth to say that there was no time for a sermon and, anyway, Parnell had preached a better sermon than he could. When the service was over, at Parnell's request, we all assembled for a church photograph. This was an important reminder of his homecoming, of the support that sustained him despite the failings of his blood kin.

TESTIFYING AND TALKING BACK

At Moth Hill Mica Company, factory workers faced crises which, if at times less extreme than Parnell's battle with cancer, also spoke to the instability of the present.[14] Like Parnell, they were forced to contend with an imperfect world where the sinners prospered and wielded undue power. They talked of the better world that lay ahead, and drew upon their religion to affirm the integrity of their own lives as measured against those who were wealthier but none the better for it.

They also called upon the tradition of testifying to articulate their concerns as individuals. In churches and in the mica factory, women invoked a language of defiance or "back talk," to depict gender relations and to assert their own authority.[15] In both settings, women did ostensibly defer to those in charge, be they plant managers or deacons. At the same time, women engaged in acts of resistance, quietly carving out their own domains within these larger hierarchies.

While such actions did not dismantle gender-based hierarchies, the force of women's dissent was evidenced not only by the dismissal of the over authoritarian pastor at Long Hill but equally through women's activities in the mica factory. They slowed down and stopped work through myriad means: refusing job assignments, performing hand labor slowly, leaving their machines to take unscheduled breaks. Women censured male co-workers when they attempted to transgress the boundaries of gender segregation by associating with women who were not kin and did not want their attention, and when the men engaged in behavior considered abusive by their female co-workers. In one instance, when I was the subject of teasing by a male worker who ran a production process in another department, Hazel interceded on my behalf by rebuking him publicly while Moth Hill employees were punching out at the end of the day. The next morning, the man came red-faced to apologize to me for his comments and for overstepping the bounds.

Women in the factory confronted managers and supervisors directly over their need for job security despite the unpredictability of production orders and for some measure of autonomy within their performance of production processes. That these actions made a difference was indicated by the fact that supervisors left women alone to do their work and, on occasion to refuse specific work assignments, as well as by the efforts of the supervisor on the Upper End to keep women employed making "stock" when there were no production orders. There were no obvious results from Frances Stokes's confrontation with one of the managers about the health problems caused by the high levels of mica dust and lacquer fumes to which workers were exposed. Nonetheless, in testifying to the manager—and grandson of the factory founder—Frances notified the owners that workers disagreed with their definition as to what constituted the necessities of production and what was a health hazard.

Fundamentalist Christianity fueled righteous indignation and formed the basis for comraderie among workers in the factory. At the same time, that sense of comraderie consolidated and collapsed along the lines of kin and church affiliation, and ultimately the class fractions with which the mica workers identified. A major effect of this tendency toward fractionalization was that gender-based concerns were not always given full recognition among women in the factory, as was the case in Sacks's study of workers at Duke Medical Center.[16] This was especially true with respect to relations *between* women of different departments, whose loyalties were determined in the first instance by departmental allegiances and production politics. These restrictions notwithstanding, women in the factory relied upon networks of female solidarity and support as a means of dealing with the vicissitudes of the mica industry and their employment at Moth Hill.

Thus, to recast this discussion in the terms of workplace resistance, the women of Moth Hill Mica Company did not embrace the militance of union organizing but neither were they complacent and passive about factory conditions. Instead, they drew upon kin groups and the traditions of the region to express their opposition to particular factory policies; to humanize the daily regimens of the factory through contact with kin located in and outside the factory, as well as through connection with co-workers who were "like family"; to fight to have owners and supervisors recognize their obligations to factory workers; and to testify to their belief in a better world. In place of strikes and formal protest, judged to be of little use, given the weakened state of the mica industry, Moth Hill workers engaged in a "routine struggle for bread and roses."[17] They fought to maintain control over the conditions of their labor, despite problematic economic times, and for respect.

But the importance of religion extended beyond the issue of activism within the factory. In my weekly meetings with the members of Long Hill Baptist Church, I learned the importance of church as "home." Both the testimony offered each week in Sunday school and Parnell's remarks before the church presented powerful evidence as to how religious belief and community networks combined in the lives of the congregation. It would be an injustice to the women I knew from the factory to see them simply as factory workers, or to understand their participation in fundamentalist Christianity only in relation to work cultures or resistance.

"Being at home" in the church, the phrase used in place of "making oneself at home," meant first and foremost being sustained by one's faith. It also meant dealing with one's circumstances, secure in the knowledge that you were supported by friends, family, and the church. Amid the consequences of economic restructuring and a class structure whose informality meant that political dealings and class differences were expressed on personal terms, "being at home" was not a simple matter. As I learned from women in the factory and at church, however, these were challenges they routinely met.

In closing, I want to note that I have not come to bury Marx in Foucauldian analysis. That exercise would hardly be possible since for Foucault, "Marx does not exist."[18] If the writings of Marx and Marxist feminists are rendered passé in some circles, they are for me seriously challenged by the post-structuralist critique to engage the concept of culture in three-dimensional form.[19] That is to say, it is clearly *not* sufficient to speak simply in terms of class or the relationship of capital to labor. However, it is equally untenable to discard these concepts for an interpretation of cultures as polymorphous texts that are ultimately undecipherable.

Nowhere is the need for a politicized, problematized reading of culture more evident than in Appalachia, eulogized by folklorists and anthropologists as "the land where time stood still." Freed from the press of history, Appalachia in this dominant interpretation is also devoid of any traces of class or gender or race. And I find no room there for the life stories of Parnell Hayes, Hazel Roberts, or Zona Watson—and their compatriots on the Upper End.

ACKNOWLEDGEMENTS

I would like to thank Ann Kingsolver, and the anonymous reviewers, for their helpful comments on a previous draft of this essay. This research was funded, in part, through an Appalachian Studies Fellowship from Berea College, a James Still Fellowship from the University of Kentucky, and a National Women's Studies Association/Pergamon Press Scholarship in Women's Studies.

NOTES

1. See Anglin (1990), especially pages 198–225 from which this analysis is derived in large part. All proper names listed here are pseudonyms to protect the confidentiality of my informants.

2. There were male workers on the Upper End as well. Their number varied from three to five, depending on production orders and the needs of the company, as well as a male supervisor who oversaw the operations of the department. Insofar as the men on the Upper End did not work jointly with the women, nor often among themselves, I do not discuss them here. However, the men of the Upper End exerted their influence, through interactions with their female colleagues and the gender differential, which underwrote Moth Hill employment policies (see Anglin 1993a).

3. Female factory operatives were routinely paid the state minimum wage, $3.35 per hour in 1987. On some productive processes, to which they were occasionally assigned, women were paid an additional $.10 per hour. All men were paid a base pay of $3.45 per hour, on top of which workers on specific productive processes might receive an additional $.10 or $3.55 per hour. Male supervisors received an additional $.20 or $3.65 per hour. I am not sure what wages the sole female supervisor received.

4. See Anglin (1990, 1991, 1993a), Benson (1978), Sacks (1988), Sacks and Remy (1984), Lamphere (1985, 1987), Zavella (1987), Westwood (1985), Terborg Penn (1985), Shapiro-Perl (1984).

5. Sacks (1988), p. 70.

6. See for example Lamphere et al. (1993), Sacks (1989a,b), and Zavella (1991).

7. For the critique offered by historians, who argued against an essentialized, ahistorical woman worker, see Baron (1991), Blewett (1988), Reverby and Helly (1992), and Scott (1990). See also Anglin (1993a) and Kondo (1990) for commentary and criticism from the standpoint of anthropology.

8. It is important to note that an understanding of culture as partial, emergent, contested, and influential derives from the insights of critical and feminist anthropologies—see, for example, Diamond (1974), di Leonardo (1991), Etienne and Leacock (1980); Gailey (1987), Nash (1979), Roseberry (1989), Schneider and Rapp (1995), Taussig (1980), Wolf (1982), Yanigasako and Delaney (1995)—as well as from the contributions of interpretive anthropology. See Behar (1993), Clifford and Marcus (1986), Limón (1994), Rosaldo (1989).

9. See Anglin (1991). In the instance of Moth Hill, at least, women moved between lines of difference and shared experience to confront institutional structures they found oppressive. See Gregg (1993) and Smith (1995) on the implications of differences in ethnicity, race, class, gender, and life experience for coalitional politics and labor activism.

10. See Ginsburg (1989:59) for a similar reading of activism, as grounded in "people's experiences of self, gender, family, community, and culture in a specific setting," albeit in the context of the politics surrounding reproductive rights.

11. I visited those churches with Hazel, in accordance with the tradition of circuit-riding preachers and church singings, where people from one church would "fellowship" with their neighbors: coming together in one location to hear the preacher or to trade hymns.

12. There was no Episcopal Church in the community and, while the exotica of Episcopalian ritual was subject for discussion when Hazel and I visited another factory department, for the most part we left my religious upbringing out of the conversation.

13. The idea of making a spiritual stand was an important theme in the year-long strike of union coal miners in southwest Virginia against the Pittston Coal Company in 1990. Striking miners sang hymns on the picket lines and erected prayer tents to keep their spirits strong and their strike nonviolent despite flagrant abuses by the Virginia state troopers called in to help the company and the company officials themselves. A year into the strike, then Secretary of Labor Elizabeth Dole forced Pittston to bargain with the union, and much was lost as well as gained in those negotiations. The miners, however, had upheld their union and their way of life against Pittston executives who openly ridiculed them. See Couto (1993), Sessions and Ansley (1993), and Anglin (1995).

14. Life-threatening illness and the loss of spouses were also significant themes on the Upper End.

15. See Kathleen C. Stewart (1990) for her development of this term. While I agree with Scott's (1994) notion of contradictory tensions between gender, class, and community in religious discourse, I disagree with her devaluation of the role of women in Pentecostal and evangelical Protestant churches. As I learned in attending church over the course of seven months and in talking with women in the factory, the situation in western North Carolina at least was much more complex than Scott's image of gender relations in eastern Kentucky where women left the church to take on jobs and "modern" lives.

16. See Sacks (1988). In this respect I agree with Friedman (1985) when she argues that the overlapping structures of churches, kin, and communities mitigated against gender-based solidarity.

17. This reworking of the famous slogan comes from Shapiro-Perl (1984). Her usage of the phrase is reflective of the emphasis on the daily, informal strategies used by workers to contest their exploitation, in contrast to the extraordinary dynamics of strikes and militant struggles.

18. Foucault (1980), p. 76.

19. See especially Haraway (1988), Hawkesworth (1989), Poovey (1988), Rabine (1988), and Scott (1990) for their perspectives on poststructuralist interpretations and their implications for feminist analyses. Where Poovey and Rabine are openly critical of poststructuralism as apolitical at best, Haraway and Scott argue that poststructuralism presents a more complicated reading of texts and sensibilities from which feminist theorists could well benefit. Butler (1993), Diamond and Quinby (1988), Nicholson (1990), and Sawicki (1994) more specifically examine Foucauldian analyses and their convergences with the concerns of feminist scholars/activists.

REFERENCES CITED

Anderson, Perry
1976–77 The antinomies of Antonio Gramsci. *New Left Review* 100:5–78.

Anglin, Mary K.
1995 Ministering to the working class: Evangelical Protestantism in rural America. In *Religion in the Contemporary South: Diversity, Community, and Identity*, O. Kendall White, Jr. and Daryl White, eds. pp. 97–105. Athens: University of Georgia Press.
1993a Strategic differences: Gendered labor in southern Appalachia. *Frontiers: A Journal of Women Studies* 14:68–86.
1993b Engendering the struggle: Women's labor and traditions of resistance in rural southern Appalachia. In *Fighting Back in Appalachia: Traditions of Resistance and Change*. Stephen L. Fisher, ed. pp. 263–81. Philadelphia: Temple University Press.
1991 The dialectics of kinship. In *Southern Women: The Intersection of Race, Class, and Gender*. Working Paper Series, Center for Research on Women, Memphis State University/Duke University/University of North Carolina at Chapel Hill, Working Paper No. 4.
1990 "'A Lost and Dying World': Women's Labor in the Mica Industry of Southern Appalachia." Dissertation. NY: The New School for Social Research.

Baron, Ava, ed.
1991 *Work Engendered: Toward a New History of American Labor*. Ithaca, NY: Cornell University Press.

Behar, Ruth
   1993 *Translated Woman: Crossing the Borders with Esperanza's Story*. Boston: Beacon Press.

Benson, Susan Porter
   1978 The clerking sisterhood: Rationalization and the work culture of saleswomen. *Radical America* 12:41–55.

Billings, Dwight B.
   1990 Religion as opposition: A Gramscian analysis. *American Journal of Sociology* 96:1–31.

Billings, Dwight B., and Robert Goldman
   1983 Religion and class consciousness in the Kanawha County school textbook controversy. In *Appalachia and America: Autonomy and Regional Dependence*. Allen Batteau, ed. Lexington: University Press of Kentucky.

Blewett, Mary
   1988 *Men, Women, Work and Gender: Class, Gender and Protest in the New England Shoe Industry*. Urbana: University of Illinois Press.

Burawoy, Michael
   1985 *The Politics of Production: Factory Regimes Under Capitalism and Socialism*. London: Verso.

Butler, Judith
   1993 *Bodies that Matter: On the Discursive Limits of "Sex."* New York: Routledge.

Clifford, James, and George Marcus, eds.
   1986 *Writing Culture: The Poetics and Politics of Ethnography*. Berkeley: University of California Press.

Corbin, David Alan
   1981 *Life, Work, and Rebellion in the Coal Fields: The Southern West Virginia Miners, 1880–1922*. Urbana: University of Illinois Press.

Couto, Richard A.
   1993 The memory of miners and the conscience of capital: Coal miners' strikes as free spaces. In *Fighting Back in Appalachia: Traditions of Resistance and Change*. Stephen L. Fisher, ed. pp. 165–94. Philadelphia: Temple University Press.

Diamond, Irene, and Lee Quinby, eds.
   1988 *Feminism and Foucault: Reflections on Resistance*. Boston: Northeastern University Press.

Diamond, Stanley
   1974 *In Search of the Primitive: A Critique of Civilization*. New Brunswick, NJ: Transaction Books.

di Leonardo, Micaela, ed.
   1991 *Gender at the Crossroads of Knowledge: Feminist Anthropology in the Postmodern Era*. Berkeley: University of California Press.

Etienne, Mona, and Eleanor Burke Leacock, eds.
1980 *Women and Colonization: Anthropological Perspectives.* Brooklyn, NY: J.F. Bergin/Praeger.

Fernández-Kelly, María Patricia
1983 *For We Are Sold, I and My People: Women and Industry in Mexico's Frontier.* Albany: State University of New York Press.

Foucault, Michel
1980 *Power/Knowledge: Selected Interviews and Other Writings, 1972–1977.* New York: Pantheon.
1975 *Discipline and Punish.* London: Verso.

Frankel, Linda
1984 Southern Textile Women: Generations of Survival and Struggle. In *My Troubles Are Going To Have Trouble With Me: Everyday Trials and Triumphs of Women Workers.* Karen Brodkin Sacks and Dorothy Remy, eds. New Brunswick, N.J.: Rutgers University Press.

Frederickson, Mary
1985 "I know which side I'm on": Southern women in the labor movement in the twentieth century. In *Women, Work and Protest: A Century of U.S. Women's Labor History.* Ruth Milkman, ed. Boston: Routledge and Kegan Paul.

Friedman, Jean E.
1985 *The Enclosed Garden: Women and Community in the Evangelical South, 1830–1900.* Chapel Hill: University of North Carolina Press.

Gailey, Christine Ward
1987 Culture wars: Resistance to state formation. In *Power Relations and State Formation.* Thomas C. Patterson and Christine W. Gailey, eds. Washington, D.C.: American Anthropological Association.

Gaventa, John
1980 *Power and Powerlessness: Quiescence and Rebellion in an Appalachian Valley.* Urbana: University of Illinois Press.

Genovese, Eugene
1974 *Roll, Jordan, Roll: The World the Slaves Made.* New York: Random House.

Ginsburg, Faye
1989 Dissonance and harmony: The symbolic function of abortion in activists' life stories. In *Interpreting Women's Lives: Feminist Theory and Personal Narratives.* Personal Narratives Group, ed. pp. 59–84. Bloomington: University of Indiana Press.

Gramsci, Antonio
1971 *Selections from the Prison Notebooks.* Quintin Hoare and Geoffrey N. Smith, eds. and translation. New York: International Publishers.

Gregg, Nina
1993 "Trying to put first things first": Negotiating subjectivities in a workplace organizing campaign. In *Negotiating at the Margins: The Gendered Discourses of Power and Resistance.* Sue Fisher and Kathy Davis, eds. pp. 172–204. New Brunswick, N.J.: Rutgers University Press.

Gutman, Herbert
1976 *Work, Culture, and Society In Industrializing America.* New York: Vintage.

Hall, Jacqueline Dowd
1986 Disorderly women: Gender and labor militancy in the Appalachian South. *Journal of American History* 73: 354–382.

Haraway, Donna
1988 Situated knowledges: The science question in feminism and the privilege of partial perspective. *Feminist Studies* 14:575–99.

Hawkesworth, Mary E.
1989 Knowers, knowing, known: Feminist theory and claims of truth. *Signs* 14:533–57.

Kingsolver, Ann E.
1992 Tobacco, textiles, and Toyota: Working for multinational corporations in rural Kentucky. In *Anthropology and the Global Factory: Studies of the New Industrialization in the Late Twentieth Century.* Frances A. Rothstein and Michael L. Blim, eds. pp. 191–205. New York: Bergin and Garvey.

Kondo, Dorinne K.
1990 *Crafting Selves: Power, Gender, and Discourses of Identity in a Japanese Workplace.* Chicago: University of Chicago Press.

Korson, George
1943 *Coal Dust on the Fiddle: Songs and Stories of the Bituminous Coal Industry.* Philadelphia: University of Pennsylvania Press.

Lamphere, Louise
1987 *From Working Daughters to Working Mothers: Immigrant Women in a New England Industrial Community.* Ithaca: Cornell University Press.
1985 Bringing the family to work: Women's culture on the shop floor. *Feminist Studies* 11:519–40.

Lamphere, Louise, Patricia Zavella, Felipe Gonzales, and Peter Evans
1993 *Sunbelt Working Mothers: Reconciling Family and Factory.* Ithaca, NY: Cornell University Press.

Lewis, Helen M., Sue Kobak, and Linda Johnson
1978 Family, religion, and colonialism in central Appalachia. In *Colonialism in Modern America: The Appalachian Case.* Helen M. Lewis, Linda Johnson, and Don Askins, eds. Boone, N.C.: Appalachian Consortium Press.

Limón, José E.
1994 *Dancing with the Devil: Society and Cultural Poetics in Mexican-American South Texas*. Madison: University of Wisconsin Press.

McDonnell, Lawrence T.
1984 "You are too sentimental": Problems and suggestions for a new labor history. *Journal of Social History* 17:629–54.

Murphy, Marjorie
1987 Work, protest, and culture: New work on working women's history (a review essay). *Feminist Studies* 13:657–67.

Nash, June
1983 The impact of the changing international division of labor on different sectors of the labor force. In *Women, Men, and the International Division of Labor*. June Nash and María Patricia Fernández-Kelly, eds. pp. 3–38. Albany: State University of New York Press.
1979 *We Eat the Mines and the Mines Eat Us: Dependency and Exploitation in Bolivian Tin Mines*. New York: Columbia University Press.

Nicholson, Linda J., ed.
1990 *Feminism/Postmodernism*. New York: Routledge.

Ong, Aihwa
1987 *Spirits of Resistance and Capitalist Discipline: Factory Women in Malaysia*. Albany: State University of New York Press.

Poovey, Mary
1988 Feminism and deconstruction. *Feminist Studies* 14:51–65.

Rabine, Leslie Wahl
1988 A feminist politics of non-identity. *Feminist Studies* 14:11–31.

Reverby, Susan M., and Dorothy O. Helly
1992 Introduction: converging on history. In *Gendered Domains: Rethinking Public and Private in Women's History*. Dorothy O. Helly and Susan M. Reverby, eds. pp. 1–26. Ithaca, NY: Cornell University Press.

Rich, Mark
1951 *Some Churches in Coal Mining Communities of West Virginia*. Charleston: West Virginia Council of Churches.

Rosaldo, Renato
1989 *Culture and Truth: The Remaking of Social Analysis*. Boston: Beacon Press.

Roseberry, William
1989 *Anthropologies and Histories: Essays in Culture, History, and Political Economy*. New Brunswick, N.J.: Rutgers University Press.

Sacks, Karen Brodkin
1989a Toward a unified theory of class, race, and gender. *American Ethnologist* 16:534–50.

1989b What's a life story got to do with it? In *Interpreting Women's Lives: Feminist Theory and Personal Narratives*. Personal Narratives Group, ed. pp. 85–95. Bloomington: University of Indiana Press.

1988 *Caring by the Hour: Women, Work, and Organizing at Duke Medical Center*. Urbana: University of Illinois Press.

Sacks, Karen Brodkin, and Dorothy Remy, eds.

1984 *My Troubles Are Going to Have Trouble with Me: Everyday Trials and Triumphs of Women Workers*. New Brunswick, NJ: Rutgers University Press.

Sawicki, Jana

1994 Foucault, feminism, and questions of identity. In *The Cambridge Companion to Foucault*. Gary Gutting, ed. pp. 286–313. Cambridge, U.K.: Cambridge University Press.

Schneider, Jane, and Rayna Rapp, eds.

1995 *Articulating Hidden Histories: Exploring the Influence of Eric R. Wolf*. Berkeley: University of California Press.

Scott, Joan W.

1990 Deconstructing equality-versus-difference: Or, the uses of poststructuralist theory for feminism. In *Conflicts in Feminism*. Marianne Hirsch and Evelyn Fox Keller, eds. pp. 134–48. New York: Routledge.

Scott, Shauna L.

1994 "They don't have to live by the old traditions": Saintly men, sinner women, and an Appalachian Pentecostal revival. *American Ethnologist* 21:227–44.

Sen, Gita

1980 The sexual division of labor and the working-class family: Towards a conceptual synthesis of class relations and the subordination of women. *The Review of Radical Political Economics* 12:76–86.

Sessions, Jim, and Fran Ansley

1993 Singing across dark spaces: The union/community takeover of Pittston's Moss 3 plant. In *Fighting Back in Appalachia: Traditions of Resistance and Change*. Stephen L. Fisher, ed. pp. 195–223. Philadelphia: Temple University Press.

Shapiro-Perl, Nina

1984 Resistance strategies: The routine struggle for bread and roses. In *My Troubles Are Going To Have Trouble With Me: Everyday Trials and Triumphs of Women Workers*. Karen Brodkin Sacks and Dorothy Remy, eds. pp. 193–208. New Brunswick, N.J.: Rutgers University Press.

Smith, Barbara Ellen

1995 Crossing the great divides: Race, class, and gender in Southern women's organizing, 1979–1991. *Gender and Society* 9(1995):680–96.

Stewart, Kathleen Claire
   1990 Backtalking the wilderness: "Appalachian" en-genderings. In *Uncertain Terms: The Negotiation of Gender in American Culture*. Faye Ginsburg and Anna Tsing, eds. pp. 43–56. Boston: Beacon Press.

Taussig, Michael
   1980 *The Devil and Commodity Fetishism in South America*. Chapel Hill: University of North Carolina Press.

Terborg Penn, Rosalyn
   1985 Survival strategies among African-American women: A continuing process. In *Women, Work, and Protest: A Century of U.S. Women's Labor History*. Ruth Milkman, ed. pp. 139–55. Boston: Routledge and Kegan Paul.

Thompson, E.P.
   1963 *The Making of the English Working Class*. New York: Vintage.

Tullos, Allen
   1989 Cultural politics and political culture in Appalachia. *Radical History Review* 45:181–86.

Westwood, Sallie
   1985 *All Day, Every Day: Factory and Family in the Making of Women's Lives*. Urbana: University of Illinois Press.

White, Caroline
   1989 Why do workers bother? Paradoxes of resistance in two English factories. *Critique of Anthropology* 7:51–68.

Williams, Raymond
   1977 *Marxism and Literature*. Oxford: Oxford University Press.

Wolf, Eric
   1982 *Europe and the People Without History*. Berkeley: University of California Press.

Yanigasako, Sylvia, and Carol Delaney, eds.
   1995 *Naturalizing Power: Essays in Feminist Cultural Analysis*. New York: Routledge.

Zavella, Patricia
   1991 *Mujeres* in factories: Race and class perspectives on women, work, and family. In *Gender at the Crossroads of Knowledge: Feminist Anthropology in the Postmodern Era*. Micaela di Leonardo, ed. pp. 312–36. Berkeley: University of California Press.
   1987 *Women's Work and Chicano Families: Cannery Workers of the Santa Clara Valley*. Ithaca: Cornell University Press.

Chapter 4

The Community as Worksite:
American Indian Women's Artistic Production

Tressa L. Berman

INTRODUCTION

In the circulation of American Indian arts, art works have generally been approached from the standpoints of production and consumption (see Mullin 1995). As outside markets move into venues of popular arts, the ways in which production and consumption implicate each other through productive sites of artistic proliferation have been shown to be a response to the expansion of capital (García Canclini 1993), and a necessary component of the informal economy (Nash 1993). Where Native American[1] artists make art objects both for their own consumption and for the market, webs of social relationships are forged that both reenforce and reshape power dynamics. These "webworks" of social relations inform what Bourdieu outlines as the "secondary properties" of class and power that occupy particular social spaces:

> This means that a class or class fraction is defined not only by its position in the relations of production, as identified through indices such as occupation, income or even educational level, but also by a certain sex-ratio, *a certain distribution in geographical space* . . . and by a whole set of subsidiary characteristics. (Bourdieu 1984: 102, italics mine)

If, as this volume suggests, "it takes more than class" to link the labor process to its product, we need to account for the ways that social relations create new social spaces (see Massey 1994). As Kingsolver notes in the introduction to this volume, using binary categories for understanding class structures in

workplaces can limit our understandings of the complexities of class posi-
tioning vis-à-vis both shifting venues of production and shifting roles within
matrices of power relations (Kondo 1990). In the world of American Indian
art and artistic production, these issues have gained a renewed saliency as
artistic images and objects become appropriated as the last vestiges of cultural
capital and identity (hooks 1995; Fusco 1995).

I consider how the effects of capitalism on artistic production and the
class-based demands created by art markets have resulted in new strategies
created by American Indian women to bridge market demands with social and
ceremonial life. By conceptualizing the *community as worksite*, I emphasize
relations of production as the "social arrangements that direct the forces of
production and allocate its output on *and beyond* the shop floor" (McCarl
1992:69, emphasis mine). I analyze shifts from kin-based ceremonial production to individual production for the market within the framework of what I
call *ceremonial relations of production* by looking at two forms of American
Indian women's artistic production, Hidatsa quillwork and Lakota quilt making. Quillwork, an indigenous ceremonial art contrasts with quilt making, an
introduced art form that incorporates utilitarian and ceremonial values.[2]

I consider the production of quilled and quilted items in several ways.
First, I show that capitalism has had contradictory effects on women's arts,
characterized by both decline and revitalization. This is demonstrated by
American Indian women's incorporation into commodity production at local
village (i.e., reservation) and world market levels where the community
remains the locus for productive activity (Etienne and Leacock 1983; Albers
1983). Ceremonial relations of production combine forms of market and non-
market activities in order to meet ceremonial commitments. Conversely, ceremonial forms of production have in some cases been taken out of ceremonial
contexts for market consumption. In these ways, ceremonial relations of production are distinct from, yet intersect with, social relations required for participation in wage labor. Finally, ceremonial forms of production and
exchange can be interpreted as symbolic acts of everyday resistance that reinforce cultural identity (Scott 1990; Caulfield 1974; Clemmer 1974).

The idea of symbolic capital of artistic and political identity can be
examined by focusing on the location of production—that is, the household,
the community hall. I address these points by analyzing American Indian
women's work activities in milieux that have been reified as peripheral to discussions of U.S. work*places*: "private" (woman-controlled) and artistic. In
both cases, I build on recent research in the anthropology of work that shows
how artistic expression serves as both a conduit and a mechanism for workers' collective resistance to unequal power relations (Calagione and Nugent
1992). Challenges to conventionally held models of power relations require a
view of the workplace beyond the shop floor, and "beyond the misidentifica-

tion of the 'informal sector' as only a product of, rather than a response to, the expansion of capitalism" (Calagione 1992:9; see Sassen 1991).

By reconceptualizing "the community as worksite," I consider "site" as not just a localized space, "but a set of social surroundings, social boundaries, and patterns of communit[y]" (Garrell 1992) that reenforce cultural identity through the social relations that give work its meanings. It is within the frame of the reservation community at large that Hidatsa and Lakota women link household and market relations by embuing the latter with kinship values that resist (and often supercede) profit-driven work incentives. Looking at the community as worksite helps us to *redefine* the workplace, and to better understand the dialectic tension between kinship and market relations that characterize women's artistic production within the reservation economy.

As feminist research has shown, we must go beyond public/private dichotomies that constrain women's roles within the "private" world of domestic life (Fraad et al. 1994; di Leonardo 1991; MacCormack and Strathern 1987). Furthermore, a privatized view of family life fails to consider the fact that since the 1960s there has been a significant increase in U.S. women's participation in the labor market (Benería and Stimpson 1987; Bose, Feldberg, and Sokoloff 1987). Reservation economies reflect this trend, both in reservation employment opportunities and in emigration that involves both men and women (Ambler 1990). Consequently, changes in household formations reflect the flexibility of family forms and a loosening of conjugal bonds that free men and (mostly young) women's labor for migratory and transitional wage work (Bureau of Indian Affairs Finance Report 1989; Berman 1994). Feminist research in areas of women's wage and nonwage work has also shed light on the dynamic relationship between global capitalist economies and changes in family forms, especially as in tandem, they transform relations of production (Enloe 1990; Nash and Fernández-Kelly 1983).

In addition, researchers can no longer conceptualize our communities of study as discretely bounded geographical spaces. For example, we must consider American Indian artists living in Paris, American Indian dancers who buy British dance shoes (assembled in Hong Kong), and German and Danish enthusiasts who come to reservations so they might learn more about how to "authentically" replicate Native American dances and art (see Trouillot 1991: 22). Yet in this global context of artistic production and exchange of materials and ideas, reservation communities themselves remain essentially kin-oriented—even when kin networks extend beyond the reservation and across the Atlantic Ocean.

However, gaps in knowledge and interest in the production of specific artistic objects has forced a reassessment of kin-based production and persistently begs the question, Who gets to count as kin? For example, Hidatsa women no longer rely on matrilineally transmitted knowledge as a requirement for production of quilled items. This is in part a consequence of differences in generational needs and interests between mothers and daughters, and the fluctuating on-reservation residency of close female kin.

Production and exchange of these items, however, was never limited to domestic (i.e., "private") spheres. Within a reciprocal cycle of gift giving, the exchange of items functions to link households. Objects themselves remain central to public rituals that involve both men and women in ceremonial and political life. The contradiction between public/private and ceremonial/political is resolved at the community level through the daily politics of American Indian women. Despite their awareness of and economic ties to a larger world market, they remain marginalized at the site of production. Yet it is there, at the level of kinship and community, that authenticity in artistic work is sanctioned, and where culturally meaningful work is accomplished.

The daily politics of Native American women cannot be separated from social life and the way that kinship relations help to spread the risks of survival by linking up household and community concerns (Stack 1975; Folbre 1988). Albers (1983:216) contends that it is the very nature of Native American women's abilities to link up "public" and "private" concerns that has allowed some Dakota women to become active leaders in tribal politics. She attributes this to women's influence and control in social networks, and the provisioning of goods that accompanies ceremonial activity. Ceremonial activities, especially the rules that govern the quantity and quality of goods, form a baseline from which women resist the devaluation of artistic production for market consumption. By setting its own standards for production and distribution, the "community as worksite" operates outside the boundaries and constraints of capitalist control over production, thereby resisting its alienating effects.

Power relations of subordinate to dominant groups often take the form of everyday resistance, whereby kinship and community ties serve as the seedbed for collective action (Scott 1990; Bookman and Morgen 1988). The notion of "everyday resistance" provides a shorthand for describing the daily strategies of the powerless and economically marginalized in their day-to-day activities of making a living (Halperin 1990; Ackelsberg 1988). This idea is particularly germane to feminist studies that seek to broaden the definition of politics by describing the everyday work lives of women (Sacks 1988; Day 1982; Kaplan 1982) and examine the ways in which community imperatives bring women into negotiating spheres of power.

CEREMONIAL RELATIONS OF PRODUCTION AND AMERICAN INDIAN WOMEN'S ARTS

Since the beginning of contact with white traders on the northern plains, Native American women have produced decorative arts for social, ceremonial, and utilitarian occasions (e.g., from clothing to household dwellings). Mixed economic strategies of the inhabitants of the Upper Missouri included horticulture, hunting, and fishing, while the Teton Sioux tribes relied more heavily on hunting and trading for agricultural products with their river valley neighbors. While the "old way" of life was disrupted by white encroachment and forced resettlement, many Hidatsa women continue to garden, and artistic production in some form or another proliferates within almost every household. Today, Hidatsa and Lakota women combine a variety of paid jobs (working for tribal governments, Bureau of Indian Affairs, Indian Health Service, or any number of private enterprises that boom and bust within reservation boundaries) with unpaid household labor, including artistic production. Artistic production commonly involves beading and sewing, especially sewing quilts for an unending cycle of ceremonial activities. Despite the constant demand on women's productive labor, most of the work that women do remains unremunerated. Lack of jobs in the formal sector for both men and women hover at an average of seventy-five percent unemployment for Fort Berthold and Pine Ridge reservations, according to labor force statistics I obtained in 1991 from the Aberdeen, South Dakota, area office of the Bureau of Indian Affairs.

Economic development strategies since the 1930s have approached problems of unemployment through social welfare programs designed to address the egregious loss of a land-based economy on reservations. One approach prompted through the efforts of the American Indian Arts and Crafts Board was to target women's skills as beadworkers, quilters, and (through missionary tutelage) lacemakers. The involvement of native Plains women in small-scale commodity production brought them into market relations where their perceived "status" has changed through time. For example, among Hidatsa women today, ceremonial rights to produce certain items are now limited to a few women, whose prestige is enhanced by their knowledge. At the same time, women who have become successful artists act as power brokers between community and market relations. In these ways, the effects of capitalism have had contradictory effects on women's arts by ascribing monetary value to scarce items that once figured highly only in ceremonial contexts.

Production-for-use and production-for-exchange have become enmeshed with ceremonial activities, so that market relations and kin-based ceremonial relations have grown interdependent and form the basis for *ceremonial relations of production*. These structural interdependencies between market relations and kin-based relations are a consequence of the increasing need for cash contributions for ceremonial events, and wealth differentials that require more prosperous families to act on their redistributive obligations by "giving away" mass quantities of both handmade objects, such as star quilts and shawls (Albers and Medicine 1983) and store-bought goods, such as blankets and commercially manufactured cloth.

The dimension of *distribution* is an important focal point for analyzing changes in the value of goods and the status of women (Klein 1980). Hidatsa and Lakota women's status is partially reckoned through their function as key distributors of gifts and producers of decorative arts that have social, ceremonial, and economic importance within reservation life (Schneider 1981; Grobsmith 1981). In their face-to-face interactions of daily life (Foster 1991), women mediate between kin groups, and weave a network of kin and friends into a web of potential resistance against exogenous forces of control (Day 1982; Joseph 1983). In the following sections, I describe how Lakota and Hidatsa women's participation in public ceremonies and the wider off-reservation art market marks them as central actors whose dealings crosscut ceremonial and market relations, making them key negotiators between these realms.

ETHNOGRAPHIC CONTEXT
OF CEREMONIAL OBJECTS

In her study of Devil's Lake Sioux women, Albers (1983) shows how the relationship of capitalism to the domestic sphere of production has not been stable through time. These effects are paralleled among the Lakota Sioux and the Hidatsa. Demands on women's labor can be evidenced as early as the eighteenth-century fur trade, where women's skills as hide tanners were highly sought (Klein 1983). In the nineteenth century, the reteaching of domestic skills to Indian women by missionary matrons affected domestic relations, and altered the sexual division of labor to reflect Anglo values. For example, Hidatsa men were taught farming—an area of productive activity previously conducted by women. Lakota women were initially excluded from tribal politics, but still held esteemed ceremonial positions (Powers 1986). Within their ceremonial exchange networks, women bridged public and private domains in efforts to respond to missionization and market conditions. Furthermore, Lakota and Hidatsa women tranformed kin-based artisan production to meet the needs of their households and families in order to face the challenge of dramatic cultural change. In this section, I outline key points of white contact that altered indigenous modes of production and the social relations that govern them.

The Lakota Sioux, representative of the "buffalo hunting / vision quest / sun dance" complex of Plains nomads, have been well placed in the ethnographic literature since the early twentieth century (Deloria 1929; Mails 1972; Meyer 1967; Powers 1977; Walker 1917; Wissler 1940; Nurge 1970). Their neighbors, the Hidatsa, were semisedentary horticulturalists, who along with other tribes of the upper Missouri region (e.g., Mandans) produced beans, squash, and corn, which served as basic trade goods (Berman 1996a; Wilson [1914] 1985; Lowie 1917; Meyer 1977; Ewers 1968; Hanson 1986; Bowers 1965). In the eighteenth century, women were involved in direct trade relations with other tribes, especially in exchanges for corn (Weist 1983). Thus, women retained distributive control over the fruits of their labor.

After the conquest of the Sioux and the 1851 Treaty of Fort Laramie, all tribes were dispossesed of their native lands and forced to live on reservations. The Fort Laramie Treaty reserved portions of North and South Dakota for Minneconju, Oglala, Brule, Hunkapapa, Sicangu, Sihasapa, and Itazipco bands of Lakota Sioux (M. Powers 1986:24). A widely bound area of north central North Dakota was also set aside for Arikaras, Awatixa, Awaxawi, and "Hidatsa Proper" Hidatsa villages, and what remained of the Mandan after smallpox had reduced their numbers to less than three hundred. The boundaries established by the Fort Laramie Treaty were redrawn two years after it was signed (Meyer 1977:103), marking the beginning of a contentious history of broken treaties. In 1870 the Fort Berthold reservation was established in western North Dakota along the upper confluence of the Missouri River. Mandan, Hidatsa, and Arikara Indians later became incorporated as the Three Affiliated Tribes under the Indian Reorganization Act of 1934. Since the nineteenth century, the "Three Tribes" have lived together and intermarried. While my discussion is limited to Hidatsa quillwork, Arikaras and Mandans share similar cultural features with Hidatsas (see Meyer 1977).

In the nineteenth century, polygynous households characterized Hidatsa social organization, with sororal polygyny as a predominant form. Kinswomen, by both proxy and necessity, cooperated in everyday household tasks (Weist 1983:42–43). The archaeological record tells us that Hidatsa women procured and processed all food resources (except killing), collected water, wood, wild plants, herbs, bark, and reeds (Spector 1993:82.) Women also worked collectively to process animal hides and to build shelters. They also spent a great deal of productive time in their gardens, for which they were responsible (Spector 1993:89–90; Wilson [1917] 1985). Lakota women were similarly industrious, but unlike Hidatsa women who had a long-standing agricultural tradition, Lakota women were in greater demand as hide-tanners in the buffalo trade. Furthermore, through matrilineal clan structures, Hidatsa women retained greater control over their productive labor, especially in relation to their agricultural work (Hanson 1986).

The incorporation of the horse into Plains societies had differential effects, marked by differences in cultural adjustments or adaptations that transformed productive relations (Hanson 1986). Klein (1980) argues that an increasing dependence on the horse and the hide trade transformed relations of production from eighteenth-century "production-for-use" to nineteenth-century "production-for-exchange." What was changing, he notes, was "access to and ownership over wealth" (1983:153). With an increase in individualism that was fostered by the acquisition of horses as status markers, women's collective work efforts became harnessed for individual men's gain.

By the mid-nineteenth century, federal Indian policy had succeeded in carving out territories by Christian denominations through religious conversion efforts sanctioned by U.S. governmental approval. Thus, it was by extension of federal policy that the first resident missionary arrived at Fort Berthold in 1865 (Case 1977). Changes in cosmological belief systems in turn affected ceremonial rules that governed production and use of ceremonial objects, as I outline below.

SIGNIFICANCE OF CEREMONIAL OBJECTS

Changes in material culture reflect adoption of new (Christian) religions and represent structural changes that followed the destruction of a native land-based economy. Lakota women figured highly in creation stories that linked the creation of the Earth (Maka Ina) to the survival of the Buffalo Nation—the first people (M. Powers 1986). This association of women's sacred mediating role between material and cosmological realms is best exemplified by White Buffalo Calf Woman, one of the most venerated cosmological figures. At a time of starvation and despair, she brings the starving Lakota people the Calf Pipe and its associated sacred rites (M. Powers 1986:35; W. Powers 1977; Walker [1917] 1980).

The relationship of ceremonial objects to spiritual practices, illustrated by the coming of White Buffalo Calf Woman to the Lakota people, bound Indian people within complex social and ceremonial constructs. For the Hidatsa, these involved kin relations within age-graded societies that fostered the persistence of native rituals. For Hidatsa women, admission to age-graded societies, such as the Goose Women Society and those associated with the Woman-Above rites (Bowers 1965), was based upon ritually prescribed behavior and life-cycle readiness. I will discuss how quillwork is linked to ceremonial prescription at greater length below; the important point here is that these complex ceremonial forms of social organization and their attendant rites of passage were forced "underground" or into extinction by foreign laws and a sense of moral superiority that was part of systematic conversion efforts:

It was April 1887 . . . that Poor Wolf proved his new faith by throwing away his old fetishes. He had a dried turtle shell, muskrat skin, mink skin, red muscles, crab's head, otter skins, six things besides peppermint and other herbs . . . such things were used at the buffalo dance for conjuring . . . all these conjuring things he took out onto a hill, talked to them, told them he did not need them anymore, and threw them away. (Case 1977:173)

The coerced abandonment of ceremonial objects struck at the core of native beliefs. The fact that certain beliefs, practices, and creation of ceremonial objects have persisted in any form is a testament to the tenacity of native people in preserving their cultural integrity. Cosmological figures, such as White Buffalo Calf Woman, reinforce women's key positions as provisioners, especially in times of scarcity.

Changes in availability of goods had an effect on the production of porcupine quillwork, especially as government-issued seed beads replaced porcupine quills. Moreover, assaults on native religious practices affected the ceremonial rites that governed quillwork production. In contemporary times, ceremonial production has shifted to secular production for some individuals; others, lacking religious knowledge, are unable to produce items at all. On the other hand, quilting, an exogenous art form, was initially a social and secular activity. Some native women have adapted its techniques and symbols and incorporated them into ceremonial spheres; others produce only for the market. The fluctuation of market demand has had the effect of intensifying ceremonial production. For example, some Hidatsa women, when faced with the unreliability of market outlets, withdrew their crafts and now refuse to produce for anyone but family for ceremonial occasions.

The intensification of ceremonial life can be interpreted as a response to the systematic and everyday domination of living within an internal colonial relationship to federal bureaucracies and policies (see Godelier in Leacock 1978:250). As a specific response to the extirpation of religious and economic practices, Native American women reformed their artistic skills to meet the needs of social and ceremonial life.

HIDATSA QUILLWORK AND
GENDER SPECIALIZATION

Gender specialization in artistic production has been prevalent since prereservation times, but was not cross-culturally uniform. For example, wooden bowls were carved by men among the Pawnee, but among the Hidatsa, both men *and* women were carvers (Schneider 1983). Quilling and quilting, however, are known throughout the Plains as arts practiced only by women.[3] While porcupine quillwork preceded colonial contact, quilting was introduced to native women by missionary matrons. In contemporary times, star quilting has taken on features of "pan-Indianism," where forms and meanings are similar across tribal groups. The religious significance of quill-work has been documented for a number of Plains tribes, and unlike that of quilting, takes culturally specific forms. Among the Mandan and Hidatsa, pro-duction of goods, including quillwork, was traditionally governed by age-graded social and ceremonial structures (Bowers 1950 and 1965). For the Hidatsa, age-graded societies involved kin relations that fostered the persis-tence of native rituals. Among these, women's quillworking societies allowed women to participate in shared ritual knowledge that included the technical craft of quilling. Although Lakota women belonged to sacred societies and guilds, the absence of age-graded societies constrained women less in the production of quilled items. A discussion of Hidatsa quillwork illustrates the decline of arts associated with age-graded societies, such as the Holy Woman Society related to the visionary experiences of quillworkers.

Hidatsa quillwork is a decorative art form that involves fastening dyed porcupine quills in geometric or floral designs to buckskin objects. The effect is similar to an appliqué. Motifs belonged to individual women who dreamed of a particular design. Techniques were learned by a girl from one of her "mothers" or other clan relatives (Wilson [1917] 1985:92).

Prior to colonial subjugation, the Hidatsa were matrilineally clan-based horticulturalists with a complex system of age-graded societies that affected all aspects of social life (Bowers 1965; Bruner 1961; Lowie 1917). Hidatsa quillwork is intrinsically tied to the ceremonial organization of women's age-graded societies associated with the Woman-Above rites (see Bowers 1965). Admission to quilling societies was determined by visions or dreams, partic-ularly those related to the mythical Holy-Woman-Above. Girls who learned how to quill shared visions that entitled them to knowledge of the ritual tech-niques associated with the technical skills. Failure to comply with proper comportment could result in blindness or other harm.

Women owned rights to production that were passed on ritually through payments (i.e, from a daughter to mother). Reciprocal deeds were also accept-able forms of payment, as noted by Bowers:

> A girl would do favors for her "grandmothers" who had made toys for her or had taught her how to decorate things with beads and quills. (Bowers 1965:131)

In this way, rights were preserved within the matrilineage of the clan through a ritualized process of kin-based production.

Quilled goods, while produced by women, had important functions in male ceremonies and village-level political spheres. As decorative arts, quilled items were used in hunting and warring ceremonies, and for alliance forming ceremonies, such as the Adoption Pipe (Bowers 1965:48). Quilled robes and elkskin dresses, made by a man's female relatives, were given by men to holy women in return for prayers for their hunting exploits (Bowers 1965:413–15). In this way, quilling arts were integral to band organization and cooperation, and functioned both within and between households as items of ceremonial exchange (i.e., "crosscutting" private and public domains). Women also accrued great prestige for their quilling skills, and kept records of their accomplishments through "quilling counts." An elder Hidatsa quill-worker told me in ranked order all of the quilled items she has produced in her lifetime.

Women were valued as productive household members, and acknowledged with gifts for the quilled items they produced (Gilman and Schneider 1987). Among the Hidatsa and the Lakota, with respect to quilling and quilting respectively, women remain the key distributor of goods for inter-household visits, communitywide events (such as powwows and honorings), and for ceremonial events (such as naming ceremonies). Despite tremendous changes in ceremonial and social activities, it seems clear that many significant features of ceremonial life persist and continue to change through innovation and experimentation. Today, most reservation Indians have adopted some form of Christianity, although its effects on what women actually do varies individually and generationally.

Missionization in the early reservation period (1879–1910) affected both men and women's productive roles. One dramatic result was a decline in age-graded societies, resulting from prohibitions and punishments against traditional dances that were integral to the persistence of native practices. Despite these assaults on native culture, women's power associated with visions related to quilling was maintained and in some cases *transferred* to other types of production. For example, Plains beadwork closely followed quilling patterns and motifs. Where men entered the cash economy through wage labor and agriculture (formerly women's domain), women entered through petty commodity production. Albers's description of the Dakota Sioux has relevance to the Hidatsa at the initial phase of capitalist penetration into the reservation economy:

> Although Sioux women were excluded from major annuity and cash-producing activities . . . *through their own initiative* . . . [they] entered into the cash economy . . . by way of petty commodity production. . . . [They] manufactured a wide variety of textile commodities suitable for sale or trade in an off-reservation marketplace. In this manufacture, Sioux women not only used traditional industrial and decorative skills (e.g., beadwork and quillwork), but also employed such newly learned techniques as quilting, crocheting, and lacemaking. (Albers 1983:187, emphasis mine)

For Hidatsa women, the relationship between decline in age-graded structures and a shift to commodity production parallels a shift to *subsistence* handicraft production. By the 1930s the reservation economy afforded few options for wage work for women. However, traditional kin networks and exchange systems continued to function, and through them women worked to meet their families' needs by designing means to supplement government rations. Although artisan production did not offer women much money, they at least continued to control their means of production and distribution.

Women's church groups, such as those formed at the Congregational Mission at Fort Berthold, taught women to produce handicrafts suited to Victorian tastes—such as lace tablecloths, napkin rings, and quilts. Additionally, the American Indian Arts and Crafts Board, as part of the New Deal era, initiated a series of craft production workshops to "reteach" beadwork and quillwork to Plains Indian women. These included art cooperatives on several reservations, including Pine Ridge and Standing Rock of South and North Dakota (Schrader 1983: 217). Although this effort was centered on Pine Ridge (B. Medicine, personal communication), the fact that the Crafts Board worked regionally to create markets and provide raw materials to Indians may have also affected Hidatsa women's access to these markets. Today, reservation cooperatives often serve as mediators between producers and the market, offering workshops and promotional assistance to native artisans. Artisan workshops, sometimes sponsored by federal job training programs (Berman 1996b), provide a place where non-kin work together in what were previously kin-based work groups.

Women have been central participants in community-based cooperatives that provide a venue for collective work projects. Their conscious efforts to improve their artistic and management skills point to an aspect of everyday resistance by which women work for "survival and uplift" within their community (see Gilkes 1988). By working together on artistic projects, American Indian women "resist" the alienating effects of capitalist industry. However, as I will show in the following section, changes from kin to non-kin production have increased the privatizing effects of market production.

LAKOTA QUILTING

Whereas quillwork and its elaborate complex of ceremonial traits functioned within an ongoing system of reciprocal exchange and kin-based distribution, quiltmaking fulfilled an important niche in reorganizing social relations. Quiltmaking was not a direct replacement, but rather allowed for *extensions* of traditional patterns of design and forms of production.

Albers and Medicine (1983:128) suggest that starquilts (eight-point star designs) are descended from traditional ceremonial hides bearing the morning star design (see also Locke 1988). While missionary matrons referred to star quilt designs as the "Bethlehem Star," Indian women transposed them ideologically to conform to traditional motifs (Albers and Medicine 1983:129). This "reintegration" of design motifs eased the introduction of star quilts into the ceremonial sphere, and resulted in a proliferation of production. This is evident in the great number of star quilts given away at public honoring ceremonies today.

The ceremonial relations of production that characterize quilting circles today have their beginnings in church-sponsored quilting bees. Initially, women's quilting groups were tightly formed alliances around church societies. These groups resembled women's sodalities that traditionally formed around quillwork (M. Powers 1986: 139–40). Later, they generally reflected kin-based groups whose membership fluctuated according to the needs of their kin. Even though quilts were introduced as a potential revenue-raising resource, native women quickly co-opted quiltmaking and imbued this art form with their own meanings and uses. Similar to quillwork, women's visionary experiences have typically influenced quilting designs (Albers and Medicine 1983). Quilting "counts" keep track of designs and quantities produced, reminiscent of quilling counts of former times.

The elevation of the star quilt as a symbol for native identity can be witnessed in a variety of native ceremonials and gatherings, such as Lakota curing ceremonies, funerals, honoring ceremonies, and secular powwows (social dances). Women perform central roles in these events and are responsible for building "collections" of items to be donated and given away. Additionally, women perform public naming ceremonies, are often key officiators of gift donations, and take responsibility for telling announcers which relatives and friends should come forward to receive their gifts. Common items at "giveaways" range from everyday household goods, such as tupperware and blankets, to rarer goods—but one of the most prestigious items, except for perhaps a horse, remains the star quilt.

While the value in the sale of hand-crafted goods has declined in more recent times, innovation in commodity production has facilitated an adaptive shift to tourist and collector markets. Changes in family and residential patterns have also necessitated a shift from strictly kin-organized production to "putting-out" systems of piecework among sought after quilters. One Lakota star quilter told me that she now works strictly as a designer, and hires other Lakota women to cut and sew the materials.

The sale of items has involved women in marketing their goods at local and regional markets, such as powwows and state fairs, and for international markets that involve museums, art shows, and fine art collectors. Star quilts, in particular, have recently been accorded status in museum collections (Coe

1986; Gilman and Schneider 1987). While women always guarded their designs, some women now compete for differential market values, with "museum quality" pieces being the most highly prized.

Thus, what was formerly a cooperative form of production has become stratified and competitive to meet the demands of the market. This has resulted in little compensation for some women when the quality of their workmanship is deemed inferior by market standards. For instance, selection processes for exhibitions exclude some women's work, even though it may be considered good by local standards. Other women have become well known for their quilting skills, and their work is in higher demand. Devaluation in market terms has resulted in a fluctuation back to domestic handicraft production for *ceremonial* use. In this way, the market has influenced both the social relations of production *and* the function and value of the item, both in market and cultural terms.

CEREMONIAL RELATIONS OF PRODUCTION AND PRODUCTION FOR THE MARKET

A few Hidatsa women continue to learn quillwork from elders who have the ceremonial right to quill. These younger women can, in turn, pass on the right if they so choose. While the technical skill has remained largely unchanged (excepting the use of commercial dyes and tools), accompanying ritual knowledge is less elaborate than in former times. In some cases, the complex of rules and rites has eased, increasing access to productive knowledge accordingly. This fact could, in time, facilitate a form of revitalization in quillwork among a younger generation of quillworkers, now in their twenties and thirties.

The clan relationship to the learner is less important than the willingness and ability to pay. Payment is ritually prescribed by tradition, and can be in the form of Pendleton blankets and food, and negotiated cash supplements. Feasting is also an understood obligation, whereby the learner prepares a meal for the quillworker at the end of initial instruction. Within this ceremonial system, however, values influenced by the capitalist economy have resulted in an inflation of the price paid to acquire quilling rights and knowledge. This means that young girls, even with their families' assistance, cannot afford to make the large payments required (e.g., hundreds of dollars in cash and goods). In this way, the market has directly affected the *cost of production* by increasing value and demand, while skewing the ability of traditional producers to satisfy that demand. Some women try to generate cash by working in wage labor, or by relying on contributions of cash and goods from close female kin.

Production of quilts persists within a ceremonial sphere of production, although inflation in star quilt giving has raised an expectation in reciprocity that was not previously part of a distributive cycle of exchange. Production for sale has changed the nature of social relations that previously governed quilting circles. Many quilters now work at home on machines. While this has the effect of privatizing production within the domestic sphere, women retain control of and are responsible for marketing their finished products, just as in prereservation times women controlled the trade of their agricultural products. One effect of capitalism, exemplified through a "putting out" system of production among some quiltmakers, is the shift from interdependent, kin-based structure to a hierarchical one among nonrelatives based on supply and demand. However, goods produced for ceremonial occasions or traditional social events (such as dance costumes) are still largely produced through cooperative kin efforts.

Differences in social boundaries created by the needs of the market result in a type of privatization of artistic skills that are themselves inextricable from the web of social relations that govern their transmission of artistic knowledge and skills. The privatization of production has the effect of separating "place" from "space." The community still serves as worksite, but social relations across space shift to meet competing demands of the market and ceremonial life.

DISCUSSION

Hidatsa and Lakota women confront market demands while simultaneously drawing on kinship relations that once formed the center of productive activity. Through time, they have resisted assimilation efforts through artistic production in several ways; first, by incorporating symbols and designs that mark cultural identity, such as the morning star for the star quilt. Second, by drawing on culture-based skills in the face of colonial domination. Examples of "culture-building" enterprises (see Gilkes 1988) include the organization of community arts and crafts guilds, and the conscious decisions that accompany the sale of particular items for the market. Cultural identity is asserted through control over artistic objects, sometimes by the *withdrawal* of those objects from circulation. In extreme cases, such as Hidatsa quillwork, where ritual knowledge confers a form of personal power, it is carefully guarded at the expense of the art itself. When viewed within the framework of an "everyday resistance" strategy, the withholding of information is a final effort to control cultural knowledge. The contradiction here is that cultural identity is maintained at the expense of transmission of cultural knowledge itself. Ceremonial relations of production distribute power by "stretching out" webs of relations across space (beyond the localized worksite) and time (as a dimension of cultural history).[4]

To offset culture loss, innovation frequently accompanies intensification efforts. Innovation in forms of production has carried over into less conventional items. Originality in star quilt design has emerged in other types of regalia, such as dance shawls and "Western" style ribbon shirts, as well as non-Indian clothing such as skirts and dresses that are sold at Indian markets and fairs to predominately white patrons. These art objects assert cultural identity as forms of symbolic capital along the borders of ceremony and commodity.

The "market," in terms discussed here, comprises a wide range of outlets that includes museums, galleries, private collectors, and regional fairs and powwows. Goods range from commissioned works to souvenirs for tourist markets, both regional and international in scope. Since Hidatsa quillwork remains subject to ceremonial constraints, it has not been incorporated as a market commodity, despite its high value in collector circles. Due to scarcity, recognition of the decline of such items has increased market values. Conversely, quillwork among the Lakota does not involve the same kinds of ceremonial restrictions, and is finding a place within contemporary art showcases. These factors have contributed to marking quillwork as a distinctive "fine art" (Schneider 1980).

Additionally, Lakotas, who do not place the same constraints upon quillwork production as Hidatsas, have revived aspects of quilling since the 1970s for a growing tourist market. Quilled bracelets and earrings are now common items at the annual Red Cloud Art Show at Pine Ridge reservation. Such efforts are often assisted by Native-run co-ops that, similar to Bureau of Indian Affairs efforts in the 1950s (Useem and Eicher 1970:14–15), provide raw materials and attempt to locate outlets for goods. Two examples are the Rosebud reservation co-op and the community-level co-op at Oglala, Pine Ridge (M. Powers 1986,199). Some Hidatsa women, in an attempt to counter the restrictions placed upon production, are assessing the viability of taking certain items outside the ceremonial spheres of exchange to produce for a Native art co-op that will market goods off the reservation.

The contradictory effects of capitalism on quillwork and quilting reflect market penetration and ceremonial intensification within the spatial webwork of social relations that straddles more than one "site." In order to make sense of the different relationships required for participating in both market and ceremonial life, Hidatsa and Lakota women engage in forms of *ceremonial relations of production*. I use this term as a purposeful attempt to embody the contradictions American Indian women face in their adaptation to commercial enterprises on the one hand, and their resistance to hegemonic domination on the other. Artistic production affords women a type of "resolution," by involving them in market activities and allowing them to create cultural identity through art objects. Hidatsa and Lakota women resist assimilation into the market by deciding when to uphold or to bend cultural rules, and how to reshape the social relations that govern production and distribution of cultural objects. At the same time, women recognize the need to modify cultural constraints in order to make a living. Divisions such as public/private, local/global, wage/nonwage fall short of describing the ways in which each informs a part of the other, both by implication and design. By conceptualizing the community as worksite in such a way that ceremonial relations of production *transform* social relations toward various outcomes (for a give-away, for an art gallery), Hidatsa and Lakota women construct new forms of class relations given value through the effects of specific practices (Bourdieu 1984). Hidatsa and Lakota women assert culture-based skills as a means to generate cash and resist hegemonic incorporation into the market through everyday activities that involve them in the production and distribution of artistic objects that symbolize their cultural identity. Recognizing that the market demands its share of cultural betrayal, American Indian artists and artisans have intensified their claims to cultural knowledge—sometimes at the expense of production altogether. While this does not exactly constitute a "work stoppage" in familiar terms, ceremonial intensification and market proliferation contribute in multiple (not dichotomous) ways to restructuring both social relations of production and the worksite(s) of the reservation by situating them beyond its shop floor.

NOTES

1. I use the term *Native American* to designate those groups of people who are indigenous to the Americas; whereas I use the term *American Indian* to refer to those groups of indigenous peoples who have distinct federal-trust relationships with the United States (per Barbara Feezor-Stewart, personal communication).

2. Data on quillwork were gathered during fieldwork with Hidatsa women at Fort Berthold reservation, North Dakota (1989, 1991–92). Data on Lakota quilting come from fieldwork at Pine Ridge reservation, South Dakota (1986), and build upon the work of Pat Albers and Beatrice Medicine (1983). I reported some of these findings earlier in *Anthropology UCLA*, vol. 16, no. 2, 1989.

3. Notable exceptions were the roles of male *berdaches* who were often gifted artists. See Collendar and Kochems (1983); Williams (1986).

REFERENCES CITED

Ackelsberg, Martha A.
　　1988 Communities, resistance, and women's activism: Some implications for a democratic polity. *Women and the Politics of Empowerment.* Ann Bookman and Sandra Morgen, eds. pp. 297–321. Philadelphia: Temple University Press.

Albers, Patricia
    1983 Sioux women in transition: A study of their changing status in a domestic and capitalist sector of production. In *The Hidden Half: Studies of Plains Indian Women*. Patricia Albers and Beatrice Medicine, eds. New York: University Press of America.

Albers, Patricia and Beatrice Medicine
    1983 *The Hidden Half: Studies of Plains Indian Women*. New York: University Press of America.

Ambler, Maryjane
    1990 *Breaking the Iron Bonds: Indian Control of Energy Development*. Lawrence: University of Kansas Press.

Benería, Lourdes, and Catherine Stimpson, eds.
    1987 *Women, Households and the Economy*. New Brunswick, N.J.: Rutgers University Press.

Berman, Tressa L.
    1996a Bringing it to the Center: Artistic production as economic development. *Research in Human Capital and Development*.
    1996b Hidatsa. In *Encyclopedia of North American Indians*. Fred Hoxie, ed. Boston: Houghton Mifflin Company.
    1994 The house of cards: Building American Indian communities in the context of HUD policies. Paper presented at the American Anthropological Association, Washington, D.C.

Bookman, Ann, and Sandra Morgen, eds.
    1988 *Women and the Politics of Empowerment*. Philadelphia: Temple University Press.

Bose, Christine, Roslyn Feldberg and Natalie Sokoloff, eds.
    1987 *The Hidden Aspects of Women's Work*. New York: Praeger.

Bourdieu, Pierre
    1984 The social space and its transformations. In *Distinction: A Social Critique of the Judgement of Taste*. Translated by Richard Nice. Cambridge: Harvard University Press.

Bowers, Alfred
    1965 Hidatsa Social and Ceremonial Organization. Bureau of Ethnology Bulletin 194. Washington, DC: Smithsonian Institution.
    1950 Mandan Social and Ceremonial Organization. Chicago: University of Chicago Press.

Bruner, Edward
    1961 Mandan. In *American Indians and Culture Change*. Edward Spicer, ed. Chicago: University of Chicago Press.

Bureau of Indian Affairs
    1989 Bureau of Indian Affairs Finance Report. Distributed by Bureau of Indian Affairs Area Office, Aberdeen, South Dakota.

Calagione, John
1992 Working in time: Music and power on the job in New York City. In *Workers' Expressions: Beyond Accommodation and Resistance*. John Calagione, Doris Francis, and Daniel Nugent, eds. Albany: State University of New York Press.

Calagione, John, and Daniel Nugent
1992 Workers' expressions: Beyond accommodation and resistance on the margins of capitalism. In *Workers' Expressions: Beyond Accommodation and Resistance*. John Calagione, Doris Francis, and Daniel Nugent, eds. Albany: State University of New York Press.

Case, Harold and Eva
1977 *100 Years at Fort Berthold: The History of the Fort Berthold Indian Mission: 1876–1976*. Bismarck Tribune Press.

Caulfield, Mina
1974 Imperialism, family and cultures of resistance. *Socialist Revolution* 4(2):67–85.
1974 Culture and imperialism: Proposing a new dialectic. In *Reinventing Anthropology*. Dell Hymes, ed. pp. 182–212. New York: Vintage Books.

Clemmer, Richard
1974 Resistance and the revitalization of anthropologists: A new perspective on cultural change and resistance. In *Reinventing Anthropology*. Dell Hymes, ed. pp. 213–47. New York: Pantheon Books.

Collendar, Charles, and Lee Kochems
1983 The North American berdache. *Current Anthropology* 24(4):443–71.

Coe, Ralph T.
1986 *Lost and Found Traditions: Native American Art 1965–1985*. New York: American Federation of Arts.

Day, Kay Young
1982 Kinship in a changing economy: A view from the Sea Islands. In *Holding on to the Land and the Lord*. Robert L. Hall and Carol B. Stack, eds. Athens: University of Georgia Press.

Deloria, Ella C.
1929 The sun dance of the Oglala Sioux. *Journal of American Folklore* 42:352–413.

di Leonardo, Micaela
1991 Gender, culture and political economy: Feminist anthropology in historical perspective. In *Gender at the Crossroads of Knowledge*. Micaela di Leonardo, ed. Berkeley: University of California Press.

Enloe, Cynthia
1990 *Bananas Beaches and Bases: Making Feminist Sense of International Politics*. Berkeley: University of California Press.

Etienne, Mona, and Eleanor Leacock, eds.
1983 *Women and Colonization*. New York: Praeger Press.

Ewers, John S.
1968 *Indian Life on the Upper Missouri*. University of Oklahoma Press.

Folbre, Nancy
1988 The black four of hearts: Toward a new paradigm of household economics. In *A Home Divided: Women and Income in the Third World*. Daisy Dwyer and Judith Bruce, eds. Stanford, CA: Stanford University Press.

Foster, Morris
1991 *Being Comanche: A Social History of an American Indian Community*. Tucson: University of Arizona Press.

Fraad, Harriet, Stephen Resnick, and Richard Wolff
1994 *Bringing it All Back Home: Class, Gender and Power in the Modern Household*. London: Pluto Press.

Fusco, Coco
1995 Passionate irreverence: The cultural politics of identity. In *English is Broken Here*. New York: New Press.

García Canclini, Néstor
1993 *Transforming Modernity: Popular Culture in Mexico*. Lidia Lozano, translator. Austin: University of Texas Press.

Garrell, Gary
1992 The curators. *Art News* Sept. 97:73.

Grobsmith, Elizabeth
1981 The changing role of the giveaway ceremony in contemporary Lakota life. *Plains Anthropologist* vol.26/9.
1981b *Lakota of the Rosebud*. New York. Holt, Rinehart and Winston.

Gilkes, Cheryl Townsend
1988 Building in many places: Multiple commitments and ideologies in black women's community work. In *Women and the Politics of Empowerment*. Ann Bookman and Sandra Morgen, eds. pp. 53–76. Philadelphia: Temple University Press.

Gilman, Carolyn, and Mary Jane Schneider
1987 *On the Way to Independence: Memories of a Hidatsa Indian Family*. St. Paul: Minnesota Historical Society Press.

Halperin, Rhoda H.
1990 *The Livelihood of Kin: Making Ends Meet "The Kentucky Way."* Austin: University of Texas Press.

Hanson, Jeffrey R.
1986 Adjustment and adaptation on the Northern Plains: The case of equestrianism among the Hidatsa. *Plains Anthropologist* 31:93–108.

hooks, bell
1995 *Art on My Mind; Visual Politics.* New York: New Press.

Joseph, Suad
1983 Working-class women's networks in a sectarian state: A political paradox. *American Ethnologist* 10(1).

Kaplan, Temma
1982 Female consciousness and collective action: The cases of Barcelona, 1910–1918. *Signs* 7(3):545–67.

Klein, Alan
1983 The plains truth: The impact of colonialism on Indian women. *Dialectical Anthropology* 7:299–313.
1980 Plains economic analyses: The Marxist complement. In *Anthropology on the Great Plains.* W. Raymond Wood and Margot Liberty, eds. Lincoln: University of Nebraska Press.

Kondo, Dorinne K.
1990 *Crafting Selves: Power, Gender, and Discourses of Identity in a Japanese Workplace.* Chicago: University of Chicago Press.

Leacock, Eleanor
1978 Women's status in egalitarian societies. *Current Anthropology* 19(2):247–55.

Locke, Kevin
1988 The star quilt in Plains Indian culture. In *Native Needlework.* Christopher Martin, ed. North Dakota Council on the Arts.

Lowie, Robert H.
1917 Notes on the social organization and customs of the Mandan-Hidatsa and Crow. *American Museum of Natural History Anthropological Papers*, vol. 21, pt. 1.

MacCormack, Carol and Marilyn Strathern, eds.
1987 *Nature, Culture and Gender.* London: Cambridge University Press.

Mails, Thomas E.
1972 *Mystic Warriors of the Plains.* New York: Doubleday.

Massey, Doreen
1994 *Space, Place and Gender.* New York: Polity Press.

Meyer, Roy W.
1977 *The Village Indians of the Upper Missouri: The Mandans, Hidatsas and Arikaras.* Lincoln: University of Nebraska Press.
1967 *History of the Santee Sioux.* Lincoln: University of Nebraska Press.

McCarl, Robert
1992 Exploring the boundaries of occupational knowledge. In *Workers' Expressions: Beyond Accommodation and Resistance.* John Calagione, Doris Francis, Daniel Nugent, eds. Albany: State University of New York Press.

McNickle, D'Arcy
　　1972 Process or compulsion: The search for a policy of administration in Indian affairs. In *The Emergent Native American*. D. Walker, ed. Boston: Little, Brown and Co.

Moore, Henrietta
　　1988 *Feminism and Anthropology*. Cambridge: Polity Press.

Mullin, Molly H.
　　1995 Making Indian art, "Art, not ethnography." In *The Traffic in Culture: Refiguring Art and Anthropology*. George E. Marcus and Fred R. Myers, eds. Berkeley and Los Angeles: University of California Press.

Nash, June, ed.
　　1993 *Crafts in the World Market: The Impact of Global Exchange on Middle American Artisans*. Albany: State University of New York Press.

Nash, June, and María Patricia Fernández-Kelly, eds.
　　1983 *Women, Men and the International Division of Labor*. New York: State University of New York Press.

Nurge, Ethel, ed.
　　1970 *The Modern Sioux*. Lincoln: University of Nebraska Press.

Powers, Marla N.
　　1986 *Oglala Women: Myth, Ritual and Reality*. Chicago: University of Chicago Press.

Powers, William K.
　　1977 *Oglala Religion*. Lincoln: University of Nebraska Press.

Sacks, Karen
　　1988 *Caring by the Hour: Women, Work, and Organizing at Duke Medical Center*. Urbana: University of Illinois Press.

Sassen, Saskia
　　1991 *The Global City: New York, London, Tokyo*. Princeton: Princeton University Press.

Schneider, Mary Jane
　　1983 Women's work: An examination of women's roles in Plains Indians arts and crafts. In *The Hidden Half: Studies of Plains Indian Women*. Patricia Albers and Beatrice Medicine, eds. Washington, D.C.: University Press of America.
　　1981 Economic aspects of Mandan/Hidatsa giveaways. *Plains Anthropologist* 26(91):43–50.
　　1980 Plains Indian art. In *Anthropology on the Great Plains*. W. Raymond Wood and Margot Liberty, eds. Lincoln: University of Nebraska Press.

Schrader, Robert Fay
　　1983 *The American Indian Arts and Crafts Board: An Aspect of New Deal Indian Policy*. Albuquerque: University of New Mexico Press.

Scott, James C.
1990 *Domination and the Arts of Resistance: Hidden Transcripts.* New Haven: Yale University Press.

Spector, Janet
1993 *What this Awl Means: Feminist Archaeology at a Wahpeton Dakota Village.* St. Paul: Minnesota Historical Society Press.

Stack, Carol B.
1975 *All Our Kin: Strategies for Survival in a Black Community.* New York: Harper and Row.

Trouillot, Michel-Rolph
1991 Anthropology and the savage slot: The poetics and politics of otherness. In *Recapturing Anthropology.* Richard G. Fox, ed. pp. 17–44. Santa Fe: School of American Research Press.

Useem, Ruth Hill, and Carl K. Eicher
1970 Rosebud reservation economy. In *The Modern Sioux.* Ethel Nurge, ed.

Walker, James R.
1980 [1917] *Lakota Belief and Ritual.* Raymond DeMallie and Elaine Jahner, eds. Lincoln: University of Nebraska Press.

Weist, Katherine M.
1983 Plains Indian women. In *Anthropology on the Great Plains.* W. Raymond Wood and Margot Liberty, eds. Lincoln: University of Nebraska Press.

Williams, Walter L.
1986 *The Spirit and the Flesh: Sexual Diversity in American Indian Culture.* Boston: Beacon Press.

Wilson, Gilbert L.
1917 [1985] *Buffalo Bird Woman's Garden.* Introduction by Jeffrey Hanson. St. Paul: Minnesota Historical Society Press.
1914 [1985] *Goodbird the Indian.* Introduction by Mary Jane Schneider. St. Paul: Minnesota Historical Society Press.

Wissler, Clark
1940 *Indians of the United States.* Garden City, N.Y.: Doubleday.

Chapter 5

Rights, Place, Orders, and Imperatives in Rural Eastern Kentucky Task-focused Discourse

Anita Puckett

The role of multiple discourses in the reproduction or transformation of socioeconomic and political economic relations within highly complex societies is now recognized as central to an anthropological understanding of power processes, wage-labor worksite dynamics, or social-stratificational issues related to constructions or critiques of class relations (Bourdieu 1984; Foucault 1973; Giddens 1984; Kingsolver, this volume; Nash 1992). As argued by others in this volume, this focus is now critical if current rapid restructurings, fragmentations, and multiple reformulations of work itself are to be understood locally and globally. Yet rather than treating "discourse" as an abstraction that organizes cooperation, contestation, resistance, revolt, or dialogic interaction, among other multivocal or multifaceted expressions of power,[1] I am instead considering discourse simply as the linguistically-based sound units that individuals create when talking to others or to themselves which express linguistic and cultural meanings through the process of talking (Duranti and Goodwin 1992; Moerman 1988; Sherzer 1987).

Discourse then becomes an empirical representation of language-in-use, which, through its complex communicative properties, will convey multiple levels of meanings as speakers address listeners over the course of the verbal interaction. The underlying patterns and regularities it exhibits in specific speaking instances then assume primacy in studying work relations.

When studied ethnographically across the full range of speakers' social interactional activity, these patterns, and the social and cultural meanings they acquire through conventionalized use, reveal core, central relations between regularized linguistic forms and basic cultural interpretive structures, including political economic ones. Such an encompassing orientation toward "talk" yields a replicable and valid approach to understanding processes of power construction or replication from the microlevel of a given instance of discourse use to macrolevels of ideology construction or implementation of institutional hegemonies (Bauman and Sherzer 1989; Gal and Woolard 1995; Gumperz and Hymes 1974).

In keeping with arguments offered by Irvine (1989) and Duranti (1992, 1994), I assert that the meanings conveyed by a subset of the full range of these regularized linguistic forms are so integrated into cultural life that appropriate use of them by cultural members is constitutive of a political economic system, necessary to its very reproduction, transformation, or creation and the power relations inherent in them.[2] Under such a view, such acts of talking construct or reconstruct political economic patterns through the communication of multiple meanings, often indexical (or context-dependent) rather than referential (or descriptive), within speaking events. Rather than viewing speech as something apart from the material world of political economic activity, political economic discourse must be understood as the central, driving mechanism effecting the maintenance, change, or dissolution of power and control relations in specific labor events. Focus on discourse as a concept has been enlightening for understanding power relations. But focus on discourse as a substance for analysis can assist significantly in revealing how and why political economic power relations assume the form they do.

Similar to scholarship that has developed Bloch's (1975) now well-known argument for understanding political relations through empirical analyses of linguistic and nonlinguistic political behavior (for example, Brenneis and Myers 1984; Paine 1981), this discussion argues for empirical analyses of linguistic socioeconomic behavior to understand the complex structuring of work relations in plural, wage-labor dominated societies such as the United States. As was Bloch's assertion for political domains, socioeconomic arguments using discourse as mode of explanation must be supported by analyses of actual representations of it. Differing from other studies of language-in-use, which have recognized the need to study structurings of work discourse instances (for example, Drew and Heritage 1992; Firth 1995), the following argues for a broad ethnography of discourse approach (Hymes 1974; Sherzer 1987; Urban 1991) both inside and outside of workplace settings to capture as many speaking practices and discourse genres as are within the verbal repertoire of those participating in work events.[3] This supports the call for full, interactive ethnographic involvement articulated by Nash (1992) from a language-in-use perspective. It is by understanding the composition, functions, and scope of the entire language-and-political economy verbal repertoire that the specific discourse configuration created in a given instance of work communication can be most fully contextualized into the matrix of cultural relations known by participants. Without such an ethnographic orientation, microanalyses of specific occasions of speech are subject to ethnocentric bias through imposition of one's own system of speech pragmatics, rather than that of the culture's (see Gumperz 1982; Hymes 1981).

An assumption in adopting this approach is that we will never fully understand why class or other key concepts in political economic theory are insufficient indicators of interpretive structures affecting power relations until we consider the form and function of all meaningful behavior in work settings, including linguistic interactions (see Gal 1989). This paper explores these claims through an analysis of two examples of the rural Appalachian speaking practice of "showing," or instructional, discourse used in situations in which someone "shows" another how to do something. Instructional discourse is at the very nexus of work relations and is likely to be a point at which culture itself is most precarious because of the need to transmit knowledge, skill, and information to the instructee.[4] Although seldom explored as overt representations of power, instructing interactions presuppose control over privileged knowledge, skill, and resources by the instructor, and disenfranchisement from the control or use of these resources by the uninitiated.[5] Understanding the language and cultural relations of instructional discourse is therefore highly significant for understanding how economic power processes are constituted and for illuminating various political economic theoretical orientations.[6]

As I participated in Ash Creek's daily life, a pseudonym for a rural eastern Kentucky community, for several years in the mid- to late 1980s (with visits up to the present),[7] I was able to note that "telling" someone how to do something was rarely done and was negatively valued. Rather, residents, both men and women, preferred to "show" someone how to do something, frequently saying that they would have to show me how to do something because they couldn't "tell" me. Consequently, "showing" someone how to do something with hands-on demonstration is a critical and central work discourse practice in Ash Creek, as knowledge and skills must be transmitted to interested members or new residents. Highly elliptic in form, often relying on deictics, such as "this" or "that," or on gestures which eliminate or minimize the need for verbal exchanges, showing discourse is always organized around a culturally dangerous grammatical form, the imperative. Unless overridden by some other speech act function, such as greetings or leave-takings, English imperatives—whether formulated as Appalachian English or other English speech varieties—are interpreted as commands or explicit directives that demand compliance from the addressee (Davies 1986; Ervin-Tripp 1976, 1982; Kramarae, Schulz and O'Barr 1984; Quirk et al., 1985). They are therefore bald statements of power in which the speaker asserts control over the addressee(s).

In Ash Creek, such assertions must be made carefully within the limited range of culturally appropriate discourse structures to avoid disruption of relationships or precipitation of negative sanctions or violence. "Showing" discourse, as a type of discourse that permits the use of imperatives under a limited range of conditions, is therefore at the center of economic, power, and linguistic intersections. Appropriate use of these forms is critical to the maintenance of socioeconomic relations and, implicationally, the cultural order.

OVERVIEW OF ASH CREEK SOCIOECONOMY

The name "Ash Creek" is an analytical term more than a demographic one. It refers to an approximately six mile by one-half mile stretch of land on either side of a creek and three of its tributaries populated by families who have regular knowledge about or interact with each other.[8] Ash Creek (population approximately 400) is typical of one type of rural eastern Kentucky community in that it is organized around family groupings (Pearsall 1959), is populated by a disproportionately high number of older residents (a result of heavy emigration), and is facing acute economic stress as coal mining and corporate logging have ceased to exist as viable industries. It has a poverty rate of about thirty-three to forty-seven percent, suffers from deteriorating economic conditions greater than the state or national average (1980–1990), and exhibits the kind of permanent, structural unemployment that currently characterizes many former monoindustrial coal counties. As with many similar rural communities, it has not benefited significantly from the growth of regional centers such as Corbin, Pikeville, and Hazard (Eller 1994).

The nearest town is eighteen miles away over a curving, mountainous road that, in severe winter weather, is often impassable except to four-wheel drive vehicles. Ash Creek is not and never was a coal camp, nor subject to kinds of community sociopolitical structuring that corporate coal mining imposed on those planned communities. Rather, it is an amalgamation of old family farming land that has been subdivided among descendants to the point of lots capable of producing only small (up to 1/2 acre) garden plots, of land owned by wood-processing companies such as Georgia Pacific but rented by a few local residents for a nominal annual rent as low as $8/year, and of land that is owned and managed by outside institutions such as churches, educational organizations, or the state forestry division. Some corporately owned land is farmed for cash-cropping; one resident owns enough acreage to market for a small profit. A few privately owned lots have been developed for churches, three ma-and-pop stores, or local business concerns such as the one automobile repair garage.

Most monetary income is obtained through activities such as family coal-mining, cash cropping of garden produce, marijuana growing or resale of other illegal substances, temporary contract labor, or transfer payments from retirement or government subsidy. Some still earn income through heavy equipment operation, coal or gravel truck driving, or perhaps manual labor at the local environmental center. A few younger men work in nonlocal corporate strip or underground coal mines, and two men work full-time as paid ministers rather than "called" preachers. A few women work in the local, consolidated elementary school nearby as teachers or teachers' aides or as teachers in the local Christian school. Other working (as opposed to the very few retired) professionals included (until 1992) a nurse practitioner not native to Ash Creek, and (up to the present) nonlocal teaching staff at an environmental center in the immediate area. For most traditional gardening and hunting activities contribute either centrally or peripherally to subsistence so that talk about and knowledge of how to use these economic resources is accessible even to young children. Strong and clear expectations of gender roles exist in terms of both economic and linguistic labor.

Changes in socioeconomic activity from 1985 to 1995 are deceptive in their apparent stability. While appearing to be slight, they represent significant processes of restructuring the value and locus of economic labor. They center around a greater entry of wives and other adult women into whatever acceptable workplace opportunities exist for women, from selling Blair or Mary Kay products locally to commuting to nearby towns for retail sales, fast food service, or one of the small number of office jobs for those few who have the skills and appropriate political network to apply. More teenagers who still live in Ash Creek graduate from high school and take community college classes under Pell Grant or student loan financial support than in the early 1980s. Most young adults move to a regional town or city such as Corbin, Lexington, or Knoxville to work; it is assumed that they must leave to "make it." Computer technology is accessible to a limited extent[9] through the elementary school and through a few pc's, in homes, or through community college classes twenty miles away. Most have no computer knowledge or access. Infrastructure support from multifamily water systems to telephone service are unevenly available. One section of the community is served by a single engine volunteer fire department as of 1995. Since the local clinic staffed by a nurse practitioner closed in the early 1990s, the nearest medical service is twenty-two miles distant.

These rural, mountain social organizational patterns promote a sociocultural separation, if not isolation, from work patterns and processes normative in urban settings such as Cincinnati, Knoxville, or Detroit. Residents come in contact with only a few formal, corporate institutions: hospitals or medical clinics, government agencies such as food stamp offices or Social Security, fast food restaurant and grocery store chains, K-Mart, or perhaps the local community college—all encountered in time-limited trips to town. All but a few residents interact most often with a finite, highly predictable set of known individuals, usually kin or kin of kin, so that life activity patterns are routine or at least highly predictable. The hierarchically structured work settings characteristic of urban labor environments, and the prolific use of imperative discourse for commands or requests within them (Ervin-Tripp 1976; Weigel and Weigel 1985), are as removed for most Ash Creek residents as the literate practices that allow them to function.

When working within the local system, Ash Creek workers may "earn" wages for performing manual, hand, or semiskilled labor according to a number of criteria, all of which reproduce reciprocity or barter exchange relations. To be hired for a "job," laborers are usually selected according to community or family knowledge of their skill at the task and the contractor's perception of the laborer's perceived need for the work. Laborers accept or reject the offer according to the amount of money offered by the individual (not a company)[10] wanting the work done, their need for money, the nature of the relationship between the contractor and the worker, or the state of the erratic market for temporary wage-labor among the higher-paying mining, gravel-hauling, or, recently, small logging businesses located within easy commuting distance. Only a handful of men labor for corporations managed outside the immediate region, whether in mining or some other industry, and they are necessarily a group marginal to community life for they are frequently away for long periods working at remote job sites. Those desiring or able to obtain this form of work frequently move elsewhere, either permanently or temporarily, to be closer to the job site. Frequently, their families move with them.

Consequently, in keeping with many Appalachian coalfield communities in the 1990s, most Ash Creek residents who do not migrate for work are beginning to resort to modes of obtaining what Lewis (1996) has called a "livelihood" economy rather than resorting on institutional sources for wage-labor.[11] "Livelihood" strategies include amalgamations of subsistence farming, cash cropping, small-scale forest harvesting (logging, ginseng harvesting/growing, or marijuana growing), barter and trade of needed goods (as well as monetary purchases), further development of preexisting reciprocity systems, and other modes of obtaining goods and services that permit residents to live in a manner that is more personally acceptable and less commodity-based than industrialization of the region had encouraged (Banks 1980; Eller 1982; Gaventa 1980). Such adaptations are not nostalgic re-creations of preindustrial modes of production, but syncretic and creative reapplications of diverse socioeconomic practices that have existed in the community area. They are most consciously resistance strategies only in the sense that most residents value family co-location more highly than precarious low-to-moderately paying employment in nonlocal businesses or industries.[12]

As a result, advanced capitalism rests uneasily upon Ash Creek socioeconomic patterns as residents interpret political relations, economic exchange activities, and employment problems in terms consistent with these diverse strategies. For those who have migrated back to Ash Creek from urban centers, terms such as "blue collar," "working class," and "labor" have meaning in everyday discourse. Dominant patterns of talking about socioeconomic stratification, however, include such dichotomies as "country" versus "city," "simple" versus "educated," and "hillbilly" versus "educated" or "city." Within the community membership itself, individuals are categorized into general categories based on family names that have political economic and prestige value. Family name AB, for example, may have higher value than family name XY. In terms of praxis, male AB members will have greater access to (but not necessarily ownership or control of) economic resources (land, money, vehicles, heavy equipment, and tools, or other needed items), political influence (access to local jobs, ability to get county money for roads or other improvements, or control of votes), and influence on community needs (infrastructure needs, educational issues, or moral/religious matters) (see Batteau 1981, 1982 for a general discussion of this system of valuation).

Similarly, individuals establish personal names, which carry political economic weight in local terms. As one older resident said, "If you have a good name, you can get anything you need." Nonnative residents must build a name, a process that is strongly gendered and requires "brokerage" using the positive valuation of an established resident(s) whose name is positively known. The process often fails and "outsiders" rarely stay in Ash Creek for longer than a few years unless they are married to a native resident. Neither family nor personal name valuation requires an individual to engage in institutional workplace systems of ranking or personal legitimization, although it is nearly impossible to avoid exposure to and adoption of some of them when most residents have worked in or have had business contact with institutional workplaces. Instead, Ash Creek community systems of valuation have scope over workplace practices in a manner similar to that described by Anglin (1992; this volume) such that interactional disjunctions and contestations regularly occur when locals "work for" nonlocals in business or industrial settings.

Therefore local interpretive structures about the nature and value of "work" tend to conform to nonindustrial and family-based patterns consistent with the cultural systems of the oldest residents reared under subsistence farming economics. In the complex but circumscribed relationships created by local residents with outside businesses and local work, these structures continue to be passed down to children, grandchildren, and great-grandchildren, who use them in local schools, the county's consolidated high school, and the regional community college where they mesh with more urban administrative patterns in syncretic and symbiotic ways (Puckett 1992; for related discussions see Keefe, Reck, and Reck 1991).

These semiotic systems of work interpretation provide meaning and organization to labor events according to a culturally recognized set of negotiated statuses and appropriate behaviors within these statuses, all of which are linked to the value of "name."[13] Individuals in Ash Creek are granted certain sets of "rights" to do culturally acknowledged activities as long as individuals are within their "place" when they perform them.[14]

RIGHTS AND PLACE RELATIONS

To use "showing" discourse, a resident must first be "right" and have "rights" to do so. As understood by most residents, "rights" are determined not by law, but by God as interpreted in local fundamentalist or Pentecostal-based churches. Predicated on gender and age status categories, not on educational levels or professional position in a company, individuals engage in labor activities or economic exchanges according to their "rights." Men can hunt in the woods (even out of season for some), for example, because it is a man's right. Women can demand that visitors to their homes eat a meal because it is a woman's right. Older women can expect donated labor from sons and grandsons because it is right for a man to honor his mother in "doing for her." When someone violates status "rights," as when a woman "works like a man," then "it's not right" and some form of sanctions, at least as gossip, are likely to follow.

Even when individuals are within their rights, they must conform to their "place" within family or community social organizational structure. "Place" criteria are often less clearly defined than "rights," in that they depend upon individuals negotiating positions within community reputations of families, gender, and an individual's personal achieved status efforts.

Similar to Kingsolver's discussion of "placing" in Cedar (1992), Ash Creek residents must orient others according their location within a kinship network or community group, often with assumptions of residence in a specific locale. "Place" in Ash Creek, however, is more geographically grounded than in Cedar, and is a central structure in providing residents with a community identity. It links residents' social activities to specific cultural transformations of land, and to the matrix of social networks that arise from these transformations.[15] Without such grounding, I quickly learned, for example, that, for one family, it was not my place to provide transportation assistance to an elderly woman family member, even though it was within my rights to do so. Likewise, if a community resident wants to "show" someone how to do something, such as deer hunting or hooking up a video cassette recorder/player to a television, it must be his or her place to do so.

Appropriate uses of the Ash Creek socioeconomic showing discourse repertoire therefore require that participants are within their "rights" and "place" to do so. From the perspective of the theoretical orientation outlined earlier, the configuration of speech event components (for example, type of speech variety, speech act forms, goals, and discourse structuring) and participant relationships within showing settings must somehow signal that such rights and place requirements are met if discourse itself is constitutive of socioeconomic relations communicated in showing how to do a task. They minimally do so by a process of indexicality[16] in which the use of expected showing discourse structures simultaneously signal, or point to, rights and place criteria associated with the use of such forms. These associations are not random, but normative, and represent a nearly invariant but learned relation between language and culture in their very construction.

It is important to note, however, that residents do not all share the exact same inventory of rights and place criteria, although the predictable and routine nature of most residents' interactions encourages consensus for most activities. A conventional showing discourse structure such as "put that here" uttered by a woman in instructing another on how to complete a job application form must index the right of woman to use "that" deictically (indexically) to reference a woman's or gender-neutral item. But whether all community residents accept that this task is "right" to do for any woman may be problematic. It is this variation in individuals' rights and place criteria that provides opportunities for labor diversity and socioeconomic change, albeit in highly constrained ways.

Consequently, in situations of use, showing discourse establishes indexical relationships with participants such that appropriate use of instructions simultaneously reproduces the rights of the speakers to use them, and, conversely, inappropriate uses of the imperatives within them produce negative or hostile responses as addressees feel "ordered" or "told" what to do. A woman, for example, cannot instruct an adult man on how to tune a car engine. "It's not right."

Likewise, participants within their "rights" to show or be shown must know their "place," meaning they must have an awareness of the power relations existing between the interlocutors. If it's not "right" for a woman to show a man how to tune an engine, it's not an adult man's "place" to show another man how to do this same task with fully developed showing discourse. The imperatives that form the basis of these developed forms create indices of social asymmetry in their expectations of compliance, inequalities that blatantly question core cultural norms of male equality. Whereas "rights" violations disrupt the social order, "place" violations weaken or break social relationships, often creating personal grudges.

While such miscommunications could be approached as politeness violations (Brown and Levinson 1987), such interactional misfires jeopardize a man's (or woman's under a different set of "place" assumptions) identity and worth (or "name") as a community member and affect the potential reproduction of the socioeconomic system. Violations of the power relations constructed by showing discourse indexicalities of place jeopardize the ability to construct exchange relations in the future.

SHOWING DISCOURSE AS CONSTITUTIVE OF SOCIOECONOMIC RELATIONS

For these reasons, fully-developed showing discourse is a marked, or notable, discourse practice, occurring only when both rights and place are appropriately indexed, an uncommon juxtaposition among adults. Instead, an occasional verbal directive may be offered in a learning situation, or, most commonly, the learner simply observes how the task is done until he or she learns by observation and subsequent practice. On the other hand, fully embellished forms of this practice are not uncommon with children, as is seen in Example 1.

Example 1[17]

Maintenance building of environmental center around 10:00 P.M. during night watchman's dinner break. Instruction in progress. Participants: woodcarver (night watchman) and local boy, nine years old and distant kin to woodcarver. Visitors: boy's parents, nonnative local couple, and myself, who are conversing among ourselves during instructional sequence. The woodcarver's son and daughter-in-law join us as the session continues. WC = woodcarver; LS = local student. Tape 8A:1986.

Sanding and pounding noises in background throughout; visitors converse among themselves periodically. Instructional session in progress. Carvers focus upon the young boy's attempts at carving a butter knife, although woodcarver also has in his hands a piece he is working on. Occasionally the woodcarver will take the hands of the boy to show him how to hold the knife or carve. Most often, he demonstrates with his own work.

WC: So (3.8) ya see, it's not wantin to . . . carve tha, that way.
When it gives you trouble, ya got to turn it around an
(come) this way. An too, (2.0)
if ya cut yourself,

you, you put your fist against you here,
an you're carvin out like this (3.0).
So when your knife flips off ya see your hand hits first.
So you don't hit yourself with your knife.
Because, it's, it's sort a automatic. (4.0)
Ya hold ya, you hold your arm real close to ya here. (3.0)
So usually . . . one side will carve one way,
An the other side'll carve the other. (2.5)
That's the way the grain . . . works.
So when you're carvin this way ya see ya don't see your mark
    here.
You carve down a little ways,
you can always glance over to see . . . where your mark is. (4.8)
Now, you make this curve. (2.0)
Put your thumb down here now,
you do everything I show you,
you won't get cut. (2.0)
Put your thumb down there ya see
an it sort a shaves down like that. (2.4)
Just let that stay.
An you shave down (2.0) (X) like,
an you back this side.
You, you'll be forgettin a lot of this stuff,
an I'll just keep showin ya. (2.0)
An you take that off.
Careful, like that ya see.
Cause ya come down against this too hard,
you'll split it off,
an then you won't cut your a,
cut your mark off. ((clears throat)) (10.0)
So when you're doin this ya see you're doin
        little sharp strokes. (5.8)
If ya git beyond your mark don't worry about it,
we'll uh.
There's a lot a people that change styles with their butter knives
((all chuckle))
Now you take this off you ya see,
You, you gone a use your thumb again for leverage. (3.0)
See there?
LB: Uh-huh.
WC: Thumb's over here.
    An your knife'll come off.

An if you have it up there too high,
It'll come off when you can't stop it.
You, you make sure your thumb is down there,
below where knife comes off. (2.0)
LB: Uh-huh.
WC: An you'll never git cut,
if you, you always remember these tips.

This segment from an hour-long instructional session is an example of appropriate and fully developed showing discourse, used in what residents consider to be a traditional manner despite the institutional setting of the environmental center's shop rather than a private home or shed. The woodcarver is on his break as a night watchman and is instructing a local boy, distant kin, in "whittlin," or pocket-knife carving. His parents, who work for the center, have brought him for lessons because of the woodcarver's reputation.

Such local man and local boy participant structuring was unusual for this setting, as residents seldom visit the center's campus at night. At this time (1985–87, but not after early 1988), the woodcarver instructed visiting nonlocal students and elder hostelers under very similar conditions. While he was sometimes paid for daytime demonstrations, these night sessions were voluntary and performed during his "lunch" hour at about 10:00 P.M. Regulars, such as a few center staff or other nonnative, younger locals including myself, often developed reciprocity bonds, or "claims," with him, resulting over time in gifts from his stock of carvings, much desired as purchases by short-term visitors, but never for sale.

In this case, the woodcarver is within his rights to instruct the boy: "whittlin" is a male task and he is known to be good at it. The boy is of course within his rights to learn, both by age and by gender, and his parents felt that is was "right" for their son to learn a traditional craft from a community member whom they could "place," when neither of them was able to carve themselves.

Each of the participants knows his place as well. The woodcarver assumes he is superior in knowledge, skill, and experience, and asserts his right to demonstrate whittling processes and talk about them, so that he controls the verbal and gestural action completely. The boy, on the other hand, grants the man control over the event, only backchanneling with "uh-huh" to confirm understanding of the directions. Nor is he ignoring the directions as he works on his own butter knife carving as he makes eye contact with the carver, nodding occasionally, to indicate understanding of a point. Otherwise he looks down, focusing on his own work, in keeping with Ash Creek rules of avoiding eye contact unless considered necessary.

Such verbal and gestural restraint is characteristic of community instructional behavior by most learners, but was very uncharacteristic of visitors who questioned, asked many questions, demanded time or help, or requested verbal directions or explanations that told them how to carve rather than demonstrating techniques, and frequently demanded eye contact. Considered "aggravtin," these interruptions showed that they didn't know their place; the boy did. The woodcarver obtained respect, influence, and a certain amount of prestige through others granting him a right to control the showing discourse so fully; the activity enhanced his name. It also granted him a modicum of influential power in the community as he built a "place" for himself, as a "teacher" of "whittlin."

The discourse itself in Example 1 appears disjointed, in fact almost nonsensical as text alone. Deictics from the beginning, such as "it's not wantin to carve that way," and "now when you make this curve" bond the text to the carving activities being performed by the participants. Pronouns such as "it" and nouns such as "wood" reference specific material items being manipulated by the carvers, creating a verbal text that illustrates the task, but is subordinate to the performance of it. Without visual support of the activity itself, the discourse is therefore meaningless or at least highly ambiguous.

Yet it is structured. Such discourse requires an early introduction of imperatives such as "ya got to turn it around an (go) this way," which index the right of the speaker to direct the action. Compliance of some form is expected through at least an attempt by the listener at performing the task, or the instruction is terminated in some culturally appropriate way. When the learner does attempt compliance, it is a response that acknowledges the speaker's place to be in control of what the listener does in the instructional session. Thus, action by the listener acknowledges that the use of imperatives as directives is appropriate and that the speaker is within his rights and his place. In this instance, the speaker marks these rights and place relations further by ending the sequence with a moral or caveat: "an you'll never git cut if you always remember these tips." This phrase is formulaic, a slight modification of closings to television, popular magazine, or agricultural extension pamphlet descriptions of household, garden, or home improvement procedures. It associates the woodcarver with those professionals who demonstrate or write these procedures, enhancing his qualifications as knowledgeable instructor further, at least from his perspective as a member of the environmental center's staff for many years.

The discourse also must gloss, or tell about, the action, giving meaning to the process of manual labor in progress. Consequently the sequencing of imperatives or other directive discourse is highly dependent upon the sequence of steps involved in the activity itself. In fact, it cannot exist as showing discourse without them. The most minute and specific tasks are as important as more general planning tasks in that each comes in an exact location in the sequence of actions. The boy cannot "make this curve" until he "put [his] thumb down here" (meaning the bottom of the piece with respect to his body). This highly specific action is as important in the sequence of steps as is putting the final oil or varnish on the finished product.

Finally, these discourse glosses, which are dependent upon the manual actions that manipulate material forms such as wood, assist in, but do not in themselves, create a new or modified product, whether it be a butter knife, a quilt, an apron, a new shed, or repair the brakes on the car. With its linguistic ability to reference specific steps and actions, showing discourse is necessary to transmitting the knowledge and skill necessary to complete a task, but it is ultimately subordinated to those nonverbal semiotic processes of simply doing it. This blending of meaningful human utterances to meaningful nonverbal actions create, in turn, a composite communication, drawing upon multiple modes of signification. No mode can be isolated from the others without altering the cultural significance of entire activity. All modes, including language, are necessary for its success. The use of language, however, infuses the entire activity with its capacity to create relations of power and control. In this case, these relations are culturally acceptable.

The relations created by the showing discourse in Example 2, however, are inappropriate to the task being instructed. It represents an occasion in which a young (23–year-old) community resident has been asked to instruct an older nonlocal woman, myself, in tasks pertinent to the performance of receptionist duties at the local clinic. I am to replace her when she is off. The clinic is a small outpost of a much larger incorporated medical care facility obligated to meet state and federal guidelines for licensed medical care. Local record-keeping and insurance procedures must be in accord with the facility's, so some knowledge of medical protocol is required.

Example 2

Reception area of regional medical center's outpost clinic, a small building of six small rooms and a larger waiting area, fall 1986. No clients are in the waiting area at this time and nurse practitioner is in her office working. Receptionist, a young married woman living and working locally, is instructing me in how to do her job as a fill-in. The following is an instructional segment occurring about one-half way through the session. Tape 10B; 1986. R = receptionist; AP = Anita Puckett.

R: Uh, but then, on the, on the Kentucky Medical Card,
       the way I do that,
       ok . . . now this is different than these kind a cards.

     See, this has got one subscriber's name.
     This is got all of them in the family,
AP: Uh-huh.
R: Covered.
     Ok.
     Whoever has come in to see Millie,
     you put their name up here.
AP: Ok.
R: hen you put their number.
AP: Got ya.
R: Now I always put KMC . . . with parenth, parentheses and then
        Medicaid.
     That way they'll know it's from Kentucky.
     I don't even know if we're supposed to take a out of state
        Kentuck, uhm, [medical] card or not.
AP: [Medicaid]
R: But I do that just in case.
     You might want a have a number.
     Uh, I don't ful, fill this out
     I don't [fool with] this.
AP: [fill that] You have to do [one]
R: [jis] start here at sex.
     ((both chuckle))
     An then go on with that.
AP: Ok.

     In this instructional discourse segment, basic participant relations are
skewed with respect to culturally normative ones. The receptionist does have
the right to instruct other women in her duties since medical care is within
women's domain and since reading and writing are women's activities (Puckett 1992, 1993). Yet she is also young, without a widely known name for herself in the community, so that, in cultural terms, her place in her family network and the community matrix of relations is less defined and still very
much open to negotiation. Therefore her place to instruct is also uncertain,
especially when the trainee is older and without place as a nonlocal outsider
as I was. Discourse segments from other occasions or from this one, which are
not included here, exhibit this problem as she giggles, apologizes, or uses
other deference behavior to not only me, but to other trainees older than herself as well.
     In addition, this task, filling out that section of a patient's encounter
form requiring reference to an insurance card, does not produce a final and
new product, only writing on a previously existing piece of paper. Seemingly

amenable to showing discourse, this shifting of manual labor from shaping or modifying material items to simply filling in blocks or sections of a form is a major one in terms of showing discourse functions. The use of oral language to explain written language activities upon a printed piece of paper creates a second order of removal from the task of paper modification for the showing discourse itself. A speaking practice created to map talk onto action now confronts an intervening level of signification, that of writing. Normative showing discourse is not structured for this conflation of semiotic systems.

In this case, the glossing, or labeling, function of normative showing discourse is reproduced, as the speaker treats each medical card according to the configuration of print on it, setting each one apart from the other by its markings in a manner similar to appliqués or quilt pieces. Each item on the card receives attention, even though such careful examination has little to contribute to the knowledge needed to fill in the form.

The imperatives, such as "you put their name up here," direct a task that is more appropriately considered as "marking" an ideograph (Ong 1982) in which one places a form rather than "writing" a text. Each name is repeated, pattern style, in the box marked "name." Finally, the text "just start here at sex" directs the trainee to begin at a particular place on the form ("sex") as if it were a point on a pattern from which to begin a manual task. None of this discourse "tells about" the medical form itself or describes abstractly the kinds of information mediated through writing that are needed to complete it. With the further omission of an appropriate standardized medical form lexicon such as "write," "enter," "box," "code," or "line" as well, this discourse segment does not meet a basic function of any instructional discourse to map speech as precisely as possible onto pertinent action within the immediate context. The speech does not use words that "gloss" the requisite literate actions required, nor does it "explain" the goals and purposes of the task at hand. This discourse segment does, however, meet the structural requirements of Ash Creek showing discourse, including the use of some imperatives and a dependency on the sequence of motor activities. In this case, speech appropriate to the Ash Creek socioeconomic discourse repertoire becomes inappropriate as the activity itself does not meet the structural requirements of the discourse, nor does the discourse meet the needs of the activity.

Such meaning disjunctions are significant in terms of "place" indexical relations and the interactive power such relations create. At a basic level, the very configuration of participant relations themselves undercuts appropriate "place" associations. More complexly, the ineffective use of showing discourse makes creation of appropriate place indexicals unlikely. The result is a failed instructional sequence in which power relations are not clear. This disjunction is interpreted by community trainees (always women) in terms of their ability to understand and do the job. They consider it hard, complex, if not impossible to understand all the "details," and many do not continue, even when literacy skills are not a factor. Yet this type of position is a prerequisite for most offices and critical for effective corporate organization, a very common type of position in most urban workplaces.

Nor is this example an isolate, encountered only with this particular clerk. In many situations involving women learning office tasks, similar discourse/activity disjunctions occur.[18] Regional analysts, businessmen, and scholars often attribute women's avoidance of such encounters to educational weaknesses, low self-esteem, or negative stereotypes (for example, Shakertown Roundtable 1987).

IMPLICATIONS OF SHOWING DISCOURSE IN WORKPLACE POWER RELATIONS

As demonstrated by this example, however, inappropriate use of showing discourse certainly plays a significant role in these workplace difficulties. When men are considered, the role is more pronounced. The rights and place relations indexed by showing discourse, and the power and control messages created through its use, are in direct opposition to the egalitarian ideology affirmed by Ash Creek men. Instructional discourse, whether as Ash Creek "showing discourse" or as the reading-dominated forms of corporate offices, is shunned by Ash Creek men as a symbolic index of nonadult status. Practiced from childhood in observing how to do things and then do them, men will frequently claim to know how to perform a task rather than admit they need to be shown "how to do" something and risk identification with children. Imperatives are powerful, and discourse that requires their use is potent in its ability to control the actions of others.

Finally, Ash Creek socioeconomic discourse has only "showing discourse" in its repertoire as a fully developed verbally-dependent means of instructing others (Puckett 1993). Bonded tightly to manual tasks that produce some product, it is structurally unsuitable for highly literate, hierarchically organized instructional sequences in corporate workplaces (for related discussions, see Ervin-Tripp 1976; Heath 1983; Linde 1994; Weigel and Weigel 1985), just as these institutional forms of discourse are minimally adapted to instructing culturally valued Ash Creek tasks. More than conflicts in task mastery, acquisition of a form of standard American English, or in work behavior patterns, Ash Creek residents in contact with formal, corporate, and more urban work contexts and workplaces are often literally at a loss for words. Often offended by violations of their rights and place, unfamiliar with the structure and function of instructional sequences or unable to apply their cultural knowledge of how to learn in verbal form, they retreat from the workplace or attempt to restructure it in a form with which they are familiar, with various degrees of success or frustration. For these individuals, the result is economic disempowerment, as access to the resources that permit full participation in workplace activities is denied. They continue to resort to known strategies, which construct identities based on noncapitalistic criteria.

Frequently, workers will develop a type of discourse syncretism in which local discourse patterns are maintained with some modification, as seen in the instructional sequence presented in Example 2. Institutional forms, such as telephone etiquette, are incorporated into workplace speaking practices. The clinic receptionist, for example, handled the routine interactions of her job well, but readily transferred extended workplace interactions with nonlocal medical personnel or other outsiders to the nurse practitioner managing the facility. Not uncommonly, male work crews will count on using a fellow worker, often a supervisor or company boss of some type, as a discourse "broker" who is an area (but not necessarily from the community) native, often from a town, who has mastered some level of nonlocal discourse patterns and who can filter, even recode administrative instructions to them, in culturally appropriate discourse usages. Such adaptation of speaking practices facilitates successful interaction, but does not demand loss of community-valued ideologies of work.

It is insufficient to suggest that problems in using instructional discourse can be addressed by companies simply offering workshops or training in how to use corporate or formal institutional instructions. Ash Creek showing discourse practices are nontrivial verbal activities in which central relations of self to culture are communicated. Yet the relations encoded in showing discourse are also constructed, albeit with different kinds of constraints, within other political economic discourse practices.[19]

The result of such multiple ways to empower individuals economically is that residents acquire norms of empowerment that are not likely to be altered by a few out-of-context encounters in the workplace. When taken as a whole, these community-based verbal processes reproduce counterhegemonies of how power and access to powerful resources are constituted. These processes are directly relevant to an individual's understanding of what economic power is or should be. Consequently, superficial changes in how typical workplace instructions are structured in attempts to train Ash Creek residents will only promote economic separation, not reduce it. As instructors bring different sets of indexical relationships associated with different instruction structures than are familiar to Ash Creek residents, some levels of miscommunication will occur, precipitating instructee withdrawal or recoding into Ash Creek intepretations of power relations.

This presentation of "showing discourse" functions from one Appalachian community implies a larger argument that rural Appalachian

socioeconomic work relationships to regional or national wage-labor corporations or businesses are ones that cannot be relegated to analytic categories
of class, educational status, or rurality, as if each concept possessed explana-
tory power ipso facto. Rather, it takes a more basic stance that the often
intangible communicative processes facilitated or created by actual utterances of one discourse practice within any work discourse repertoire need to
be investigated and understood in their multicontextual significations within
the wider cultural matrix in which they occur. In this case, this assertion suggests that such ethnographic knowledge of discourse practices reveal how
cultural members construct instructional discourse when they use it and what
meanings such emergent systems of learning convey to them. These structurings are patterned, polysemous, and multifunctional. Among their structurings are constructions of socioeconomic power or powerlessness. What
types of power, under what conditions, and why, are manifestations of the
discourse-in-use; the discourse is constitutive of them. As more of these
types of investigations emerge, it is certain the language and political economic relations revealed by them will foster significant changes in theory.
For it is by such ethnographically based investigations that empirical, replicable, and culturally meaningful interpretations can be given to the linguisti-
cally based dialogic (in the Bakhtinian sense) and multivocal expressions of
power and powerlessness people themselves use to construct that contemporary complex of changing labor interactions in which they always find themselves.

NOTES

1. Notable exceptions to this conceptualization of discourse in terms of linguistic approaches to political economy are represented by works such as Duranti (1994),
Gal (1979, 1989), and Woolard (1989).

2. This linguistic anthropological perspective resonates with Giddens'
(1995:237) general observation that "ordinary language is the medium whereby social
life is organized as meaningful by its constituent actors: to study a form of life involves
grasping lay modes of talk which express that form of life." Of course analogs or sympathetic formulations are present in contemporary political economic theory as well
(for example, Bourdieu 1991; Foucault 1973, 1977; Habermas 1979). From a linguistic anthropological perspective, however, it is important to ground these observations
in actual instances of speaking, a process that requires sensitivity to the multilayered
and multistructural aspects of any segment of talk.

3. Such a methodological demand is more easily met in communities such as
Ash Creek, which are relatively homogenous in their discourse practices repertoire
than in culturally diverse settings such as are found in large corporations in highly
urban areas. Nevertheless, as the Ash Creek case illustrates, an ethnographic under-

standing of workplace interactants' discourse practices repertoire yields results that are generative, meaning they offer high levels of explanation which can be reapplied in new instructional discourse situations to provide more culturally sensitive interpretations.

4. Anthropologically sensitive studies of instructions in workplace settings tend to focus upon issues related to "learning" organizational skills, information, or ideologies (for example, Linde 1994; Orr 1995; see also Zuccermaglio et al. 1995) where their central role in organizational continuity is recognized. Discourse-focused studies of instructions (for example, Goldberg 1974 and Collins 1986) offer excellent analyses of how specific instructional interactions are structured in specific settings or reinforce organizational norms of learning competency. This discussion is based on developing studies in language and political economy that affirm broad-based ethnographic observations across the full range of participants' interactions. In this case, focus is upon rural Appalachian "showing" occasions both inside and outside organizational workplaces. This orientation toward the ethnographic process is more in keeping with works such as Briggs (1986), Duranti (1992), and Rosaldo (1982) and is indebted to studies such as Gumperz (1982), which recognize that the discourse created in a social interaction can communicate very different contextual meanings to participants according to their cultural presuppositions about how to interpret a particular type of speech event.

5. This sentence is deliberately general with respect to its implications for or dependence upon particular political economic theory. Habermas's conceptualizations of how societies address learning problems (1979) and Giddens (1982) critique of them, for example, are particularly relevant to developing the implications of this statement in the Ash Creek case. From a linguistic anthropological perspective, however, it is important to focus upon the communicative aspects of the discourse first and their relationship to language and power relations before relating them directly to social theory. To do so prematurely is to risk inaccuracies in how power is constructed across the full range of cultural members' communicative repertoires.

6. As noted in Kingsolver's "Introduction" (5), Colson (1977) makes a clear distinction between evidence of power and sources of power. This discussion of rural eastern Kentucky instructional discourse focuses upon how uses of this discourse function to control access to resources, and is therefore evidential of power rather than a source for it. It is in this sense that I use the term economic or socioeconomic rather than political economy in the following analysis.

7. The actual length of time spent in Ash Creek was 26 months, 1985–87. This portion of the research was supported by a National Science Foundation dissertation grant, BNS 8516273 and by Berea College through a Melon Foundation Appalachian Studies Fellowship. I lived in the immediate area, however, from 1987–89 and 1990–93, teaching at a local community college. During this time, I made periodic visits to the community, while becoming socially familiar with many who lived in a different part of the county or in an adjoining county and who shared may of the same verbal repertoire speaking practices. I last visited Ash Creek in August 1995. When I

actually lived in Ash Creek, I assumed the role of "teacher," teaching extension classes for a regional community college. This role allowed me to visit with most community women and to assume duties having some value to many residents.

8. Residents actually consider this area to consist of at least four different locales defined historically by such indicators as a post office, a church, or a local store. With extensive loss of population over the last 25 years, clear demarcation of these locales as communities has broken down so that residents may claim residency in more than one unit depending upon the conversational topic. Hence, I created a general community name to capture a more realistic picture of local interactional patterns.

9. Knowledge and skill to use even simple programs is very uneven within educational institutions, and upgrading of equipment is problematic, particularly in the local grade school. Consequently those exposed to computer technology are significantly behind in their integration into current technological capabilities. Telephone service is through a small, local company whose infrastructure does not permit internet linkage.

10. Even if an organized company, such as the environmental center, makes a job offer, the laborer will couch the offer in personalized terms so that clauses such as "Joe Smith needs me to lay some pipe" are more likely than "Massey Ferguson needs me to lay some pipe."

11. Lewis (1996) makes the point that, if local communities in Coalfield Appalachia are to survive, they must begin to engage in economic activities that are not "job" oriented, but "livelihood" focused, as coal reserves deplete and the cost of coal mining escalates into nonproductivity. Although Ash Creek residents are not consciously adopting the kinds of strategies noted by Lewis, they are in many cases recognizing the need to be eclectic in ways in which they obtain necessary goods and services. With most young adults migrating elsewhere in attempts to engage in class-based wage-labor work, it would be incorrect to assert that these livelihood strategies are necessarily adaptive for those left in Ash Creek. It is too early in this process to suggest that residents' efforts will actually succeed in supporting those remaining and in retaining a young population.

12. Of course, more abstract arguments (for example, using Bourdieu 1984 or, particularly, Habermas 1972, 1979) for viewing such strategies as resistance are suggested by these current economic activities, but most residents view such activities as ways of "getting by" rather than efforts at restructuring organizations or the regional economy. Furthermore, these adaptational strategies are nascent, evolving and shaping in highly diverse and not necessarily adaptive ways at the time of writing (June 1996).

13. As used here *status* is not to be considered a static term in the sense of Ratcliffe-Brown or Talcott Parsons; nor should is it intended to echo Weber's arguments for class formation. Rather, it is intended to encompass dynamic, negotiated categories of personality assessment by residents that are constantly reinterpreted and reassessed through discourse (for related discussions, see Duranti 1992; Woolard 1989).

14. The terms *rights* and *place* are derived from metacommentary about discourse about peoples' actions and behavior. Much community conversation is about what other people are doing or have done. Residents, in talking about these actions, will frequently assess the narrative by a phrase such as "that's not right," or "she's not actin right." Likewise, "place" is used to situate someone within the matrix of actors in a conversational narrative or face-to-face interaction—for example, "I can't place her," or "it's not your place to do that."

15. Although extraneous to the central development of this discussion and therefore not elaborated upon, Ash Creek constructions of "place" directly address the kinds of environmental and cultural relations issues illuminated by Rodman's (1992) discussion concerning the centrality of place and space in cultural life. Throughout much of rural Appalachia, "place" and its concomitant compound "homeplace" are central, core symbols permeating the entire verbal repertoire, functioning in part to organize all social life.

16. As used here, index is a type of semiotic sign in which there is a spatial and temporal co-presence between the sign itself and what it signifies (after Peirce 1931; see Silverstein 1979). Given the theoretical and methodological orientation of this discussion, an indexical sign is always presumed to be verbal, if not actually linguistic. For a comprehensive and exceptionally insightful discussion of the role of indexicals in Mayan deictics, or those grammatical forms that shift meaning according to context such as "this, that, here, "and "yonder" in English, see Hanks 1990.

17. Most Ash Creek residents depend upon the grammar and accentual patterns of Appalachian English (Wolfram and Christian 1976) for oral communication, although many, usually women, are familiar with basic standard written English conventions and may incorporate many standard forms into their speech. The transcription system adopted for this discussion is derived from those used by conversational analysts, in particular that method described by Du Bois et al. (1993). Here, notation has been simplified to capture only intonational contour units transcribed as line and those recognized phonemic differences between pronounciation of standard written American English and Appalachian English. Numbers in parentheses indicated pause lengths greater than two seconds. Two periods indicate pauses longer than required for a comma or period, but less than two seconds. An X in parentheses indicates an unintelligible syllable. Underlined words received special emphasis, while brackets [ ] indicate speaker overlap. No transcription can ever capture the full range of meanings communicated by the multichanneled modes created in oral face-to-face speech events. No attempt to do so is offered here. Rather, only those features minimally necessary to convey something of the emotive richness and communicative complexity in showing discourse are attempted, in addition to noting those major markers of the sound features of this speech variety.

18. In the course of living and teaching in the area for an extended period, requiring that I engage in encounters with local medical facilities, businesses, educational institutions, churches, and other institutions in the area, examples of workplace instruction were readily and frequently observed. In efforts to comply with federal and professional guidelines regarding consent in audio recording, few of these encounters were recorded.

19. In community-recognized terms, distinctly recognizable practices include, but are not limited to, "makin a deal," "takin care of," and "helpin out" somebody (Puckett 1993). It is important to note that constructions of personal or community empowerment constructed by the use of one political economic discourse practice can of course be reproduced or redefined through the indexical properties created in another. The result is intersecting and crosscutting views of personal identity that are constantly emerging in similar or different ways through the process of talk.

REFERENCES CITED

Anglin, Mary
   1998 Looking beyond the factory: Regional culture and practices of dissent. In
        More than Class: Studying Power in U.S. Workplaces. Ann Kingsolver, ed.
        pp. 53–72. Albany, N.Y.: State University of New York Press.
   1992 A question of loyalty: National and regional identity in narratives of
        Appalachia. *Anthropological Quarterly* 65:105–16.

Banks, Alan
   1980 The emergence of a capitalistic labor market in Eastern Kentucky.
        Appalachian Journal 7:188–98.

Batteau, Allen
   1981 Appalachia as a metropolitan problem. *Social Analysis* 7:3–23.
   1982 Mosbys and Broomsedge: The semantics of class in an Appalachian kinship
        system. *American Ethnologist* 9:445–66.

Bauman, Richard, and Joel Sherzer, eds.
   1989 *Explorations in the Ethnography of Speaking*. 2nd ed. New York: Cambridge
        University Press.

Bloch, Maurice, ed.
   1975 *Political Language and Oratory in Traditional Society*. New York: John
        Wiley and Sons.

Bourdieu, Pierre
   1991 *Language and Symbolic Power*. Cambridge: Harvard University Press.
   1984 *Distinction: A Social Critique of the Judgement of Taste*. R. Nice, trans. Cam-
        bridge: Harvard University Press.
   1977 *Outline of a Theory of Practice*. New York: Cambridge University Press.

Brenneis, Donald, and Fred Myers, eds.
   1984 *Dangerous Words: Language and Politics in the Pacific*. New York: New
        York University Press.

Brown, Penelope, and Steven Levinson
   1987 *Politeness: Some Universals in Language Usage*. New York: Cambridge Uni-
        versity Press.

Collins, James
1986 Differential instruction in reading groups. In *The Social Construction of Literacy.* Jenny Cook-Gumperz, ed. pp. 117–37. New York: Cambridge University Press.

Colson, Elizabeth
1977 Power at large: Meditation on "The Symposium of Power." In *The Anthropology of Power: Ethnographic Studies from Asia, Oceania, and the New World.* Raymond Fogelson and Richard N. Adams, eds. pp. 375–86. New York: Academic Press.

Davies, Edward
1986 *The English Imperative.* London: Croom Helm.

Drew, Paul, and John Heritage, eds.
1992 *Talk at Work: Interaction in Institutional Settings.* New York: Cambridge University Press.

Du Bois, John et al.
1993 Outline of discourse transcription. In *Talking Data: Transcription and Coding in Discourse Research.* Jane Edwards and Martin Lampert, eds. pp. 45–89. Hillsdale: Lawrence Erlbaum Associates.

Duranti, Alessandro
1994 *From Grammar to Politics: Linguistic Anthropology in a Western Samoan Village.* Berkeley: University of California Press.
1992 Language and bodies in social space: Samoan ceremonial greetings. *American Anthropologist* 94(3):657–92.

Duranti, Alessandro, and Charles Goodwin
1992 *Rethinking Context: Language as an Interactive Phenomenon.* New York: Cambridge University Press.

Eller, Ronald
1982 *Miners, Millhands, and Mountaineers: Industrialization of the Appalachian South, 1880–1930.* Knoxville: University of Tennessee Press.

Eller, Ronald et al.
1994 *Kentucky's Distressed Communities: A Report on Poverty in Appalachian Kentucky.* Lexington: Appalachian Center.

Ervin-Tripp, Susan
1982 Structures of control. In *Communicating in the Classroom.* L. Cherry-Wilkinson, ed. pp. 27–47. New York: Academic Press.
1976 Is Sybil there? The structure of some American English directives. *Language in Society* 5:25–56.

Firth, Alan, ed.
1995 *The Discourse of Negotiation: Studies of Language in the Workplace.* Tarrytown, PA: Pergamon.

Foucault, Michel
   1977 *Language, Counter-memory, Practice: Selected Essays and Interviews*. Donald Douchard, ed. and trans. Ithaca: Cornell University Press.
   1973 *The Archaeology of Knowledge and the Discourse on Language*. A.M. Smith, trans. New York: Pantheon Books.

Gal, Susan
   1989 Language and political economy. *Annual Review of Anthropology* 18:345–67.
   1979 *Language Shift: Social Determinants of Linguistic Change in Bilingual Austria*. New York: Academic Press.

Gal, Susan, and Kathyrn Woolard, eds.
   1995 Special issue on constructing languages and publics. *Pragmatics* 5(2).

Gaventa, John
   1980 *Power and Powerlessness: Quiescence and Rebellion in an Appalachian Valley*. Urbana: University of Illinois Press.

Giddens, Anthony
   1995 *Politics, Sociology and Social Theory: Encounters with Classical and Contemporary Social Thought*. Stanford: Stanford University Press.
   1982 *Profiles and Critiques in Social Theory*. London: MacMillan.
   1984 *The Constitution of Society*. Berkeley: University of California Press.

Goldberg, Jo Ann
   1974 A system for the transfer of instructions in natural settings. *Semiotica* 14(3):269–96.

Gumperz, John
   1982 *Discourse Strategies*. New York: Cambridge University Press.

Gumperz, John, and Dell Hymes, eds.
   1974 *Directions in Sociolinguistics: The Ethnography of Communication*. New York: Holt, Rinehart and Winston.

Habermas, Jürgen
   1979 *Communication and the Evolution of Society*. Boston: Beacon.
   1972 *Knowledge and Human Interests*. Jeremy Shapiro, trans. Boston: Beacon Press.

Hanks, William
   1990 *Referential Practice: Language and Lives Space among the Maya*. Chicago: University of Chicago Press.

Heath, Shirley Brice
   1983 *Ways with Words: Language, Life, and Work in Communities and Classrooms*. New York: Cambridge University Press.

Hicks, George
   1976 *Appalachian Valley*. New York: Holt, Rinehart and Winston.

Hymes, Dell
1981 *In Vain I Tried to Tell You*. Philadelphia: University of Pennsylvania Press.
1974 Models of the interaction of language and social life. In *Directions in Sociolinguistics*. John Gumperz and Dell Hymes, eds. pp. 35–71. New York: Holt, Rinehart and Winston.

Irvine, Judith
1989 When talk isn't cheap: Language and political economy. *American Ethnologist* 16:248–67.

Keefe, Susan, Una Mae Reck, and Gregory Reck
1991 Family and education in Southern Appalachia. In *Appalachia: Social Context Past and Present*. Bruce Ergood and Bruce Kuhre, eds. 3rd edition. Pp. 345–52. Dubuque: Kendall/Hunt.

Kingsolver, Ann
1992 Contested livelihoods: "Placing" one another in "Cedar," Kentucky. *Anthropological Quarterly* 65:128–36.

Kramarae, Cheris, M. Schulz, and William O'Barr, eds.
1984 *Language and Power*. Beverly Hills: Sage Publications.

Lewis, Helen
1996 *Coal and After Coal. April in Appalachia Lecture*. Blacksburg: Virginia Tech University.

Linde, Charlotte
1994 "I don't wanna be computer literate": Group construction of workplace learning. Paper presented at the 92nd American Anthropological Association annual meeting, Washington, D.C.

Moerman, Michael
1988 *Talking Culture: Ethnography and Conversation Analysis*. Philadelphia: University of Pennsylvania Press.

Nash, June
1992 Interpreting social movements: Bolivian resistance to economic conditions imposed by the International Monetary Fund. *American Ethnologist* 19:275–93.

Ong, Walter
1982 *Orality and Literacy*. London: Metheun.

Orr, Julian
1995 Ethnography and organizational learning: In pursuit of learning at work. In *Organizational Learning and Technological Change*. Cristina Zucchermaglio, Sebastiano Bagnara, and Susan Stucky, eds. Pp. 47–60. Berlin: Springer.

Paine, Robert
1981 *Politically Speaking: Cross-cultural Studies of Rhetoric*. Philadelphia: Institute for the Study of Human Issues.

Pearsall, Marion
  1959 *Little Smoky Ridge: The Natural History of a Southern Appalachian Neighborhood.* Tuscaloosa: University of Alabama Press.

Peirce, Charles S.
  1931 *Collected Papers* vol. 2. Cambridge: Harvard University Press.

Puckett, Anita
  1993 *Seldom Ask, Never Tell: Speech Acts and Economic Relations in a Rural Eastern Kentucky Community.* Dissertation. University of Texas at Austin.
  1992 "Let the girls do the spelling and Dan will do the shooting": Literacy, the division of labor, and identity in a rural Appalachian community. *Anthropological Quarterly* 65:137–47.

Rodman, Margaret
  1992 Empowering place: Multilocality and multivocality. *American Anthropologist* 94(3):640–56.

Rosaldo, Michelle
  1982. The things we do with words: Ilongot speech acts and speech act theory in philosophy. *Language in Society* 11: 203–37.

Quirk, Randolph et al.
  1985 *A Comprehensive Grammar of the English Language.* London: Longman Press.

Shakertown Roundtable
  1987 The State of the Commonwealth: A Report of the Shakertown Roundtable Conference. Pleasant Hill, KY: Shakertown.

Sherzer, Joel
  1987 A discourse-centered approach to language and culture. *American Anthropologist* 89:295–309.

Silverstein, Michael
  1979 Language structure and linguistic ideology. In *The Elements: A Parasession on Linguistic Units and Levels.* P.R. Clyne, W. Hanks, and C. Hofbauer, eds. Pp. 193–247. Chicago: Chicago Linguistic Society.

Urban, Gregory
  1991 *A Discourse-centered Approach to Culture: Native South American Myths and Rituals.* Austin: University of Texas Press.

Weigel, M., and R. Weigel
  1985 Directive use in a migrant agricultural community: A test of Ervin-Tripp's hypotheses. *Language in Society* 14:63–80.

Wolfram, Walt, and Donna Christian
  1976 *Appalachian Speech.* Arlington: Center for Applied Linguistics.

Woolard, Kathryn
  1989 *Double Talk: Bilingualism and the Politics of Ethnicity in Catalonia.* Stanford: Stanford University Press.

Zucchermaglio, Cristina, Sebastiano Bagnara, and Susan Stucky, eds.
  1995 *Organizational Learning and Technological Change.* Berlin: Springer.

Chapter 6

Moving Up Down in the Mine: The Preservation of Male Privilege Underground

Suzanne E. Tallichet

INTRODUCTION

Due mostly to the antidiscrimination litigation of the late 1970s, an appreciable number of women have joined the underground coal mining workforce. However, as the institutional barriers to their entry were greatly reduced, those affecting their integration into that workforce were hardly eliminated. According to Blau and Ferber (1985:44), in many nontraditional blue-collar occupations, "hierarchical differences between the sexes still appear quite pronounced. It may be that the resistance to upward mobility of women is even greater than their entry."

When members of a previously excluded group, such as women, gain entry into a workplace where managers felt initially pressured into hiring them, job-level sex segregation typically results (Harlan and O'Farrell 1982; Reskin 1988). Thus, coal mining men continue to dominate the channels of upward mobility and to retain the better jobs, while women are disproportionately found in jobs that are lower-paying, feature less autonomy and status, and allow fewer chances for promotion due to both the organizational and cultural practices of the workplace.

Members of work organizations experience both formal and informal types of contact with one another through which conflicts develop and are resolved based on the parties' differing interests and amounts of power (Etizoni 1964). Men have greater access to organizational resources because they occupy positions of authority at work. As a result, both formal and informal processes and structures found there are biased in their favor (Taylor 1988), making them relatively more powerful than women in the workplace. Thus, despite the emphasis on the consistency of organizational rules that are assumed to have universalistic consequences, internal labor markets are disparate in terms of their impact on the sexes (Hartmann 1987). Indeed, the very creation of an internal hierarchy provides the tools necessary to discriminate, either on the basis of merit or on other worker characteristics, such as gender.

For example, in previous studies, women miners have complained about not getting the on-the-job training they needed to advance based on the qualification requirements of the seniority system (Mahoney 1978; Yount 1986; Moore and White 1989). Having the necessary skills also affects their subsequent work assignments when management periodically realigns the underground working force (Tallichet 1991).

Formal barriers do not operate alone in order to constrain women's advancement. Informal processes can directly and indirectly alter "the machine-like structure of the formal organization to fit the very human proclivities of its members, especially those in dominant organizational positions (that is, men)" (Taylor 1988:181). Numerous studies have focused on the nature of women's informal relations with co-workers and supervisors as central to understanding their relative lack of success (For a review, see Roos and Reskin 1984). Specifically, men's gendered expectations and reactions to women and women's social accommodations to a male-dominated workplace are essential for understanding the emergence of a sexual division of labor underground (Tallichet 1995).

The research findings presented in this chapter consider how the formal procedures of the internal labor market upon which the job hierarchy is based and the informal relations that reflect the effects of gender in the workplace combine to result in job-level sex segregation among underground coal miners. The analyses of data demonstrate the problematic nature of women's struggle to prove themselves to men, other women, and themselves, as competent for performing male-identified work in a male-dominated work setting. They also reveal the power of males' negative stereotyping of female work behavior sustained by men's (and sometimes women's) sexualization of the workplace (Enarson 1984; Swerdlow 1989) as results in the twin processes of "objectification" and "stigmatization" (Schur 1984) of women miners. These processes affect the structure of women's opportunities for advancement as they are mediated through the formal procedures of the mining establishment's internal labor market.

METHODOLOGY

Primary data were collected through from in-depth, semistructured interviews, informal conversations, on-site nonparticipant observation, and archival research done at a large coal mine in southern West Virginia during October and November of 1990. Fieldwork lasted one month. All of the afore-mentioned techniques were used together in order to crosscheck data gathered from multiple sources. My goal was to gain a full understanding of the women miners' beliefs, values, and perspectives about their work, their advancement, and their experiences with co-workers and supervisors. Thus, the case study design and the techniques used were best suited for this investigation because they allowed me to get close to the data and develop explanations directly from them. These techniques also provided an understanding of culturally prescribed and temporally bound social phenomena resulting from the con-stant flow of interaction based on the power relations between actors within the context of the workplace.

I first learned of the case study site from a contact, a former miner her-self, at the 1990 annual Coal Employment Project's national conference of women miners held in Norton, Virginia, in June. After writing the coal com-pany's human resources officer and receiving permission from the home office in a neighboring state, I was given access to restricted areas at the site, such as the women's bath house and the miner's lamp house, where miners gathered between shifts. I was also granted tours of the compound and a tour of the mine.

Before the early to mid-1970s, women's inroads into mining were slow and sporadic. However, in 1978, lawyer Betty Jean Hall, then director of the Coal Employment Project (CEP), successfully filed with the Office of Federal Compliance Contract Programs a massive lawsuit against 153 coal compa-nies. As a result, women who had previously and unsuccessfully applied for coal mining jobs were awarded back pay and along with other women were hired according to newly established affirmative action quota guidelines. Sim-ilar to other large coal companies involved in the hiring discrimination litiga-tion of 1978, the case study company did not begin employing women in appreciable numbers until it was forced to do so. In 1975, only three women were working there. By the early 1980s, out of 800 miners, between 80 and 90 were women. However, several years later, the industry's economic slump forced the company to lay off almost half its miners, including more than two-thirds of the women. Thus, at the time of the study, the company employed 466 miners, including 23 women. All the miners were members of the United Mine Workers of America (UMWA). The company also employed approxi-mately a dozen men as assistant foremen or "bosses." Their duties under-ground were strictly supervisory, so they were not members of the UMWA.

Based on my observations, the case study mine, like any coal mine, was a dark and damp environment where miners were working side by side often in cramped areas. Shift work was performed on several different sections simultaneously. Miners depended on each other for their collective safety and productivity, and miners and their foremen were mutually dependent. Foremen counted on their crews to meet production quotas in exchange for fair treatment and occasional favors.

During their first few months on the job, new miners were considered trainees and were assigned to grade 1 jobs, such as general inside (GI) labor or beltman. At the end of this period, they received their miner's certificate, meaning they could go on to bid on any newly posted higher-graded jobs in the mine. Jobs in grades 2 through 5 required operative skills usually, but not exclusively acquired on the job. By UMWA contract, jobs have always been awarded by seniority defined as length of service and a miner's ability to perform the bid job. However, since the mid-1980s, new job postings had been infrequent and realignments of the work force were occurring regularly. At the time of the study, the concentration of women in grade 1 jobs at the mine was substantial. Eighteen of the 23 women miners (78 percent) were so classified compared with 148 (33 percent) of the men.

All my interviews with the women were solicited in the women's bath house, usually before rather than after their shifts. My contact at the women's conference strongly advised against the latter since tired miners coming off their shifts might be less cooperative. Sampling among the women miners was a combination of snowball and purposive techniques. The snowball technique was used when I asked the first few women I interviewed to give me the names of other women. From these names I used the purposive techniques by selecting certain women to be interviewed by virtue of their tenure, job rank, or other job-related experiences, such as sexual harassment or discriminatory treatment. All of these women consented to be interviewed. Every effort was made to conduct interviews in quiet private settings, such as my motel room or in the womens' homes, at times when the respondent would be at ease and feel free to provide information and her opinions about sensitive topics.

The in-depth interviews with the women lasted up to two hours. All except two of the interviews were taped with the interviewee's consent as the setting would allow. One of these interviews was conducted in a diner and the other took place in the women's bath house. In both cases, I decided not to tape-record these interviews in order to avoid intruding upon others' privacy or to call attention to the interview process and those involved.

The first few interviews were crucial to establishing rapport and trust with the women in the sample because, as I learned from women interviewed later, the earliest interviewees assured the others that their interview experience had not resulted in any ill consequences. Moreover, from the earliest interviews, I attempted to diffuse any class-based social distance that might also lead to resentment or distrust between us through my dress and demeanor.

Being a woman in my early thirties whose usual dress was a faded army jacket, flannel shirt, jeans, and boots, facilitated my initial contact with the women miners. Most of the women were my age and dressed in a similar manner. I asked for interviews by explaining that I was a graduate student working on my thesis and not a representative of either the company or the union. By making the women aware of my student status from the outset, I literally established myself in the role of "student" eager to "become educated" about mining from my interviewees whom I dubbed "my teachers." I also likened getting my degree to them getting their "mining papers," the certificate of training needed to become a coal miner. Those women who granted interviews were often as curious about me as I was about them. After some discussion about the rigors of mining, two of the women in the sample, noting my interest in mining and my "athletic build," exclaimed that with the required training, "you could be on our crew!"

In total, interviews were conducted with ten women. Additional contact with them was initiated either by me or the women themselves. Moreover, on numerous occasions brief twenty–minute discussions were held with seven more women who were either unable or unwilling to speak at greater length. These women were willing to discuss various topics briefly in the bath house, but begged off in-depth interviews fearing possible reprisals from the company. Their classic response was: "Sorry, but I need this job." Only a few women flatly refused to be interviewed.

The women in the sample were diverse in terms of their age, education, marital status, and child bearing. The youngest woman in the sample was twenty-nine; the oldest was fifty. One woman finished the tenth grade, seven had high school diplomas, and two had attended college. At the time they were hired, six of the women were either single or divorced. Four of these women had children. All of the women in the sample said they needed a coal-mining job to support either themselves or their families. By the time of the study, two of the divorced women had remarried and one married woman had divorced, so that half the sample was married with children. Three of the other five single women had either one or two children to support. Two had remained single and childless. The youngest woman, one of the single mothers, was African American. The rest of the women in the sample were white.

As previously mentioned, coal-mining jobs are arranged according to five ranks each containing job families. Grade 1 jobs are laboring jobs usually involving mine maintenance. These jobs require few skills and more physical strength and endurance.[1] Higher grade jobs are more closely involved with coal production and require operative skills or certification, or both. Six of the ten women in the case study sample were classified in laboring jobs, three of whom were certified for higher grade jobs. The four other women held jobs in each one of the higher grades. The women's experience in mining ranged between nine and fifteen years. Two of the women in the sample had been working together. The rest were working as token members of their crews, as did most women at the mine.

Unlike interviewing women miners, interviewing the men was considerably more difficult. Thus, sampling among men was based solely on convenience. As one man told me, they believed I was only interested in "women's problems" and not in their experiences. This was not surprising given that I was referred to repeatedly by the secretary who initially showed me around the compound as "the lady here to talk to our lady miners." Nonetheless, I was able to have brief conversations with several different male miners and the local union president in and around the lamp house, which was the common meeting area for all miners because it was accessible from either the men's or the women's bath houses. It was also where miners congregated before shifts because it opened out onto a large porch from which miners got into the "buses" that took them into the mine.

The union president agreed to speak with me in lieu of granting me admittance to a union meeting because of what he termed the "controversial" nature of the topics on the agenda. One of those topics was the company's plan to lengthen shifts from eight hours as provided in the current contract to ten hours. However, one woman told me that the union president did not want me to observe him make a fool of himself which she and other (male) miners felt he often did. Finally, I also interviewed and had repeated conversations with the mine superintendent in his office.

My own field experiences gave me insight into the highly segregated and male-dominated nature of the workplace. It was made clear to me that certain places were "off limits," but more importantly, certain people were unavailable to me because I was a woman. For example, during my initial contact with company personnel I was warned to stay clear of the men's bath house because, as it was implied, I might get "more than I had bargained for." Likewise, several of the women told me that impromptu union meetings were often held in the men's bath house which insured their exclusion, as well as mine, unless we were willing to take on the challenge such an action posed. During one of my tours around the mine compound, my guide, a male security officer, took me through the the empty men's bath house at his suggestion. He indicated that he had done so as a special favor to me.

Another male-identified place was underground at the face where coal was actually being sheared from the seam. When I requested to go there during my underground tour, the miner who was giving me my gear tried to talk me out of it. He asked several times why I wanted to go there seeing how it was dirty and cold, and he said if I was going that far underground for that long I would be cold, hungry, and uncomfortable.

THEORETICAL PERSPECTIVE

Social closure theory asserts that "a status group creates and preserves its identity and advantages by reserving certain opportunities for members of the group" (Tomaskovic-Devey 1993:61) using exclusionary and, thus, discriminatory practices. Based on the concept of patriarchy, Reskin and Roos (1987) have developed a theoretical perspective for examining how men act to preserve their privileged positions in the workplace. In a given culture, status hierarchies are systems of stratification "prescribed in a supporting ideology and maintained by mechanisms that physically or symbolically set apart members of dominant and subordinate status groups" (Reskin and Roos 1987:5). Physical segregation is one such mechanism, which literally sets dominant and subordinate group members apart. However, when physical segregation breaks down, other mechanisms, such as functional differentiation, operate to reestablish the existing status hierarchies found in the larger culture.

When the sexes are physically integrated in a single work environment, functional differentiation leads to a sexual division of labor that is "grounded in stereotypes of innate sex differences in traits and abilities" and operates through "various social control mechanisms" (Reskin and Roos 1987:9). Under these conditions, "men will tolerate women in predominantly male work settings if they work in 'women's' jobs . . . but resist women doing traditionally male jobs in male work settings" (Reskin 1988:67). Thus, although women are accepted into the hierarchy, they still occupy subordinate positions that require their deference to males and create a social separation of the sexes.

The gendered status hierarchy is preserved through certain "social practices that create or exaggerate the social distance between status groups" (Reskin and Roos 1987:7). These practices dictate subordinates' behavior in the presence of dominant group members and shape the casual interaction between them. When gendered status hierarchies are maintained this way, they are usually seen by both men and women as natural and, thus, appropriate, because they re-create gendered social relations occurring in the larger culture. Because women who do "men's jobs" are challenging the routinization of the presumably natural order of gendered relations, they are "at risk of gender assessment" (West and Zimmerman 1987:136). They are held accountable for engaging in gender inappropriate behavior through other women's and men's (as well as their own) evaluations of their behavior based on "normative conceptions of appropriate attitudes and activities" for their gender category (West and Zimmerman 1987:139). Thus, these women are under pressure to prove their femininity, particularly as it is defined by the standards of womanhood and manhood in more traditional rural Appalachian culture.

Kanter (1977a,b) was among the first to document that token women's conspicuous presence leads to men's exaggeration of the differences between them. Men's behavior toward token women leads to the establishment of gendered boundaries. Such polarization can result in a token woman's social and physical isolation on the job. According to other researchers, polarization is accomplished via men's "sexualization of the workplace" meaning that work relations between men and women are "sexualized" (Enarson 1984; Swerdlow 1989).

Sexualizing the workplace and work relations consists of behaviors that express "the salience of sexual meanings in the presumably asexual domain of work." (Enarson 1984:88). As the literature on women in nontraditional blue-collar occupations has shown, most men engage in at least one of several forms of workplace sexualization using sexual harassment, sexual bribery, gender-based jokes and comments, flirtatious behavior, and profanity in order to make sex differences a salient aspect of work relations (Enarson 1984; Gruber and Bjorn 1982; Swerdlow 1989). These behaviors, according to Enarson (1984:109), "consitute a continuum of abuse" and reflect "a cultural tradition which sexualizes, objectifies, and diminishes women."

Men's sexualization of work relations directly expresses the expectation that women should "act like women" by making their integration into a sexualized workplace contingent upon their production of gender as they interact with men. Because men's sexualization of work relations identifies women primarily by their gender category and not by their work roles, it objectifies them. As Schur (1984) has pointed out, this "objectification" of women workers leads to their stigmatization by men about their work-related inferiority.

Objectification and work-related trivilization are mutually reinforcing processes (Schur 1984:142), which is how women workers are "appropriately" matched with gender-typed jobs requiring few specialized skills. Often jobs to which women are assigned mirror their relations with men in that these jobs require women's support and service to men occupying more skilled jobs. Because there are simply too few women present in a workplace dominated by men, women are usually unable to directly counter men's expressions of the negative stereotypes upon which this gender-typed matching process is based (Kanter 1977a).[2]

Studies have shown that men's gender-role expectations of women as workers negatively affect their success in nontraditional employment because these expectations color the men's perception of either women's potential for, or actual, job performance (Reskin and Padavic 1988). Those women who disconfirm the stereotypes by successful advancement have been regarded by men as "exceptional." But for most women, the stereotypes for their presumed incompetence can also affect how some of the women have come to perceive themselves and each other. Accordingly, "male workers may inhibit integration both by their ability to shape employer's decisions and by affecting the preferences of female workers" (Reskin 1993:248).

In examining women miners' day-to-day social relations with male co-workers and supervisors in several western states, Yount (1986:29) found that "women are assigned to positions that are conducive to perceptions of sex-stereotypical traits. In turn, these perceptions (based on the work they perform) provide legitimation for the assignments." That is, jobs underground become gender-identified and workers are matched accordingly through the operation of the formalized provisions of the workplace.

FINDINGS AND ANALYSES

Beyond the physical challenges they faced in the workplace, the women miners had to adapt to the male-identified culture of mining by establishing and maintaining cooperative, if not amicable, work relations with male co-workers and supervisors. Although most of the men treated them with some measure of respect, all the women in the sample reported that during their first few years underground they encountered men's sexualization of work relations in the form of either sexual harassment, propositioning, or sexual bribery. In particular, some foremen misused their authority by initiating sexual bribery in exchange for easier work assignments. In response to the women's complaints about the men's behavior, the company issued a formal set of rules forbidding the use of obscene or abusive language. According to the women, these more direct forms of sexualization became less prevalent, in part, because of the men's fear of sanctions. However, other forms of workplace sexualization, such as sexual jokes and comments, flirtatious behavior, and profanity, have persisted.

These conditions, the women said, have contributed to the endurance of the negative stereotypes that were the basis for assigning women to lesser-skilled lower status jobs involving manual labor. Moreover, these gender-typed assignments, which severely reduced the women's promotion prospects, were made according to several formalized procedures of the workplace, such as training opportunities, seniority, posting and bidding practices, temporary assignments, and realignments of the working force.

Sexualization of Work Relations and the Workplace

Half of the women in the sample said they had been sexually harassed by either male co-workers or foremen (bosses), using verbal innuendo and body language to convey a sexual message (Gruber and Bjorn 1982). For example, one woman reported an incident of homosexual buffoonery with a particularly potent message exaggerating men's sexuality and solidarity because of its contamination by an intruding female:

They was pretending they was queers in front of me. It was like one was humping the other one, but they had their clothes on. And the boss said, "You scared of us, ain't you?" I said, "No, I'm not scared of you all." And he said, "Well, this is our little world down here and you don't belong."

Some male co-workers and foremen either directly solicited sexual favors from the women or repeatedly asked them for dates. When women first started working at the mine, one woman said that they were treated "like a piece of pussy." Another recalled that "a boss (once said) all the women made beds out of rockdust for the men. You know, like that's all we did was go in there to sleep with them?"

Because of the power differential, sexual propositioning by foremen posed a much greater threat to a woman's work status than propositioning by men co-workers. It was well known by women in the sample that when a woman failed to capitulate to a foreman's sexual demands, she usually faced the prospect of getting a more difficult work assignment. One woman who had been reassigned for such an offense was told by a male co-worker "if you let these bosses pinch your titties, you'll get along. If you don't, you'll get the awfullest job that ever was." She allowed that she preferred the "awful" job every time.

Another form of punishment used by a foreman was social derogation designed to humiliate the woman who refused his sexual requests:

One time [the foreman] told the guys behind my back that I had sucked his dick, is the way he put it. It came back to me about a week or so later. I went through pure misery for about a year because the boss lied to the crew that I worked with, telling them [other] stuff. I didn't even know why everybody all of a sudden quit speaking to me, giving me the cold shoulder.

In front of her male co-workers, she retaliated:

I walked up to him and I said, "When did I suck your god-damned dick down the jackline?" He goes, "I don't know what you're talking about." I said, "You're a god-damned liar. You told everyone of them and you didn't think that they'd find out I'm not doing the shit you said I was doing and come back and tell me things, did you?" Right there it proved to the guys [he was lying] because some of them actually believed it!

In the above case, the foreman's rumors led to her isolation by virtue of her co-workers' lack of on-the-job cooperation. But even in the absence of rumors, the women's potential for becoming socially isolated was especially great because of their token status. This seriously hindered their ability to do their jobs adequately and made them vulnerable to the perception that they were incapable of doing the work.

A miner's reputation is important not only for being respected and appreciated by co-workers, but also for gaining the opportunities necessary for advancement, such as temporary assignments. Thus, men's sexualization of work relations underscored the women's sexuality at the expense of their work role performances and promotion potential.

When the company issued its mandate against harassment, the superintendent told me it was necessary to "teach the men what harassment was." His remark implied that the men were so accustomed to regarding women in terms of their sexuality that they would find it difficult, if not unnatural, to develop egalitarian work relationships with them. Although the rule has effectively eroded these incidents, the women added that its enforcement has a double binding or "damned if you do, damned if you don't" quality because it was the women themselves and not men in the mines, such as foremen, who were solely responsible for reporting harassment. Those women who reported infractions said that it was they, not their harassers, who ended up being transferred to other work locations. Other women indicated that they were often reluctant to do so because it created tension among crew members.

Moreover, it violated a UMWA oath of solidarity, thus defeating the women's attempts to become socially integrated underground despite the union local's lackluster support for the women and the workplace issues that directly affected them. In sum, the women miners were caught in the power struggles between the sexes and between labor and management in ways that doubly disadvantaged their own ploys for gaining power in the workplace.

Even though the women in the sample recognized that the men's sexual harassment was usually unprovoked, some of them tended to place the responsibility for the men's actions on themselves and each other. This was especially true for those women who had received little or no sexual harassment. According to one woman:

> The majority of the men up there are good to you if you let them. But they'll treat you how they see you act. See, men, they tend to watch women more, I believe it's just the male in them.

When the women were treated as sex objects, each woman was regarded by the men as a representative of her gender category. Hence, each women was made to feel that she had a moral responsibility to all the other women for avoiding "loose" behavior.[3] As a result, some of the firmest friendships and the bitterest of ongoing battles between them have been over the sexual indulgences of other women, particularly when any one of these women was perceived as "sleeping her way to a better job."

In order to thwart the men's sexual advances and uphold the image of fidelity, several of the women reported doing the following:

> When I first came here I set myself up right away. I've made it known: Don't bother me, I'm here to work. I'm not here for romance, [but for] finance. Once you establish yourself, they know your boundaries and they respect them.

Because of her behavior, this single and childless woman had challenged the men's heterosexist beliefs about women's sexuality. As a result, a male coworker once asked her if she was a lesbian, to which she responded: "What difference does it make what I tell you? You already have your mind made up." She was never asked that again. She explained that not only were the men intimidated when women could handle coal mining jobs, but they were also intimidated by the possibility of a woman's homosexuality. In this case, a woman could remain not only financially independent, but also sexually independent of men and their control.

But typically, men will continue to relate to women in sexual terms as long as the division of labor provides the potential for women to be equal to men (Reskin and Roos 1987). When women are present, men have a "status stake" in the sexualization of the workplace and work relations (Swerdlow 1989). Thus, over time it had become clear to the women that although the men had accepted them, their presence had done little to seriously disrupt men's sexualization of the work place. As one woman put it:

> It's a man's world. And when I started I knew I was going into a man's world and men have their ways. When the first women went into the mines, it was hard for a man to change his ways.

Continuing to relate to women in sexual terms reinforces gender-based boundaries and reasserts male solidarity underground. As one woman explained:

> It's the pal system, like if there're two young men, they stick together, and they stick up for the boss. I found out if you knowed a lot about football, baseball, basketball, how to deer hunt, or how to go to a club and drink a lot of booze [said grinning]—if you was a man [chuckles]— well, that's what the bosses like.

Types of men's behavior that contributed to the sexualization of the workplace were sexual jokes and comments, flirting, and profanity. Gutek

(1985) has concluded that sex in the forms of grafitti, jokes, comments, and metaphors for work, are a part of workplaces dominated by men regardless of women's presence. However, as women enter the work setting, they are obligated to set limits on some of the men's activities in order to avoid being degraded. Sometimes the male miners were careful about telling jokes in the women's presence. At other times the women found themselves in the position of having to "draw the line" on men's unacceptable behavior.

On her crew, one woman said that although she generally "laughs stuff off," she was careful not to "get rowdy with them" because invariably the action would escalate. She commented that occasionally if they got carried away, she would "make them stop." Another woman tried to curb the men's "sex talk":

> They would start making sexual remarks about their girlfriends and women and I'd say, "Hey, you shouldn't talk like that! What's the matter with you guys? You ought to be ashamed of yourself," just to get them to watch what they say.

Another of the women's social accommodations that marked their gendered acceptance by male co-workers was flirting. As one woman explained:

> See, I get along with the guys really good. We harass each other. We joke and we're a little bit flirty, but teasing. And with two women? They love having us up there because it's a different atmosphere.

Flirtatious behavior allowed the men to reassert their masculinity in the presence of female co-workers who might otherwise have threatened their notions of themselves as miners and, therefore, as men.

Similar to other workers employed in dangerous occupations, coal miners are notorious for using profanity. The women said that men would apologize if they thought a woman had overheard them using foul language. Their apologies strongly imply that there is a difference between men's and women's language. Language serves to maintain role boundaries. If profanity is not fit language for a woman to hear, then certainly she should avoid using it. The women varied considerably in their use of foul language and in their willingness to tolerate it from others. A few women did not swear and had no tolerance for it. However, most of the women miners admitted to using what constituted "men's language," but said they were careful to conceal or curtail their profanity in it. For example:

> There's a lot of stuff I will say. I used to not cuss too bad, but I'll cuss now. I'll say it under my breath. I don't think they've ever heard it. They'd die if they heard me say what I say to myself.

Another said: "I cuss some when I get mad, but I always try to watch what I say because I'll lose that edge." That "edge," she explained, was the men's respect.

The emphasis some men place on sexuality and gender differences in the workplace reasserts the subordinate status of women by focusing on their gender role behavior at the expense of their work role performances. As one woman put it: "The men look at our bodies and not at what we can do." Thus, the sexualization of work relationships and the workplace had the effect of stigmatizing women as a group, allowing the imputation of stereotypes about women's inferiority relative to men when it came to doing "men's work."

Stereotypes and the Sex-typing of Jobs

In a masculine-identified workplace, men's sexualization maintains the gendered relations between women and men. But it also defines women's appropriate positions in the work hierarchy based on the culturally defined stereotypical differences in women's and men's respective abilities. In the Appalachian coal fields, gendered interaction based on gendered "ways" is highly "conventionalized" and "dramatically performed" according to universal claims about gender differences (Stewart 1990). All of the women in the sample identified men's negative stereotypes as a means for justifying women's work assignments. These stereotypes were expressed verbally by some male co-workers, but were also demonstrated by foremen's behavior toward the women. In turn, the women perceived limited opportunities for advancement, emphasizing the power foremen and other managerial personnel had for either directly or indirectly determining their status in the job hierarchy.

During their first few years at the mine, all of the women I interviewed complained that at least some male coworkers had made derisive remarks questioning the appropriateness of their presence:

> Even some of our union brothers [said] I don't think women ought to be in here. They ought to get out of here and let a good man have this job. They said we should be home cleaning house, raising kids.

Several of the women also said that when they first started working, some of the men told them that mining jobs were too physically difficult for them. One woman was asked why she had taken a coal job if she couldn't do the work. She said "they didn't want you to (work). They don't even want you to try because you're crowding in on their turf." Other women also reported that their male co-workers made their jobs unnecessarily difficult by ignoring them or reducing their own efforts. Other men responded in a chivalrous fashion by offering women unnecessary assistance. The women recognized the implication this had for their presumed inadequacy and refused their help. Moreover, even at the time of the study, male miners were still expressing the same views. The women felt that these men had exaggerated their claims and likened these ideas to the superstition that women were bad luck in a coal mine. Under these circumstances, most of the women agreed that establishing a good work reputation was harder for women than it was for men. Thus, in order to avoid fulfilling the men's prophecies about their presumed incapability, the women felt they had to constantly prove themselves.

Some foremen gave the women the more physically demanding jobs underground, imposed higher work standards on them, or tried to mar the women's work reputation as described below:

> I had put up some ventilation [but] the curtain wouldn't reach the bottom. So I went off hunting another piece to attach to it. [The foreman] came up and I wasn't there. I got my ventilation and put it across the bottom. It was quitting time. Everybody was going [out], so I got my stuff. [The foreman] didn't say nothing to me. Outside he told [the superintendent] that I didn't do my job right. I never had this problem with nobody except [the foreman] and you couldn't please the man no matter what you did or how hard you worked. He just had this thing against women coal miners. Wouldn't never admit it, but it was obvious.

Other foremen communicated to the women that they were not suited for running machinery. Half of the ten women I interviewed in depth said that they had been passed over for a man when skilled work was being assigned. As one woman commented:

> We've had a couple of bosses up there that thought that women could do nothing but shovel. I had one foreman [who] had me on a section as an extra person to hang rag. I roof bolted before that and roof bolters would be off. He would send the other [male] GIs to roof bolt. Well, I went to the union to file a grievance on it. After that night I roof bolted until they sent me to [another shift].

And:

> This one boss just bypassed me on a job he knew I could do for another guy who never even run a motor. He just looked at me and went on. Now I've been on a motor; taking it in and out wasn't a problem. The boy that I work with just looked at me after we got around to the other side and started laughing. He understood. Most of the men [co-workers] did.

Finally, not only did foremen "have it in their minds that we are the weaker sex," as one woman miner said, but the superintendent insisted that "men had a more mechanical approach" to their work and the women had more menial mining jobs due to "the natural settling of their skills and their application."

As documented elsewhere in the literature on women in nontraditional occupations (Deaux 1984; Harlan and O'Farrell 1982), the women miners perceived having less opportunity for advancement than men. Before the company implemented its training policy, getting on-the-job training on mining machinery was almost impossible according to one of the earliest women miners. Although she had heard that some women had been shown how to run equipment, like others, she had not:

> I was put on the beltline shoveling and then on the belthead running the coal into the cars. As far as running equipment, I didn't get that [because] we were kept out of the face. They didn't offer us any chance to run any equipment. I don't know how to today and I don't care. I like my job. Stay where you're at and you really know what you're doing.

But even after the policy instructing senior miners to honor new miners' requests for on-the-job training was established, the women said that getting the training or the temporary assignment to get the experience was rare. Male co-workers and foremen "think women are harder to train," one woman said, "like we're dumb or something."

Three grade 1 women in the sample said they had the skills to run machinery, but were not really interested in bidding on higher grade jobs requiring operative skills. They said that the few higher grade operative jobs that were posted were on night shifts and conflicted with their family responsibilities. Others indicated that they did not want the added pressures and responsibility that those jobs entailed. As one woman explained:

> Sometimes a general inside labor job [grade 1] is not easy, but there's no pressure. There's no major head busting decisions to make. Somebody else tells you what to do and takes the blame if it does not get done right. Sometimes it's easy to fall into a situation where I don't have to make any decisions. If you don't advance you don't take a chance on being wrong or messing up.

She added that when a woman did operate machinery and made "a mistake, [the men] really don't let you live it down." She concluded by saying that the women were less likely to take such a chance "probably because we are women and we're feeling inferior." Likewise, those women who had jobs operating machinery said they were more closely scrutinized than the men working in similar jobs.

Some women who had once held operative jobs had been reassigned to grade 1 jobs as the result of workforce realignments. They contended that women were disproportionately downgraded relative to men. Like these women, another woman miner who had once bid unsuccessfully on a higher grade job had become discouraged at the prospect of trying again. Another said that one time she had bid on a job knowing that she had the necessary seniority and skills, but was turned down. When she complained to the foreman who had assigned a man in her place, "he went over [to the posted assignment sheet] and rubbed his name off there and put mine on it." As another woman who had advanced concluded: "The women have to stand up for their rights. If you wanna advance, you got to make waves." Most of the women, she contended, weren't willing to risk the men's hostility by doing so. Thus, even when these jobs came up for bid, they did not bid on them. As one woman miner said about most of the women in Grade 1 jobs:

> I think they just accept theirself in that position. They like it [or] they don't like it, but they're there, and they're afraid to advance theirself.

About herself she said:

> For the past ten years I felt like I was the underdog, that I shouldn't be stepping on their toes. I haven't felt like I was a person. They tell me to go shovel and I used to stand back and let things [jobs] go by. If there was a top paying job, if I thought I could do it, most of the time I'd say let him do it.

Some of the grade 1 women also said they could not compete with the men's greater seniority. However, one woman who had advanced said that "a lot of them women got the seniority to bid over half them guys out." Mine employment data I looked at substantiated her claim. As previous studies on women in occupations dominated by men has shown, "the perceptions of opportunities are in part dependent on evidence that members of one's own group occupy particular positions within the organization" (Deaux 1984:292). Indeed, the women in grade 1 jobs were unable to name any, or only one or two, more advanced women at the mine, even though there were five women so classified at the time of the study.

The sex bias occurring at the mine also substantiated the suitability of assigning women to certain jobs requiring those characteristics that women are presumed to possess in relation to men. During one of my conversations with several men miners, one exclaimed that "there are some jobs women can do in the mines!" According to women in the sample, they were often expected to perform duties that mirrored the work they traditionally performed in their homes in service to or in support of men:[4]

> Sunday I carried cinder block and rockdust behind them, I cleaned up the garbage, I carried their junk to them if they wanted it. It's just like you're a gofer or something. When they set up, they throw down everything. It's up to us to go clean up their mess. I know all the women experience the work discrimination because most of us are gofers, hard manual labor.

And:

> I've had bosses that treat you worse than the men. They make you go pick up things. When I was general inside labor it didn't matter what section I went to, they'd expect me to clean the dinner hole.

When I asked one woman if there were "women's jobs" in the mine, she exclaimed: "Oh yeah! You got yourself on the belt, that's a woman's job. You go shovel the belt, you help the mason build stoppings." Conversely, these jobs, such as general inside labor and beltman, carry a certain stigma. The same woman told me: "[As a GI] you're the flunkie. I mean you're the gofer. It's real hard." And another said: "It's just like you don't have no sense to do nothing else."

Over time the men's, particularly foremen's, gendered stereotyping about women's work capabilities have remained prevalent, making a token woman's negotiations with men over how she evaluates herself and other women as miners highly problematic. Moreover, their expectations that women should perform gender-appropriate support activities requiring few, if any, technical skills have resulted in the sex-typing of jobs at the mine. Using the formalized procedures of the workplace, foremen and other managerial personnel have successfully acted to restrict the women's advancement by redefining the sexes' respective places in the underground work hierarchy.

Additionally, because those men in control of the local union have continued to regard the women with whom they work as women first and miners second, several of the women recognized that their sole remaining source of power in the workplace would only come from one another. However, as previously mentioned, serious social cleavages have developed between some of the women over each other's real or perceived laziness, infidelities, and preferential job assignments. As one woman told me:

> If the women would stick together we would be recognized as different people. There would be new meaning up there and the men know that, too. But right now, I don't know what they think of us.

Still, friendships have flourished and enough of a sense of camaraderie was in evidence in order to foster a collective consciousness regarding their subordinate status as women doing a "man's job." The women's resistance was reflected in their awareness of the consequences of men's negative stereotypes and of the process by which the gender-typing of jobs occurred. In this case, their continued individual efforts to prove their competence as coal miners represented their solution to a collective dilemma.

CONCLUSION

As the women pointed out, men's sexualization has reinforced men's, particularly supervisors,' stereotypical beliefs about women's incapability of doing more masculine-identified work. Stereotypes, they said, have influenced foremen's job assignments and have contributed to the gender-typing of jobs. The women's perceptions of opportunities and, for some women, the availability of necessary training and experience also constituted barriers to their advancement. Moreover, certain organizational constraints, such as realignments of the workforce and shift work have negatively influenced their advancement decisions.

Specifically, women's initial work assignments, and subsequent physical or social isolation, affected their on-the-job training opportunities. Having the necessary training, according to seniority provisions, virtually eliminated the possibility for women to get temporary assignments to jobs requiring operative skills. Finally, realignments of the working force tended to disadvantage women who did possess the necessary training and experience for the better jobs.

Accepting the differences between women's and men's capabilities as natural implies that their consequences, such as job-level gender segregation, are beyond organizational control. But as the findings of this research have shown, sexualization, along with the resulting stigmatization of women as inferior to men, maintains the potency of sex stereotypes about women's competence that affect their employment histories. The strength of job-level gender segregation rests upon the endurance of men's stereotypical beliefs about women's capabilities for doing "men's work." These beliefs, behaviors, and corresponding organizational outcomes constitute the preservation of men's privilege. As long as these beliefs are also supported by management in the form of reactive as opposed to proactive antidiscriminatory policies and their enforcement, advancement for women miners will continue to be difficult.

Over the years, despite their pessimistic advancement attitudes, the women have been resisting men's attempts to stereotype their abilities by simply remaining on the job through their own hard work. To varying degrees, they recognize the prevalence of gender bias and the resulting work-based inequality at the mine and in other workplaces where women are similarly disadvantaged.

However, their resistance can be strengthened in two possible ways. First, the women could gain an even greater collective consciousness by forming a support group at the mine. By discussing their common issues and experiences, they could develop a greater understanding of the men's perceptions by which gender inequality in their workplace is maintained. This way, they could at least overcome the workplace-imposed isolation among themselves. As one woman told me, then "we'd be a force to be reckoned with." Second, there was also strong evidence that nonsexual, egalitarian relationships had developed between at least some of the male miners and their female co-workers. Despite the women's disillusionment with weak local leadership, their allegiance to the union and their union brothers has remained strong. Thus, the bonds between women and men miners could be furthered through union solidarity.

Hard times in the coal fields have changed miners' definition of a "good union man" (Yarrow 1991). During the more prosperous and turbulent 1970s, it meant standing up to the boss. Since the bust of the 1980s, marked by greater cooperation between operators and miners and management's co-optation of local union leaders, being a good union miner is now based on her or his willingness to work hard. This is much to the women's advantage because it allows them to separate the connection between manliness and unionism (Yarrow 1991). Today, being union means being a good union brother or sister.

Conversely, the women could also remind their less accepting union brothers that their entry represents the inevitable changes in the larger culture; that their presence should be regarded as a source of strength and not weakness; and that while some men are busy looking at women's bodies, management is busy using all miners' bodies to its own advantage. Specifically, management's use of making selective job assignments has always been a powerful tool for dividing and controlling miners. The belief that an injury to one is an injury to all needs to be reasserted because the exclusion of women as union members diminishes the potential effects of union solidarity. Together, miners could pressure the company to more vigorously enforce its own policies for all miners thereby recognizing that women deserve to be accepted as competent and not merely tolerated as "here to stay."

NOTES

1. Typically, the jobs to which beginning miners are assigned consist of rock-dusting, hanging ventilation curtain, setting timbers for roof support, shoveling coal along a beltline, moving the beltline structures and power cables, laying track, and keeping the mine free of debris. Many of the structures and equipment manually disassembled, moved, and reassembled by general inside laborers (GIs), are heavy and

cumbersome by any standards. Top rollers on a beltline weigh 150 pounds and power cable, which relays approximately 7,000 volts of electricity to heavy coal-cutting and loading machinery, is 750 feet long.

2. When women's resistance to men's stereotypically negative expectations for their work behavior is minimal or nonexistent, they often fall victim to what Kanter (1977a,b) calls "role entrapment" and Nieva and Gutek (1981) have labeled "sex-role spillover." Sex-role spillover begins when "a high percentage of one sex in an occupation leads to the expectation that people in that occupation should behave in a manner consistent with the sex role of the numerically dominant sex. . . . Thus, people in men's jobs are expected to 'act like men' to be perceived as good workers" (Gutek 1985:133). The inherent dilemma for women in nontraditional jobs is that in order to be perceived as competent, they are expected to act like men, which directly contradicts the behavioral expectations based on their gender (Gutek and Dunwoody 1987). Because men are viewed as "natural inhabitants" of organizations, there is no comparable phenomenon operating for them (Gutek and Dunwoody 1987).

3. Not only do the women miners place the burden of sexual responsibility upon themselves, but miners' wives' opposition to women miners reinforces it and may also partially account for these men's behavior toward the women with whom they work. This finding is substantiated by other current research on the topic, particularly by Giesen (1995).

4. A few women in the sample likened their crew membership to being in a family, a social unit in which patriarchal power and control and women's resulting subordinate status have already been defined (see Crull 1987: 233–34). Only one woman in the sample was married to a miner and, interestingly, she was the one quoted here. Two others were married to foremen and both declined to be interviewed citing their husband's position with the coal company.

REFERENCES CITED

Blau, Francine D., and Marianne A. Ferber
    1985 Women in the labor market: The last twenty years. In *Women and Work: An Annual Review*, volume 1. Laurie Larwood, Ann Stromberg, and Barbara A. Gutek, eds. Beverly Hills, CA: Sage.

Crull, Peggy
    1987 Searching for the causes of sexual harassment: An examination of two prototypes. In *Hidden Aspects of Women's Work*. Christine E. Bose, Roslyn Feldberg, and Natalie J. Sokoloff, eds. New York: Greenwood Press.

Deaux, K.
    1984 Blue-collar barriers. *American Behavioral Scientist* 27:287–300.

Enarson, Elaine Pitt
    1984 *Woods-working Women: Sexual Integration in the U.S. Forest Service*. Birmingham: University of Alabama Press.

Etizioni, Amitai
1964 *Modern Organizations*. Englewood Cliffs, NJ: Prentice-Hall.

Giesen, Carol A. B.
1995 *Coal Miners' Wives*. Lexington: University of Kentucky Press.

Gruber, James S., and Lars Bjorn
1982 Blue-collar blues: The sexual harassment of women autoworkers. *Work and Occupations* 9:271–98.

Gutek, Barbara A.
1985 *Sex and the Workplace: The Impact of Sexual Behavior and Harassment on Women, Men and Organizations*. San Francisco: Jossey Bass.

Gutek, Barbara A., and Vera Dunwoody
1987 Understanding sex in the workplace. In *Women and Work: An Annual Review*, vol. 2. Ann H. Stromberg, Laurie Larwood, and Barbara A. Gutek, eds. Beverly Hills, CA: Sage.

Harlan, Sharon L., and Brigid O'Farrell
1982 After the pioneers: Prospects for women in nontraditional blue-collar jobs. *Work and Occupations* 9:363–86.

Hartmann, Heidi
1987 Internal labor markets and gender: A case study of promotion. In *Gender in the Workplace*. Clair Brown and Joseph Pechman, eds. Washington, D.C.: Brookings Institution.

Kanter, Rosabeth Moss
1977a Some effects of proportions on group life: Skewed sex ratios and responses to token women. *American Journal of Sociology* 82:965–90.
1977b *Men and Women of the Corporation*. New York: Harper and Row.

Mahoney, Constance
1978 Appalachian women's perception of their work experiences as underground coal miners. Master's thesis. East Tennessee State University.

Moore, Marat, and Connie White
1989 *Sexual Harassment in the Mines*. Knoxville, TN: Allied Printing.

Nieva, V. F., and B. A. Gutek
1981 *Women and Work: A Psychological Persective*. New York: Praeger.

Reskin, Barbara F.
1988 Bringing the men back in: Sex differentiation and the devaluation of women's work. *Gender & Society* 2:58–81.

Reskin, Barbara, and Irene Padavic
1988 Supervisors as gatekeepers: Male supervisors' response to women's integration in plant jobs. *Social Problems* 35:536–50.

Reskin, Barbara F., and Patricia A. Roos
   1987 Sex segregation and status hierarchies. In *Ingredients for Women's Employ-
        ment Policy.* Christine Bose and Glenna Spitze, eds. Albany: State Univer-
        sity of New York Press.

Roos, Patricia A., and Barbara F. Reskin
   1984 Institutional factors affecting job access and mobility for women: A review of
        institutional explanations for occupational sex segregation. In *Sex Segrega-
        tion in the Workplace: Trends, Explanations, and Remedies.* Barbara F.
        Reskin, ed. Washington, D.C.: National Academy Press.

Schur, Edwin M.
   1984 *Labeling Women Deviant: Gender, Stigma, and Control.* Philadelphia: Tem-
        ple University Press.

Stewart, Kathleen Claire
   1990 Backtalking the wilderness: Appalachian engenderings. In *Uncertain Terms:
        Negotiating Gender in American Culture.* Faye Ginsburg and Anna Tsing,
        eds. Boston: Beacon Press.

Swerdlow, Marian
   1989 Entering a nontraditional occupation: A case of rapid transit operatives. *Gen-
        der & Society* 3:373–87.

Tallichet, Suzanne E.
   1995 Gender relations in the mines and the division of labor underground. *Gender
        & Society* 9:697–711.
   1991 Moving up down in the mine: Sex segregation in underground coal mining.
        Dissertation. Pennsylvania State University.

Taylor, Patricia A.
   1988 Women in organizational structural factors in women's work patterns. In
        Women Working: Theories and Facts in Perspective. Ann Helton Stromberg
        and Shirley Harkness, eds. Mountain View, CA: Mayfield.

Tomaskovic-Devey, Donald
   1993 *Gender and Racial Inequality at Work.* Ithaca, NY: ILR Press.

United Mine Workers of America
   1988 National Bituminous Coal Wage Agreement. Indianapolis: Allied Printing.

Walshok, Mary L.
   1981 *Blue Collar Women: Pioneers on the Male Frontier.* New York: Anchor
        Books.

West, Candace, and Don H. Zimmerman
   1987 Doing gender. *Gender & Society* 1:125–51.

Yarrow, Michael
   1991 The gender-specific class consciousness of Appalachian coal miners: Struc-
        ture and change. In *Bringing Class Back In: Contemporary and Historical*

Perspectives. Scott G. McNall, Rhonda F. Levine, and Rick Fantasia, eds. Boulder, CO: Westview Press.

Yount, Kristen
1986 Women and Men Coal Miners: Coping with Gender Integration Underground. Dissertation. University of Colorado, Boulder.

Chapter 7

Creen Que No Tenemos Vidas:
Mexicana Household Workers
in Santa Barbara, California

María de la Luz Ibarra

Nestled alongside the Pacific Ocean, Santa Barbara, California, is home to millionaires and movie stars. Every year there are food, music, and wine festivals, art openings, parades, and solstice celebrations, all of which attest to the city's glamour and entice thousands of visitors. There is another side to Santa Barbara, however. Beneath the glittering hills are working-class neighborhoods where the women live who bathe and feed other people's children, provide companionship to elderly residents, and clean kitchens and bathrooms. These women are mostly Mexican immigrants *Mexicanas*—who labor as waged household workers.[1]

Although they are a prominent part of the labor force, Mexicanas and their work are virtually invisible outside their neighborhoods. They often live clandestinely in Santa Barbara without official documents, and their employers do not record employment. Census and Department of Labor data underestimate growth within the occupation because they do not accurately capture occupations dominated by "under the table" pay arrangements and undocumented immigrant labor. Their invisibility within society was aptly captured by a worker who said, *creen que no tenemos vidas*—they think we do not have lives.

This invisibility forms part of many Mexicanas' everyday reality and is reproduced in the academic literature where a complex range of work activities and life circumstances are conceptualized as a single homogenous category: that of household or domestic worker. In order to deconstruct the multifarious activities subsumed in the term *household worker* and to gain some sense of the meaningful dimensions of this work in Mexicanas' lives, I have undertaken anthropological fieldwork among Mexicanas employed within the informal household work sector in Santa Barbara.[2]

To untangle this web of activities, we need to study the labor process and the power relations imbedded within it. Household work—like all work— is characterized by a wage relationship wherein the employer attempts to extract as much work as possible for as little money as possible. Unlike many other worksites, however, research access and observation are problematic. The principal method I used to study the labor process and the power relationship within the workplace is that of life history.

This chapter is divided into several sections. First, I contextualize Mexicanas within a global and a local economy, and briefly review the academic literature on waged household work. Second, I describe my fieldwork methods and the theory of power used in the study. Having sketched the background of the study group, I present three life histories in which Mexicanas speak about migration, recruitment into household work, the daily routine, and the meaning of household work in their lives.

WAGED HOUSEHOLD WORK, MIGRATION, AND THE RESTRUCTURED U.S. ECONOMY

Research suggests that the demand for waged household workers has increased in the United States and in other First World countries (Sanjek and Colen 1990; Enloe 1990; Bakan and Stasiulis 1995). Sanjek and Colen point out that "as capital grows and recomposes . . . builds cities and depopulates villages . . . it shapes local demand for labor" (1990:117). Thus if work structures and wages change, households may be transformed, leading to changes in internal demands for household workers. In California there is now a "booming market" for Mexicanas and other domestic workers to iron, clean houses, and care for children (Cornelius 1992; Solórzano-Torres 1987, 1988; Hondagneu 1994).

This hiring preference coincides with the growing settlement, since the 1970s, of Mexicanas from diverse backgrounds and sending areas (Woodrow and Passel 1990; Cornelius 1992; García y Griego 1994; Hondagneu 1994). Both the increased employment and immigration of Mexicanas are explained as part of a complex set of changes that in turn has led to a new international division of labor and a restructured U.S. economy (Sassen-Koob 1988).

Prior to the 1970s, Chicanas and Mexicanas labored in white middle- and upper-class homes as housecleaners, laundresses, cooks, and ironers (Camarillo 1979; Romero 1992; Deutsch 1987; González 1985; García 1981) and assumed an important proportion of the domestic labor market throughout the southwest (Salmon 1911; Nakano-Glenn 1986). Chicanas and Mexicanas, however, were not generally hired to care for children. In fact, throughout the 1930s and 1940s "Chicanas and Mexicanas were considered too inferior to care for children" (Romero 1992:84), and during the 1950s many middle-class employers "imported" nannies from Europe, particularly Britain.[3] By the 1960s, however, white middle-class employers voiced dissatisfaction with European employees because they tended to gravitate toward better work or get married. Then in 1965 changes in the Immigration and Naturalization Act made it easier to hire a Latin American household worker than a European worker. Thus many white, middle-class housewives in California began hiring Mexicanas not only as housecleaners, but as live-in childcare providers as well (Martin and Segrave 1985). Concurrent with the beginning of this hiring practice, there were dramatic changes within the structure of the U.S. economy.

In an attempt to increase their profits, corporate managers began a process of "deindustrialization," a transfer of industrial production from the U.S. to Mexico and other Third World countries. In this process many of the middle-class jobs that had provided a family wage were eliminated, and real wages declined for most people (Bluestone and Harrison 1988). At the new core is a service-dominated economy comprised of a polarized income and occupational structure with high-wage professional and technical jobs on the one end and low-wage, seasonal or part-time jobs on the other (Sassen-Koob 1988; Fernandez-Kelley and Sassen 1995). High-wage jobs are concentrated within banking, management, administration, and research, while low-wage jobs are concentrated within clerical, sales, and personal services (Abel Kemp 1994). Many of the new jobs have been filled by white, Chicana, and African-American women trying to maintain a middle class standard of living or wanting to work outside their homes (Amott and Matthaei 1991). Thus more than at any other time in U.S. history, women are employed outside their households.

An important characteristic of this new female workforce is that many women are married and are employed during childbearing years (Hartmann 1987) when household social reproductive needs are highest. This change is most pronounced for white women, who at the beginning of the century were the least likely group to be in the labor force (Amott and Matthaei 1991). Moreover, women's increased participation in the waged labor force has not been met with a concomitant increase in participation of males within housework (Abel Kemp 1994). Therefore, many women face what Arlie Hochschild has referred to as the "second shift" (1989).

While these trends were developing, U.S. investment in production for export disrupted local economies in Mexico by channeling resources to a few key areas and reducing the land and labor available for subsistence agriculture

(Sassen-Koob 1990). This process was further exacerbated when a severe economic crisis in 1982 caused the Mexican government to declare it could not meet its external debt (Green 1995). The U.S.-dominated World Bank and the International Monetary Fund then imposed neoliberal measures that resulted in massive job losses, a reduction in wages, and a severe restriction of social welfare programs (Nash 1995). Thus, while U.S. corporations profit from investment in the Mexican economy, they simultaneously create the conditions for emigration from Mexico. The poor economic conditions in Mexico, however, are not by themselves sufficient to explain migration to the United States. According to Sassen-Koob, the continuing and growing migration of people from Mexico is directly tied to the new work structure in the U.S., as many low-wage jobs specifically target immigrant workers (1988). One of these low-wage jobs is household work, for which employers prefer immigrant women (Repak 1995; Ruiz 1987; Colen 1986).[4]

As white, Chicana, and black women "go out" to work, and as men continue to resist a more egalitarian distribution of housework chores (Berk 1985; Hartmann 1981; Ammot and Matthaei 1991), many Mexicanas "come in" to perform those tasks once undertaken in households by mothers and wives. Mexicanas are no longer solely employed by white middle-class and wealthy households, however, nor are they solely cleaning, ironing, and washing. Within the restructured economy, Mexicanas are hired by a cross-class, interethnic group of employers and their employment increasingly consists of taking care of children. Moreover, as is typical of all postindustrial societies, there is a growing elderly population in the United States with varying social reproductive labor requirements (Salzinger 1991; Hayes-Bautista 1986) which Mexicanas (in the area I work in) also fulfill. Thus "emotional labor" or "the management of feeling to create a public, observable facial and bodily display" (Hochschild 1983:7) is an important part of the labor process.

In spite of the fact that household work is a crucial growth occupation, labor historians (Gomez-Quiñones 1994; Foster 1982) continue to give little attention to this fundamental labor and to the women who undertake it in the United States. In part, this lack of attention is a result of the prevailing notion that the private home is not a workplace and that housework is not real work but rather a natural extension of femininity (Berk 1985; see Berman, this volume). Sociologists and anthropologists have written more extensively on waged domestic labor, particularly about how the work is regarded as one of the most menial in our society, how the intersections of race/ethnicity, class, gender, and migration status determine who enters this devalued occupation, how the work itself reinforces a woman's degraded status, and how women confront dehumanizing aspects of the employer-employee relationship (Colen 1986, 1989; Dill 1994; Nakano-Glenn 1986; Rollins 1988; Romero 1992).

Nonetheless, this literature tends to naturalize domestic labor by not paying enough attention to the surprising diversity of tasks undertaken by workers. More fundamentally, there is a general disregard in the literature for Mexicanas as workers, and specifically as household workers.[5] Thus both the labor history literature and the sociology/anthropology literature point to a need for empirical data on the labor process—for ground-level studies of what workers, especially Mexicanas, actually do.

As an anthropologist, I am attentive to the economic context that helps shape households and their social reproductive labor requirements. But I am also particularly concerned about how women survive, live, labor, and feel within that context. The goal, then, of this research is to elicit qualitative data about Mexicana household laborers and their work by inquiring into the details of the daily routine, and also into the meaning and effects of household work careers in women's lives.

The notion of power that I use within the context of the household derives from Marxist analysis. The reproduction of capital is based on an unequal relationship between employers and workers: employers exploit workers through the extraction of surplus value from them. Dialectically, however, while the employer may attempt to extract as much labor from workers for as little reward as possible, workers resist these attempts (Marx 1959). Workers are alienated to the extent that they do not have control over the labor process or over the product of their labor. This process of alienation is often intensified by the reduction of contact with other workers (Marx 1967). These ideas of power and alienation in the workplace, however, tend to underrate the fact that not all work produces a commodity, not all work takes place in a factory, and not all work is performed by men. It is particularly difficult to think of domestic services as commodities in Marxist terms. In the case of household workers, then, what does it mean to be alienated?

FIELDWORK METHODS

Because the purpose of the fieldwork was to obtain data on the labor process as well as to understand the meaning of household work in women's lives, I originally planned to use three principal research methods. First, to engage in participant-observation within households in order to document the labor process and the social relations surrounding housework; second, to conduct structured and informal interviews with as many workers as possible in order to get a sense of the diversity within employment as well as of the workers themselves; and third, to compile life histories in order to understand the meaning of the daily routine in Mexicanas' lives. After two attempts, however, the first method proved to be problematic and I decided not to persist with it.

Prior to undertaking "participant-observation" within households, I knew that it would have to be carefully constructed so that neither employer nor employee were offended or hindered by my presence. With the employer and employee's permission, then, I first planned to work as an "apprentice" alongside the household worker. This, I thought, would allow me to observe the labor process and gain a sense of the verbal and nonverbal interaction between employer and employee. It was important to me that I work along-side my informant so that she could teach me without being distracted too much. I hoped that this arrangement would equalize the power imbalance between us. What I did not anticipate was that the employer would make repeated efforts to conduct a friendly conversation with me in English, while I was attempting to be an apprentice. Since in both cases where I attempted participant observation the worker did not speak English, the relationship between me and the employer made the worker visibly uncomfortable. When I later asked the workers if in fact they had been uncomfortable, both responded in the affirmative. Thereafter, I continued with the other two methods and utilized life histories to obtain descriptions of the labor process.

I used the "snowball" sampling technique in order to gain access to as many household workers as possible. Social service workers, acquaintances, friends, and household workers themselves were asked to introduce or refer me to a household worker. I conducted general and in-depth interviews with fifty Mexicanas.

The general interviews provide a sketch of the diversity among women and about the diversity of household employment. All of these were structured interviews since I was attempting to elicit the same information from each of the workers. The in-depth interviews, on the other hand, provide detailed descriptive life histories. I regard the life history as any retrospective account by the individual of her life "in whole or in part, in written or oral form that has been elicited or prompted by another person" (Watson and Watson-Franke 1985). Each life history in this study was comprised of at least twelve hours of semistructured and unstructured interviews during which I focused my questions on details about (1) the life cycle, (2) migration, (3) her employment history, (4) her household work career history, and (5) the labor process associated with her current or most recent household employment. In many cases, each of these categories of life history overlapped, but this was often helpful for me and for the worker as details that had been left out were remembered as the interview went on.

Shortly after I began fieldwork for this project, the then-senatorial candidate and Santa Barbara resident Michael Huffington made headlines for hiring an undocumented Latina childcare provider (Wilson 1994). The worker's name appeared in the media, and many women expressed their fears of being fired or, worse, deported for not having legal documentation. The issue of deportation is not new in Mexican neighborhoods (Gutierrez 1995; Balder-rama and Rodríguez 1995), but within the last ten years newspaper articles and community organizations have documented that border patrol agents have entered private homes by intimidating individuals and patrolled bus stations and streets in search of persons who "looked" illegal in the city (Sadler 1989; Parks 1994). During these episodes many women stayed indoors hoping that the detentions and searches would not reach them.

Being sensitive to the fact that many Mexicanas felt particularly vulnerable during the period of time I undertook fieldwork, I conducted the interviews in a variety of places based on where the worker felt most comfortable. The interview took place at her home, at her workplace, at my home, or at a public place like a park, a social service agency, or a restaurant. The interviews were sometimes recorded on tape, if informants allowed it; during other conversations, I took notes and then went home and wrote up the interview from memory.

In each case, I told the worker that I considered household work to be valuable and important, and that I wanted to understand what she did from day to day and what it meant to her. At first, many women looked at me as if their work should be quite obvious, particularly to a university student. When I explained that it was not obvious, most women took great pains to describe their routines, and what they considered to be fair or unfair, wrong or fulfilling.

Some of the women who form part of this study talked to me in return for assistance in filling out official forms, while others wanted an opportunity to vent their frustration. But most of the women who talked to me did so because they felt that their story might help someone else.

Life histories have proven in this project to be a useful method for studying the labor process, and thus the power dynamics within households, because Mexicanas themselves define their sources of oppression. In so doing, however, they also speak about a different conceptualization of what work should be. Thus Mexicanas' life histories are useful at two levels. First, life histories extend our limited academic knowledge about Mexicanas' working lives, about the domestic labor process, and about very basic notions of power. Secondly, life histories serve as political testimonies, empirical sources for public policy aimed at creating a fair and safe work environment for both employees and employers.

THE FIFTY WOMEN AND CATEGORIES OF WORK

All of the fifty Mexicanas I interviewed had migrated to Santa Barbara within the last ten years, and variously cited domestic violence, lack of job opportunities at home, and family reunification as the principal reasons for doing so.[6] Thirty percent of them are single without children; forty-five percent are married with children; and twenty-five percent are single with children. Most of them migrated from the northern and western Mexican states of Chihuahua, Sinaloa, Jalisco, Durango, Michoacan, and Guerrero; thirty percent migrated from Mexico City and Oaxaca. All the women speak little or no English, and their ages range from twenty-one to sixty-two. The sample includes both documented and undocumented women.

In regards to household work, Mexicanas were very aware of differences within the labor process. They divided the many types of work and the various living arrangements into six distinct categories: (1) housecleaning contractors and (2) the women they contract to work for them; (3) independent, live-out workers; (4) live-in, all-purpose workers; (5) women who either live in or out and whose principal responsibility is caring for another human being; and (6) housekeepers for absentee home owners. These "emic" distinctions serve as analytical constructs—that is, as a guide for pinpointing the skills, responsibilities, and tasks that distinguish one category from another. The wage range spanned a low of two hundred dollars to a high of two thousand, four hundred dollars per month.

Because it is impossible to encapsulate the breadth of their life, migration, and work experiences, in this chapter, I focus on the careers of three women who are presently employed in two of the above-mentioned work categories: a live-out childcare provider, a labor contractor, and a live-in convalescent care provider. These life histories illustrate how household work is structured and how women move from one sort of labor arrangement to another during the course of their lives in Santa Barbara.

HOUSEHOLD WORKER LIFE HISTORIES

I use pseudonyms in the following life histories for several reasons, most importantly because of the possibility that some of the women interviewed did not have a legal status in the United States. Although I never directly asked a worker if she was legally documented, the details of the life history reveal that some of those in this study were not when they entered the United States.

Elida: Live-out Childcare Provider

Women in this category are hired to provide emotional care, supervise, feed, nurse, entertain, dress, and clean children—particularly children under six years of age.

Elida Perez is 36 years old, and was born in Fresnillo, Zacatecas, but lived with an aunt in Juarez, Chihuahua, until she was eight. At that time she was "abandoned" and "adopted" by a neighbor who took her to Guadalajara, Jalisco, and periodically hired her out as a household worker. In spite of the early age at which she began laboring, she still managed to acquire a high school level education and an elementary school teaching certificate. She speaks a little English and currently lives in an apartment with her seven-year-old son. Elida migrated to the United States in 1990 when she was forced to resign from her teaching job in Guadalajara, after being accused of stealing materials from one of the classrooms. She says she is innocent, but was unable to prove it to a supervisor. She felt "shame" and thought that the best way to "start her life over" was to go to a different place, where no one knew of the events in Guadalajara. Because she felt it would be more difficult to find a job in Mexico, Elida decided to migrate to California. Here, she thought, her estranged father who lives in Los Angeles or her sister who lives outside of Santa Barbara might be able to help her settle.

She and her son took a bus to Tijuana, Baja California, and there paid a coyote—a person hired to smuggle people into the United States—to take them to Los Angeles. The crossing was terrifying, filled with the apprehension and fear that comes from running in unknown territory on a cold night with a child crying in your arms. When two of the migrants crossing with Elida did not have either the appropriate fee or someone who would "respond" for them in the United States, the coyotes made examples of them—"to show people what happens when someone tries to cheat them." The woman was repeatedly raped while the man was beaten and scalped.

In Los Angeles, her father who now had a "new family" wanted nothing to do with Elida, so she continued north to Santa Barbara, where her sister Mati was not as happy to see her as Elida had hoped. Nonetheless, Mati allowed Elida to stay for a few days while she looked for a job. Following Mati's advice, Elida went to a church where the priest was helpful in obtaining jobs for new immigrants. Thus Elida found her first household job through a church referral.

This first employer offered her two hundred dollars a month, and room and board, in exchange for taking care of three kids and cleaning the house. Elida notes that it was not a lot of money, but that at least "I had a place for me and my son, and food." After a year of working for this family, however, they moved and Elida was left "on the street," until she learned about a homeless shelter where she and her son could spend the night. Thereafter, through a referral from this shelter, she obtained employment cleaning apartments in an adjacent college community. Elida describes this work as "very tiring," and the labor contractors as "abusive," and so at that time she began to look for alternative household work.

From March 1994 to May 1995, Elida had the following types of household employment: cleaning houses for four dollars an hour, whenever she could find the work through word of mouth; working for a labor contractor and cleaning houses for fifteen dollars for a ten-hour day; and, finally, working as a childcare provider/housecleaner eight hours a day, five days a week for eighty dollars. During this time she said it was a "torture" traveling to and from work on the bus. She expected to be detained and deported by the border patrol who had that year conducted raids at the principal bus depot. Her fear was not only for herself, but for her son who would not know where to find her.

When I met Elida in June of 1995 she was actively looking for employment, since her only source of income at that moment was the weekly cleaning of one house for which she was paid twenty dollars for an eight-hour day. During the following two-week period she worked with a labor contractor four times. The labor contractor did not pay her full wages, however, because Elida offered to work "for free" for two days so that the contractor could observe her skills, and (she hoped) hire her on a regular basis. The labor contractor did not hire her, and soon thereafter, Elida began cleaning apartments in the small college community again, working ten to twelve hours a day for a month.

During this one-month period, she left her seven-year-old son alone in their apartment, and a neighbor reported her to the Child Protective Services. When Elida explained her situation to the case worker, "she was sympathetic, but told me to find a job with better wages so that I could afford to pay for childcare." She did not find a better paying job, but she did find one with fewer hours. Through an ex-employer she, ironically, found employment as a childcare provider. Elida was hired to take care of a two-month-old baby and a two-year-old girl nine hours a day, five days a week, for one hundred thirty dollars.

In the months of August and September, her daily routine was to get up at 5:00 A.M. and make her son's breakfast, lunch, and dinner. She then would get ready and take the bus to work at 6:15 A.M. She arrived at her employers' home by seven in the morning, when they would both leave for work. Promptly upon arriving, she telephoned home to wake up her son and tell him to get ready to go to school. She then gave both her employers' children their breakfast, and then put the baby to sleep. At 7:45, she again called her son to tell him to go down to the bus stop. Between eight and two, she played with both children, put the baby down for a nap every two hours, prepared and gave them their lunch, consoled them when they cried, changed their diapers, and at two in the afternoon she called home to make sure her son was there. She then gave both children a bath and, when she had time, cleaned up a little around the house or took the children to the park. Then two new problematic responsibilities were added: working on the weekend, and taking care of a third baby during the week.

In a recent interview, I learned that Elida has been asked to work on some weekends because her employers are both trying to earn extra money by working themselves. The third child belongs to one of her employers' neighbors who is not able to find affordable childcare. Elida "thinks" she will be earning an additional seventy dollars per week—which she needs—to take care of the third child, but the drawback is that she will be getting home much later as the new employer does not get off work until six o'clock. Elida plans on accepting the new responsibility, however, since her present employers are getting home much later than promised anyway. Elida is currently working between 45 and 72 hours a week.

Although the job description has changed considerably in only two months, Elida is not thinking of looking for another job, because in terms of the labor process and employers this is the "best" situation she has found in the last four years. She says she likes the "liberty" that she did not have when she was cleaning houses. Liberty means that no one is watching over her while she works, no one is telling her how to do her job, or pressuring her to hurry up and finish. If she could change anything about her workday, it would be to get some time off to rest because she gets very tired and worries that she is not as attentive as she "should be" to the children. "My worst fear," she says, "is that the children might hurt themselves." She regards her employers as "good people—especially her." She says that she also has a feeling of security here because her female employer tells her that in the future they will build her a room in the back of the house so that she can be with the baby twenty-four hours a day. As for the work itself, she says:

> I feel like I am doing something useful, something that deserves respect. It makes me feel good to know that people see that I work well with children. What I don't like is that people forget that I also have a responsibility to my son—that's why I'm working here. And I get this feeling that I'm split in two: here I am loving these babies and giving them my attention, while my son, who really needs it, is waiting for me to come home. I sometimes wonder why it is so hard to work.

Guadalupe: Labor Contractor

The second case is that of a labor contractor. These are women hired to clean houses, but they in turn employ other women to perform some or all of the work. In most cases, contractors provide their employees with transportation to and from the work site.

Guadalupe Nora is thirty-two years old and was born and raised in Zocotlán, Jalisco. She has a seventh-grade education, speaks some English, and was never employed outside her home in Mexico. She says she grew up in a very strict household raised primarily by her grandmother, as her mother and father divorced when she was very young. After the divorce, Guadalupe never saw her father again, and because her mother worked in Mexico City, she only occasionally saw her. Guadalupe says it was the strictness in her grandmother's house that led her to "rebel," and a few months before she turned thirteen, she found out she was pregnant. At this same time her mother migrated to the U.S., and Guadalupe moved in with her boyfriend and his family.

At age fifteen Guadalupe left her boyfriend, whom she now refers to as her "first husband" and thereafter "remarried" two more times in Mexico.[7] She now lives with her fourth common-law husband and four children in a two-bedroom apartment. She migrated to Santa Barbara ten years ago after separating from her third husband. She recalls:

> After he hit me the second time, I told him, if you hit me again, I'll leave you. And I think he thought that I was kidding. But the third time he hit me, I walked out the door.

She left the house with her three children and temporarily moved in with her grandmother. Guadalupe knew, however, that her grandmother could not financially support her and it would not be long before her husband came looking for her, so she decided to migrate to Santa Barbara where her mother was working as a live-in housecleaner for a wealthy family. She, two cousins, and her children (aged eight, three, and one) took a bus to Tijuana, Baja California, and there paid a coyote to help them cross the border. She says, "I have no words to describe the pain I felt when I saw my children scared, dirty, and tired. What I can tell you is that under no circumstances would I do it again."

Upon arriving in Santa Barbara, she and her children stayed with her mother for one week and then moved forty miles north to Santa Maria where there was agricultural work picking strawberries. Guadalupe stayed for three months, but did not like the arduous, hot work in the fields and returned to Santa Barbara where her mother arranged for her to stay with an uncle and his wife. Her mother paid him a small amount for rent and food, and Guadalupe slept in a room with her children. During this time, she says *yo me granjeaba*—I earned my way: "I prepared meals and cleaned the house, since I didn't have any work. Sometimes he would help me find work cleaning houses, but kept the money." She said tension built up because she and the children were always in the apartment. "I was afraid of being stopped by the *migra* and didn't want to go outside." Her uncle repeatedly reprimanded her children, and one day she asked him not to talk to her children so harshly:

Well, he got angry, we argued, and at one point he came over and kicked me. He then told me to leave. And so with my mother's help, I found a room for me and my children.

After she moved out, she found a day job and felt "proud" because she could say she had work. But with this employer, she suffered her first employment "disillusionment": after working an entire day cleaning, washing, cooking, and ironing she was paid barely enough to buy dinner for herself and her three kids. This experience helped her decide to take a full-time job as a janitor with a large cleaning company. She refers to these cleaning companies as "abusive" because they pay workers thirty to forty dollars for an eight-hour day, while they keep more than half of the earnings and "do nothing." But at least the money was secure and steady. It was here, too, that she "learned the business," and obtained her first "real independent" house cleaning job through a co-worker. Thereafter, it was this employer who referred Guadalupe to others so that she was able to build up her cleaning business, and leave the janitorial job after a year.

Guadalupe considers herself to have been lucky during this period because she was able to afford childcare at an in-home daycare center while she was working. She says they took "pity" on her and only charged twenty to thirty dollars a week to take care of her children. It was a "difficult" year of working all the time, and saving money to buy a car and put a deposit on an apartment. "My mother wanted to help, but I told her it was not her responsibility. It was I who had a responsibility to my children, and with my own hands, I worked to care for them."

For three years, Guadalupe cleaned houses by herself and "acquired a reputation as a good worker." Thus, when female relatives who had recently migrated asked her for assistance, she hired them as "helpers" and with her reputation obtained more cleaning jobs. She now has twenty regular clients, and on any given day, Monday through Saturday, she cleans two to four houses. She also cleans a dentist's office on Friday evenings, and irons for another client on Thursday afternoons. On average, she works nine hours a day.

As an employer, she describes herself as being "strict" in that she insists the work be done in the manner preferred by the employer. When initially training helpers, she shows them what this is and also warns them not to steal. "In my business," she says, "trust is everything."

In spite of the problems associated with the kinship/work relationship, she prefers to hire family members because nonkin have underbid her price or offered more services, and have thus "taken" houses from her. She says the kinship/work relationship has often been problematic due to the "position of authority" she has to assume, and so from the outset tells her helpers "that within work we have to forget kinship or we'll have problems." Once helpers are trained, she transports them to the houses to be cleaned and individually assigns them rooms and a specified period of time to clean them, while she goes off to clean "her" rooms. Thereafter, she does not check on their work, because she herself does not like it when people check on hers. When she cleans two houses in one day, she takes one helper, and when cleaning four, she takes two.

When asked about the labor involved in cleaning houses, she says it always varies. "In general, clients want a basic cleaning. This does not include washing windows, dusting blinds, or ironing." The first time she goes in to clean a house, she may spend the whole day there with a helper to get everything well cleaned. Thereafter, a weekly basic cleaning means she will spend two hours at that house with one other worker.

> We clean every room well, but the bathrooms and kitchen take the most time because you have to use different chemicals and you have to sweep and mop. . . . Dusting varies from house to house, because some people have a lot of little things, and you have to pick each one up individually. In the bedrooms we change the sheets, make up the beds, and then vacuum.

With her regular clients she also has a weekly focus so that special attention will be given to one part of the house. For example, if her clients have a wooden staircase she may polish the wood, while the next week she may dust books on shelves. She says she gets tired during the workday, but she likes what she does: "sometimes it gets boring, all routines are boring, but then we joke around and get through the day."

Prior to beginning work on any house, she provides potential employers with an estimate. She says that the estimate is usually high, and then if it doesn't take as long as she thought it would to clean the house, she lowers the price. She began doing this because she wasn't always able to properly estimate, and so she had underbid her work. A general price for a basic cleaning is sixty-five dollars for a three-bedroom, two-bathroom house. She says sometimes people don't like to pay what she charges, and sometimes she has to "lose" these houses. These employers may initially agree to the price, thinking they can add more tasks. This is such a widespread problem that she recently made up a flyer, in which she lists prices for extra services. One of the services for which she now charges is conversation. She says that many of the women who hire her to clean want to talk, and that makes it harder to finish the house during a two-hour time frame. Since people want that service, however, she is willing to provide it for what she thinks is a fair price.

In regards to her employers she says:

> I have worked with people who have a lot of money, and they don't look
> at me as if I were a nobody, as if I were a service. They don't look at me
> like a person who does not belong here—they treat me like a person. If
> I did this very same job in Mexico, the women would abuse me. This
> job that I do here—although it is not humiliating or dishonest in Mex-
> ico—is a job where people think they are above you. Here I have not
> personally seen that, although I have heard of people who are despots.
> To those people I would say, people come here because they have to and
> most of them work. So, don't look at women as a service, but as human
> beings.

Teresa: Live-in Convalescent Care Provider

Convalescent care providers are women who nurse and provide companionship to people who are ill or incapacitated because of an injury.

Teresa Sierra is twenty-nine years old and was born and raised in Mexico City. She is single, has a high school level education, no children, and
lives with her employer. She started working at age fifteen, helping her parents with the family vegetable vending business. Subsequently, she worked as
a cosmetic salesperson at a department store, sold cars, and then was a receptionist at a Nissan plant. She migrated to Santa Barbara three and a half years
ago, for both personal and economic reasons. "I was laid off from my job at
Nissan, and my ex-boyfriend said he would kill me if I didn't go back to him."
Her options were limited in Mexico City because she did not want to live with
her father and stepmother, who disapproved of her lifestyle and who would in
addition be subjected to problems caused by her ex-boyfriend. Her ex-
boyfriend had taken to following Teresa and demanding entry into her home.
Moreover, she said there were "no jobs." So she took her savings, obtained a
tourist visa, and flew into Los Angeles for a vacation with a friend, as well as
to see what job opportunities there were. After a month, however, she could
no longer stay with her friend and she was almost out of money.

An acquaintance offered Teresa a space in her living room for three hundred dollars a month, and also offered to help Teresa get a job. The acquaintance kept her promise and found Teresa a job selling burial plots, but she also
expected Teresa to clean the house and take care of her kids. Teresa didn't
mind the work, but she did mind that the woman did not like her talking to
anyone, nor learning to speak English.

Teresa then met sixty-five-year-old Sarita who offered to find her
household employment in Santa Barbara for a small fee. Teresa gladly
moved from Los Angeles to Santa Barbara. Sarita found Teresa a job by tak-

ing out a newspaper advertisement, screening calls, and speaking to potential employers on her behalf. After two weeks, Sarita chose what she considered the "best" situation for Teresa: a position as a live-in childcare provider. After only one week of work, however, Teresa left. She left because this employer wanted her to not only care for his three- and five-year-old children, but also to clean the house, cook, wash the car, take the dogs out for walks, clean the pool, and run errands—all for six hundred dollars a month. The day the children's mother came by for a visit, Teresa just walked away and returned to Sarita's. Her only fear was that Sarita would be angry about losing her commission. The commission was to have been Teresa's first paycheck. Sarita was indeed angry, but within two days found her another job. This time, Teresa was to work as a convalescent care provider to fifty-two-year-old Frank.

Teresa was hired by Frank's seventy-three-year-old mother and business partner. This employer, to whom Teresa refers as "grandma," told her that her responsibilities would consist of putting Frank to bed and getting him up and dressed every morning. The job description was that at 9:00 P.M., Monday through Saturday, she would undress him, clean his leg wounds in the manner described by a nurse, put on his pajamas, get him to the bathroom, and then back to bed. The process would take approximately two hours. Then, between 6:00–8:00 in the morning, she would repeat the process and get him dressed. By 8:30 A.M. she was to have breakfast ready, because Frank left for physical therapy at 9:00 A.M. Once Frank left, she was to wash and put away the breakfast dishes. Her total work hours per week were to be thirty. The salary offered her was eight hundred dollars a month plus room and board.

Almost immediately, she says, the job description changed. Frank does not always want to get ready for bed at 9:00 P.M., and "sometimes he makes me wait until 11:00 P.M. or midnight, because he is watching television—that means I won't be done until one or two in the morning." On those rare Friday or Saturday nights when she does finish by 11:00 P.M. and makes plans to go out, Frank tells her she is a "whore," while her employer pleads with Teresa not to go out because she needs companionship. Teresa often obliges.

She says she has cried in front of her employers more than once, as Frank alternately makes sexual innuendos and then tells her she is stupid. He also thinks it is funny to tell Teresa racist jokes, and tries to goad her into reacting. His mother, "to detract from what she knows is wrong on his part," blames Teresa by saying he only says these things because he is in a wheelchair and because Teresa is lazy.

She is now also working on Sunday "for free" because she feels "obligated." She feels obligation because her employer tells her that she and her son are having financial difficulties, and that on the day Teresa is not there they have to pay a licensed provider to assist Frank. Teresa reasons:

When you live-in you don't dispose of your own time—your life
revolves around other people. It doesn't matter how much you work, it's
never enough, and you have to pretend that you don't mind doing it.

Teresa estimates that she works sixty hours a week.

Teresa says that when she first started talking about attending the city
college, her employers would try to dissuade her by making "friendly threats"
about how she might lose her job or be deported. They continually tell her that
she should spend her time working and be happy with that, because they have
heard rumors of border patrol agents asking students for their papers. They
also warn her against talking to the woman who comes in once a week to
clean the house. Teresa thinks it is because her employers fear that she and the
housecleaner "will learn from each other."

In addition to the emotional distress she suffers, Teresa is not happy with
her job for two other reasons: one is the fact that she is experiencing back pain
from helping her six-foot tall, one-hundred-eighty-pound employer to and
from the bathroom. Teresa is 5' 2" and weighs one hundred four pounds. Secondly, she is never paid on time or for the full amount. She showed me a recent
paycheck and indicated that her employer had not written in her name, because
even after having worked for her and Frank for three years, they forget it.
Moreover, the check was made out in the amount of only one hundred dollars.
Teresa is afraid they will never pay her what they owe her, and that they may
suddenly decide to dismiss her. She has been thinking about these possibilities
because Frank was hospitalized for two weeks, and Teresa was not paid since,
according to the employer, "she was not doing anything." Nonetheless, she was
still required to make breakfast and stay in the house at night.

Teresa's isolation and desire to find a better job motivated her to sign up
for English classes at the city college. She thereby began to build up her network of acquaintances and friends, and it was through this network that she
began to hear about other household employment. She obtained two daytime
cleaning jobs. At one of these jobs where she cleans for four hours a week, her
employer has a sign on the bottled water that says, "this costs seven dollars a
bottle—bring your own." Commenting on household work she said:

> I am not ashamed of my work—it's honest and I help people. The prob-
> lem is that employers forget you are a person, and that you have needs
> just like them. If I were to change anything, it would be not so much the
> money—although that wouldn't hurt—it would be the amount of hours
> worked. That people respect your hours, and remember that you get
> tired too. Also that people respect you as a person, because I'll tell you
> one thing, people don't let insults stay inside them—one way or
> another, it comes out.

CONCLUSION

Although waged household work has been a constant feature in U.S. history, in the present period of global and local restructuring, new forms have emerged. In California, part of what is new is that employers are no longer primarily upper- and middle-class white women, but rather a cross-class, interethnic group of women who are often employed outside the household. These women increasingly hire Mexicanas who, in turn, come from different states in Mexico, have different life experiences and ages, as well as differing family obligations. Like the Mexicanas who perform the work, household labor itself is not homogenous. In Santa Barbara, employers have varying labor requirements that include cleaning, residential caretaking, washing and ironing, cooking, and the physical and emotional care of humans. The varying labor requirements, in turn, create different categories of work, each of which has a specific labor process.

Waged domestic work is embedded within a power relationship typical of capitalist relations of production, but unlike many other worksites, observation of the domestic labor process is not easy. Thus, I relied on life history as a method for studying power within this work relationship. Specifically, through life histories, women spoke about what it meant to be alienated from the labor process, the product of their labor, and from other workers. Ultimately, they also spoke of the effects of these three aspects of alienation on their persons.

A new category of work for Mexicanas is the caring for the bodies and emotions of human beings. Although most types of work have "emotional labor" as a component, in this category of household work it is the most fundamental aspect. The irony of the work relationship is that while it is deeply personal, workers are at the same time depersonalized. Elida, who is a childcare provider, likes her employers because they appreciate her work, yet she is not seen as a whole person: her role as a mother is ignored, and she is in fact expected to put the needs of her own child on hold as the workday and the work week have progressively gotten longer. Thus, she speaks about feeling "split" as she has to provide the mothering tasks of affection, patience, and attention to other people's children so that she is able to earn enough money to provide basic material necessities for her own child.

Teresa, who cares for the body of a convalescing adult as well as taking care of his elderly mother's need for companionship, is expected to be at their disposal at any time, while her own needs for friendship and learning are characterized as indicative of being lazy. Incongruously, she is asked to call the elderly woman "grandma," while they often cannot remember her name. Moreover, her employer makes thinly veiled threats about deportation to obligate her to stay and work for them for longer periods of time.

These various actions on the part of employers lead Mexicanas to say that they feel like "objects" or "things" within a labor process where they have little control, where they have few interactions with other workers, and where at any moment their jobs can be taken away from them. It is little wonder, then, that more experienced laborers prefer a more impersonal work situation. Guadalupe, the labor contractor, recognizes that just as cleaning homes is work, so are the tasks of listening and being empathetic. She has thus put a price on conversation—clearly signaling to employers that emotional labor is work proper.

Life histories also allow us to look at another dimension of power. This dimension of power is Mexicanas' resistance to economic insecurity, gender conflict, and dehumanization in the workplace. We are able to see how women had the courage to leave their households in Mexico, in some cases putting themselves in grave danger as they clandestinely crossed the U.S.-Mexico border. Once in the United States, they negotiated with family members, friends, acquaintances, and employers in order to obtain better living and working conditions. In the workplace, strategies include not only finding better employers and better pay, but also better categories of work. For some women, this may mean cleaning rather than engaging in human care.

That Mexicanas of the class position I describe "resist" demeaning or exploitive situations is not to say that they always succeed in their efforts. Their failures, however, also allow us to see the problems and obstacles stacked against them. The life history approach extends through women's words a recognition that household work is not only what these Mexicanas do with their days, but is in fact what they do with their lives.

ACKNOWLEDGMENTS

This chapter is dedicated to the women who so graciously and patiently shared their precious time with me. Partial funding for the research was provided by U.C. MEXUS. An earlier version of this paper was presented at the 'Latinos in California' Conference, U.C. Riverside, in 1995. I thank David Crawford, Edward Hagen, and A.F. Robertson for editorial suggestions.

NOTES

1. In this chapter, the term "Mexicanas" refers to women who were born and raised in Mexico and who emigrated to the United States as young women or adults. Mexicanas may not have official residency documents. "Chicana" refers to women of Mexican descent born in the United States. "Latina" is a broader term that refers to women of Latin American origin living in the United States.

2. The informal economic sector refers to a process of income generation "characterized by the fact that it is unregulated by the institutions of society, in a legal and social environment in which similar activities are regulated" (Portes, Castells, and Benton 1989:2).

3. In addition to a cultural preference for British domestics, U.S. employers discovered that these workers could obtain visas much more quickly than women of other nationalities. Before October 1965, immigration into the United States was controlled under a national origins quota system, which maintained the ethnic balance that existed, based on the 1920 census. Thus it was easier to obtain visas for people from the British Isles (Martin and Segrave 1985:96–104).

4. One hundred years of Mexican migration to the United States has also created extensive social networks that facilitate migration (Massey 1988).

5. Mary Romero's important study of Chicana domestics in Denver purposefully excluded Mexicanas because she wanted to avoid "bringing into the analysis immigration issues that increase the vulnerability of the women employed as domestics" (1992:7) so that the women in her study could be compared to those in Rollins' (1988) and Nakano-Glenn's (1986) studies. Vicki Ruiz (1987), Rosalia Solórzano-Torres (1988), and journalist Debbie Nathan (1991) have all written articles addressing the problems faced by Mexicana domestic workers in El Paso, Texas. Rita Simon and Margo DeLey note that work in private homes is an important occupation for undocumented Mexicanas in Los Angeles (1984), while Hondagneu-Sotelo (1994) includes household workers in her study of Mexican settlement in Redwood City. Nonetheless, to this day there is no long-term study that focuses exclusively on Mexicana household workers in the United States.

6. The reasons Mexicanas migrated specifically into Santa Barbara varies, but it is almost always associated with having a friend or family member in the city. However, although women come here because of social networks, they stay because of the possibility of finding employment. Santa Barbara is primarily known as a tourist, retirement, and university city. In fact, during the last twenty years, the service industry has provided the greatest number of jobs with the majority being in business, health, educational, and personal services (U.S. Census 1990). Agriculture and light manufacturing are also important in the local economy. Since the 1980 census, the Latino population grew by 63%, so that by 1990 there were 26,920 Latinos in a city of 85,000. The vast majority of the Latinos, 88%, are of Mexican descent. The unprecedented growth in the Mexican population reflects in great measure the growth in the service industry. The majority of Mexican service, agricultural, repair, and manufacturing workers live on the lower "east" and "west" side of State Street, where 60% or more of the population on every block is Latino. In fact, two-thirds of the total Latino population lives in these two neighborhoods (Barber 1995). Here the vast majority of people are renters, and it is common for individuals and families to live in unorthodox housing such as garages, subdivided houses, and even subdivided rooms, in order to keep housing costs down. Subsidized government-owned and nonowned housing are also prominent in these two areas.

7. Guadalupe noted that only one of her "marriages" in Mexico was sanctioned by the state. The other two relationships in Mexico and her present relationship in the United States, are common-law marriages.

REFERENCES CITED

Amott, Teresa, and Julie Matthaei

1991 *Race, Gender, and Work: A Multicultural Economic History of Women in the United States*. Boston: South End Press.

Abel Kemp, Alice

1994 *Women's Work: Degraded and Devalued*. Englewood Cliffs, N.J.: Prentice Hall.

Barber, Bob

1995 Overview: The Minority Communities of the South Coast. Unpublished manuscript prepared for the Multicultural Community Partnership, Santa Barbara, California.

1990 *Demographic Data Report compiled for the Multicultural Community Partnership*. Santa Barbara, California.

Bakan. B. Abigail, and Daiva K. Stasiulis

1995 Making the match: Domestic placement agencies and the racialization of women's household work. *Signs: Journal of Women in Culture and Society* 20(2).

Balderrama, Francisco E., and Raymond Rodriguez

1995 *Decade of Betrayal: Mexican Repatriation in the 1930s*. Albuquerque: University of New Mexico Press.

Berk, Sarah Fenotermaker

1985 *The Gender Factory: The Apportionment of Work in American Households*. New York: Plenum.

Bluestone, Barry, and Bennett Harrison

1988 *The Deindustrialization of America*. New York: Basic Books.

Camarillo, Albert

1979 *Chicanos in a Changing Society: From Mexican Pueblos to American Barrios in Santa Barbara and Southern California, 1848–1930*. Cambridge: Harvard University Press.

Colen, Shellee

1989 "Just a little respect": West Indian domestic workers in New York City. In *Muchachas No More*. Elsa Chaney and Mary García Castro, eds. Philadelphia: Temple University Press.

1986 "Working for the green card": Voices of West Indian childcare and domestic workers in New York City. In *All American Women Lines that Divide, Ties That Bind*. Johnnetta Cole, ed. New York: Free Press.

Cornelius, Wayne
  1992 "From sojourners to settlers": The changing profile of Mexican immigration to the United States. In *U.S.-Mexico Relations: Labor Market Interdependence*. Jorge Bustamante, Clark W. Reynolds, and Raul Hinojosa Ojeda, eds. Stanford, CA: Stanford University Press.

Deutsch, Sarah
  1987 *No Separate Refuge: Culture, Class, and Gender on an Anglo-Hispanic Frontier in the American Southwest, 1880–1940*. New York: Oxford University Press.

Dill, Bonnie Thornton
  1994 *Across the Boundaries of Race and Class: An Exploration of Work and Family Among Black Female Domestic Servants*. New York: Garland Publishing.

Enloe, Cynthia
  1990 *Bananas, Beaches, and Bases: Making Feminist Sense of International Politics*. Berkeley: University of California Press.

Fernández-Kelly, M. Patricia, and Saskia Sassen
  1995 "Recasting women in the global economy": Internationalization and changing definitions of gender. In *Women in the Latin American Development Process*. Christine E. Bose and Edna Acosta Belen, eds. Philadelphia: Temple University Press.

Foster, James
  1982 *Labor in the Southwest*. Arizona Board of Regents.

García, Mario
  1981 *Desert Immigrants: The Mexicans of El Paso, 1880–1920*. New Haven: Yale University Press.

García y Griego, Manuel
  1994 "History of U.S. Immigration Policy." California Immigration, Conference Proceedings. Sacramento, California. California Policy Seminar. April 29.

Gomez-Quiñones, Juan
  1994 *Mexican American Labor, 1790–1990*. 1st ed. Albuquerque: University of New Mexico Press.

González, Deena
  1985 *Spanish-Mexican Women on the Santa Fé Frontier: Patterns of their Resistance and Accommodation, 1820–1880*. Dissertation. University of California–Berkeley.

Green, Duncan
  1995 *The Silent Revolution: The Rise of Market Economics in Latin America*. London: Cassell.

Gutierrez, David
  1995 *Walls and Mirrors: Mexican Americans, Mexican Immigrants, and the Politics of Ethnicity*. Berkeley: University of California Press.

Hartmann, Heidi
1987 "Changes in women's economic roles in post World War II United States." In *Women, Households, and the Economy.* Lourdes Beneria and Catherine R. Stimpson, eds. New Brunswick, N.J.: Rutgers University Press.
1981 The family as the locus of gender, class, and political struggle: An example of housework. *Signs: Journal of Women and Culture and Society* (6).

Hayes-Bautista, David, Werner O. Schink, and Jorge Chapa
1986 *The Burden of Support.* Stanford, CA: Stanford University Press.

Hochschild, Arlie
1988 *The Second Shift: Working Parents and their Revolution at Home.* New York: Viking.
1983 *The Managed Heart: The Commercialization of Human Feeling.* Berkeley: University of California Press.

Hondagneu-Sotelo, Pierrette
1994 *Gendered Transitions: Mexican Experiences of Immigration.* Berkeley: University of California Press.

Martin, Linda, and Kerry Segrave
1985 *The Servant Problem: Domestic Workers in North America.* Jefferson, N.C.: McFarland and Co.

Marx, Karl
1967 Economic and philosophical manuscripts. Complete translation. In *Writings of the Young Marx on Philosophy and Society.* L. Easton and K. Guddatt, eds. New York: Doubleday.
1959 *Capital.* Vol. III. Moscow: Foreign Languages Publishing House.

Massey, Douglas
1988 *Return to Aztlan: The Social Process of International Migration from Northern Mexico.* Berkeley: University of California Press.

Nakano-Glenn, Evelyn
1986 *Issei, Nissei, War Bride.* Philadelphia: Temple University Press.

Nash, June
1995 Latin American women in the world capitalist crisis. In *Women in the Latin American Development Process.* Christine E. Bose and Edna Acosta Belen, eds. Philadelphia: Temple University Press.

Nathan, Debbie
1991 *Women and Other Aliens: Essays from the U.S.-Mexico Border.* El Paso, Texas: Cinco Puntos Press.

Palmer, Phyllis
1989 *Domesticity and Dirt: Housewives and Domestic Servants in the United States, 1920–1945.* Philadelphia: Temple University Press.

Parks, Rhonda
1994 Latinos protest raids by INS agents, *Santa Barbara News Press*, 1 June, p. B1.

Portes, Alejandro, Manuel Castells, and Lauren Benton
1989 *The Informal Economy: Studies in Advanced and Less Developed Countries.* Baltimore: Johns Hopkins University Press.

Repak, Terry
1995 *Waiting on Washington: Central American Workers in the Nation's Capital.* Philadelphia: Temple University Press.

Rollins, Judith
1988 *Between Women: Domestics and Their Employers.* Philadelphia: Temple University Press.

Romero, Mary
1992 *Maid in the U.S.A.* New York: Routledge.

Ruiz, Vicki
1988 "And miles to go . . .": Mexican women and work, 1930–1950. In *Western Women: Their Land, Their Lives.* Lillian Schlissel, Vicki L. Ruiz, and Janice Monk, eds. Albuquerque: University of New Mexico Press.
1987 "By the day or the week": Mexicana domestic workers in El Paso." In *Women on the U.S.-Mexico Border: Responses to Change.* Vicki Ruiz and Susan Tiano, eds.

Sadler, Martha
1989 Ain't no border wide enough. *Santa Barbara Independent*, 2 August, p. 34.

Salmon, Lucy
1911 *Domestic Service.* London: McMillan Co.

Salzinger, Leslie
1991 A maid by any other name. In *Ethnography Unbound.* Michael Burawoy, ed. Berkeley: University of California Press.

Sanjek, Roger, and Shellee Colen
1990 At work in homes I: Orientations. In *At Work in Homes: Household Workers in World Perspective.* Roger Sanjek and Shellee Colen, eds. American Ethnological Society Monograph Series, no. 3. Washington, D.C.: American Anthropological Society.

Sassen-Koob, Saskia
1990 U.S. immigration policy toward Mexico in a global economy. *Journal of International Affairs* 43(2) Winter.
1988 *The Mobility of Labor and Capital.* New York: Cambridge University Press.

Simon, Rita, and Margo DeLey
1984 The work experience of undocumented Mexican women migrants in Los Angeles. In *International Migration Review* 18(4).

Solórzano-Torres, Rosalía
1988 Women, labor and the U.S.-Mexico border: Mexican maids in El Paso, Texas. In *Mexicanas at Work in the U.S.* Margarita Melville, ed. Houston: Mexican American Studies Program.

1987 Female Mexican immigrants in San Diego County. In *Women on the U.S.-Mexico Border: Responses to Change.* Vicki Ruiz and Susan Tiano, eds. Boston: Allen and Unwin.

U.S. Bureau of the Census
1990 *Population and Housing Report.* Santa Barbara, California.

Watson, Lawrence, and Maria Barbara Watson-Franke
1985 *Interpreting Life Histories: An Anthropological Inquiry.* New Brunswick, NJ: Rutgers University Press.

Wilson, Scott
1994 Huffington concedes he broke law in hiring alien. *Santa Barbara News Press*, 28 October, p. A1.

Woodrow, Karen A., and Jeffrey S. Passel
1990 Post IRCA unauthorized immigration to the United States: An assessment based on the June 1988 CPS. In *Undocumented Migration to the United States: IRCA and the Experience of the 1980s.* Frank Bean, Barry Edmonston, and Jeffrey Passel, eds. Santa Monica, CA: Rand Corporation.

Chapter 8

Seeing Power in a College Cafeteria

Daniel Cogan

In the spring of 1994, I produced A COLLEGE CAFETERIA, a documentary video about the workplace experiences of nonstudent food service workers at one of four cafeterias at a university in northern California. Throughout the production of the video, I worked from a central question: Why is there a physical and social separation between workers and students? On a campus removed from the town, the collective labor of food service workers makes it possible for some two thousand on-campus students to eat two to three meals daily. Yet, this community of workers is largely ignored by, and invisible to, these same students who see the university as a location for higher learning as opposed to a site where labor occurs. This case study examines the use of documentary video as a visual tool in the exploration of power in a service-oriented workplace.

SERVICE WORK IN A UNIVERSITY

I participated in the cafeteria first as a student customer consuming the food services and then as a student worker contributing to the production of the food services. These two distinct experiences in the same institution exposed me to the ways in which institutional power (Foucault 1979) functions to differentiate the experience of students from nonstudent workers. The Bartlet Corporation (a pseudonym), a large food service corporation that currently operates food service at the university, has in place a formalized system to distinguish the student workers from nonstudent workers. "In institutional settings, stratification is built in to organizational structures, including lines of authority, job descriptions, rules and spatial and temporal segregation" (Nakano-Glenn 1992:32). For instance, student workers, like myself, are generally assigned jobs that specifically entail interacting with student customers in the service encounter. Nonstudent workers, on the other hand, are relegated to fill positions that isolate them in the kitchen.

Through its student educational program, Bartlet privileges student workers by offering them quarterly book-aid bonuses, by continuing employment beyond one year, and by allowing them to work a minimum of eight hours each week. Student workers, moreover, have the opportunity to advance in the cafeteria hierarchy by applying for positions reserved for students as shift-leaders, supervising other student workers, and as student manager, assisting the two cafeteria managers. For workers distinguished as non-students, only seven full-time jobs are available in the cafeteria—the cook, pantry, and utility positions. While the full-time positions include a benefits plan, the rest of the nonstudent workers are limited to work under thirty hours per week as part-time employees ineligible for any bonuses or benefits plan.

If it is in the corporation's interest to provide student workers with book-aid bonuses for working food service at a university, then why doesn't this corporation provide educational bonuses or opportunities to its non-student workers who want to pursue higher education? The privileges bestowed upon student workers in the workplace of the cafeteria reinforce their position as trainees of the university and nonstudents as reproductive laborers at the university.

While the segmentation of student and nonstudent workers is a formal designation of power based on an educational relationship to the university, other factors of socioeconomic experience (e.g., education, race, gender, migration, language, and citizenship) function to further complicate the relationships of power between managers, students, and workers in the cafeteria. Of the nonstudent workers, only two possessed a bachelor's degree. Three were Mexican migrant workers of seven years; two worked part-time as dish-washers, and one held the full-time position as utility worker. Speaking primarily in Spanish, these workers were spatially segregated by the architecture of the cafeteria into the dishroom. Their tasks included washing the dishes and cooking utensils, throwing out the garbage, cleaning the floors between meals, and stocking the deliveries. Most student-workers did not work these physically demanding jobs from which the Mexican workers made their living. While this work is considered unskilled in comparison with the cooks,' these workers provided the vital daily reproduction of the cafeteria services.

The overrepresentation of women and migrant workers from Mexico in the workplace of the cafeteria requires us to examine the ways in which reproductive labor is defined by race, gender, citizenship, and language. Evelyn Nakano-Glenn (1992) documents the ways in which workers of color, specifically women of color, are historically overrepresented as reproductive service laborers in institutional settings. In this institutional site of food service, male migrant workers have been constructed as those who reproduce the services of the workplace. In California, migrant workers from Latin America and elsewhere overwhelmingly fill the need in our service-oriented economy for social reproductive labor.

Because of the constructions of race and cultural difference in the U.S. shaping views of Latino workers specifically, they have been stereotypically hired to work in physically demanding positions as dishwashers, as farm workers, as domestic workers, and the like. In an interview in the video I made, one of the migrant workers discusses his own analysis: as a migrant worker, he is forced to work as a dishwasher because of the unwillingness of other groups of workers—students, for example—to perform these physically demanding jobs. The passing of Proposition 187 in the state of California in 1994, in part, reflects the racist attitudes of other workers in the state who cling to their position of power over migrant workers, undocumented and documented, by asserting their perceived "legitimate" claims to higher paying and more prestigious jobs based on notions of whiteness (Roediger 1991), citizenship, and language.

In an increasingly changing service-oriented economy, institutions of higher education function to facilitate, more so than in the past, the training of a sought-after "educated" class of white-collar workers. At the same time, this institution necessitates the services of a large number of clerical, janitorial, maintenance, and food service workers from outside the university to service and maintain the daily reproduction of the university:

> . . . the population no longer relies upon social organization in the form of family, friends, neighbors, community, elders, children, but with few exceptions must go to the market and only to the market, not only for food, clothing, and shelter, but also for recreation, amusement, security, for the care of the young, the old, the sick, the handicapped. (Braverman 1974:281)

A university is an institution that functions within the parameters of a service-oriented marketplace. It is important to recognize it as a site where reproductive labor enables the institution to function, even though that labor is often overshadowed by the dominant perception of the university as a place for higher education. While food service workers serve the personal needs of student customers, the relatiohship between these groups in the cafeteria is quite detached.

SEGREGATION OF LABORERS FROM CONSUMERS

In the cafeteria, walls physically separate the eating area from the serving area, and the serving area from the kitchen. This demarcation of space not only designates specific spaces for particular activities, but also visually hides the labor of nonstudent workers in the kitchen from the student customers in the serving and dining areas. Student customers and nonstudent workers almost never see each other because of the wall that separates the kitchen from the serving area. Rarely do nonstudent workers have time during the meal to come out and watch the students. Similarly, students almost never freely walk back into the kitchen; if they do, it is to talk to management. Within the kitchen itself, work stations are separated and hidden from one another by ovens, refrigerators, and walls. Yet the managers' office, which sits in one corner, oversees to some extent all the work spaces. The architectural design of the kitchen limits the ways in which individuals see within this institutional workplace. It functions as a panoptic mechanism in the way Foucault described it: "This architectural apparatus should be a machine for creating and sustaining a power relation independent of the person who exercises it" (Foucault 1979: 201). The physical and social division between students customers and nonstudent workers empowers management in a position of power to control the operation in the workplace.

As a way of further disempowering workers in the workplace, the Bartlet Corporation encourages student customers to use comment cards in order to have a voice about the food services they use daily. The managers, in their responsibility to the customer, reply to all suggestions that customers make about food quality and choice, including the humorous and off-the-wall ones. Because the management responds to consumer demands, managers in turn use these comment cards to reflect input from customers in changing certain aspects of production.

At the beginning of an extensive customer survey conducted on campus by the university food service, students were asked to fill it out so that the management could improve food services to better meet students' dining desires. This survey, along with the comment cards, officially seeks student customers' participation in improving food quality and the execution of food service. Yet, only two boxes in the nine-page survey asked student customers to evaluate worker performance. This would seem to affirm for student customers the notion that the workers in the dining hall are inconsequential in the production and reproduction of food services. The relationship the management dictates to student customers through the use of customer surveys and comment cards disenfranchises the role of the worker in his or her job. However, in spite of their stated efforts to improve food and service quality, after one of the cooks left in the middle of the term, the managers refused to hire another chef at the request of the full-time workers to ease their work load and improve food and service quality.

The facade of a dialogue between student customers and management not only excludes workers, but deems them to be invisible participants in the production of food services. In omitting a significant analysis of workers from the customer survey, the Bartlet Corporation is able to develop its own standards for worker performance. In cafeterias that produce food for over five hundred students per meal, service quality is difficult to evaluate outside of customer replies. Because the labor which goes into the service production of food occurs periodically, it leaves few traces and is invisible as a product produced by workers. Student customers tend to evaluate food not on its utility in their lives, but rather on its quality at the point of consumption.

CONTROLLING SERVICE WORKERS

Reflecting its broader corporate philosophy, the Bartlet Corporation employs specific language in reference to labor relations that creates a facade of workplace equality. For instance, all the workers in the dining hall are called associates. Moreover, the full-time nonstudent employees and management have a biweekly meeting to discuss changes that need to be made. However, with a corporation opposing its workers' right to organize as a collective body, disgruntled employees who do not feel heard by management have few recourses but to move on and find another job. Four of the workers I videotaped in the spring of 1994 ended their working relationship with the university food service soon after, for a variety of reasons. Their horizontal movement to other service jobs represents the high turnover characteristic of unorganized, low-paying service work.

Clearly, in its relations with labor, there exist economic and political motivations of a university that contradict its primary, acknowledged purpose as an institution for the reproduction of knowledge. By contracting the food service responsibilities out to a corporation, the university removes its responsibility from managing the food service workers directly. While it is not uncommon for universities to subcontract out maintenance work or food service, subcontracting to Bartlet not only saves the university money, but also undercuts the relationship that workers might have with the university as well as with students.

This practice of subcontracting social reproductive labor has been a strategy of other corporations to undercut the rights and wages of service workers perceived to be manipulable. In the face of this corporate strategy, Justice For Janitors, as a union and social movement, has fought and continues to fight against the ways in which subcontracting undercuts the wages, benefits, and collective power to which a group of workers is entitled.

The university has proven to be quite powerful in undercutting the power of organized workers. UPTE, the Union of Professional and Technical Employees, and ASE, the Association of Student Employees—which repre-

sents graduate students and undergraduate students at the University and has
sister unions at four other California campuses—are still struggling to gain
formal recognition from the university.

In spite of their lack of collective representation, food service workers
who service the needs of the university, have spaces in which to contest the
institutional power of the university. For instance, as sites of higher education,
universities usually lack the ability to move production and reproduction of
education from the already established campus community. As Giarini and
Stahel (1989:80) point out, "service activities often face less international
competition because they have to be performed where the need is." This
inability to move production and reproduction contrasts with the trend of
many industrial manufacturing corporations to move operations overseas in
search of cheaper labor sources. While reproductive service labor, as an essential aspect of the U.S. increasingly service-oriented economy, is largely considered to be unskilled and low-paid employment, with high turnover, its per-
manence as a fixture in the economy instills this sector with a strategic place
for collective organizing.

The 1984–85 clerical and technical workers strike at Yale University
demonstrated the collective power that service workers possess at a work site
that is publicly visible and from which production cannot be relocated. In
that strike, the clerical and technical workers (mostly women, many of them
women of color) fought the Yale corporation for better wages, comparable
worth, and respect as workers and won their demands (Gilpin et al. 1995). An
understanding of the differences among workers at an institution such as a
university, where workers are divided by language, immigration status, race,
and gender poses a great challenge to understand how they collectively are
disciplined in an institution of higher learning. As Scott and Storper have
said:

> With the diversity of labor processes . . . we are perhaps observing the
> end of the "mass collective worker." Not only is labor demand differ-
> entiated by industry, occupation, skill, age, gender, and race, but also by
> geographical affiliation. Add to this the often complex loyalties that
> individuals have to their communities, and the ways in which experi-
> ence and world-views cut across these social divisions within specific
> regions, and an extremely complex mosaic of social life in capitalism
> suggests itself. (Scott and Storper 1986:13)

In a university community as worksite, the social division between students
and workers relies upon the consent of student customers to treat workers as
nonhuman beings. As "it is not possible to totally separate production workers (service providers) from customers" (Czepial et al. 1985:80), the service

encounter remains a potential site for political action for both customer and worker, with the possibility of drawing on other sets of alliances within the community than those emphasized by management.

SEEING POWER

The fact that relations of power in the hierarchical workplace I observed remained so hidden provided the impetus to use documentary video as a medium through which to visually authenticate the experiences of nonstudent workers in their work spaces. The genre of documentary video, in its many contexts, provides a myriad of examples for its application both in the actual process of videotaping and in the editing of a final representation. Sarah Elder discusses the technique of collaboration in her article "Collaborative Film-making" (Elder: 1995) as a method by which to more ethically produce documentary films by providing those filmed with choices about how they want to participate. At the start of the project, I approached individual workers and the management with the proposal of making a documentary about the cafeteria, to obtain permission as well as to establish with them, as participants, the parameters of the project.

Several workers, in their responses, expressed apprehension and ambivalence about taking part in the making of a videotape. In spite of the prevalence of video technology in our society (or perhaps because of it), many people have reservations about their own lives being recorded visually. After I obtained permission to shoot selectively in the cafeteria, it became more comfortable for those who originally felt apprehensive about being in front of the camera. In part, this was because of how we collaborated in selecting what questions they felt were important and wanted to address in the interviews. The methodology of collaboration not only provided an ethical approach to this documentary project, but also helped to inform me as the videographer about the participants' insights into the project.

By bringing video technology into the workplace with the goal of creating an ethnographic documentary video, I—as a student—was employing a technology of power to which those I was videotaping did not have access. As a result, I framed the process of videotaping from my perspective as a student worker, whereby I was not just an outsider attempting to understand the workplace, but someone who could relate to workers' insights about management, bureacracy, student workers, student customers, and the daily trials of the mass reproduction of food service. "Participation is no longer seen as just a technique that yields objective data; it is a distinctive mode of creating data" (Hastrup 1992:12).

While my use of the camera would allow the hidden work spaces of the cafeteria to be seen in a final edited piece, during the process of collecting

footage and conducting interviews the camera altered the normative configurations of power and perception among the participants, because I primarily
focused the camera and my inquiries on nonstudent workers as opposed to
management or students. As a form of surveillance, the presence of the camera created a heightened sense of awareness for workers about how power
relations influence how they perform their jobs. Similarly, we might consider
the effect upon workers and managers in their workplace if an academic, a
union representative, or a state safety inspector entered the location of work
with the specific purpose of conducting a study.

As the videographer, I found that my approach of collaboration with the
nonstudent workers allowed them to feel empowered in front of the camera as
opposed to a manager who felt untrusting of my use of the camera. Still, I was
doubly situated as a worker and a student, and had a privileged position in
relation to the nonstudent workers featured in the documentary video. Collaboration did not, then, mean complete equality in terms of power and voice
in the workplace or in some aspects of the project.

John Gaventa, a political scientist, in his book *Power and Powerlessness* (1980), provides the example of creating visual represenations by using
the technology of video democratically—so that the participants act not
merely as subjects or objects of an ethnographic gaze, but become more significantly involved in the entire production process. "Videotape technology
provides a medium that can be used as a tool for alternative communication
amongst 'disconnected' communities" (Gaventa 1980:221). In his study of a
coal mining community in Appalachia, Gaventa explains that the use of this
collective process enabled the people within that community to feel empowered as a result of their participation in the production of a self-representa-
tional documentary video.

Democratizing the production of video allows a space for oppressed
people to not only create a positive self-image, but to also form critical consciousness through participation (Freire 1989). As I gathered footage of the
cafeteria and began interviews, I began to see how the use of the camera contributes to a process of self-examination among the participants.

Ideally, the use of a democratic production process, suggested by
Gaventa, acts to empower participants in the crafting of a representation.
However, in many documentary projects full participation from all participants is difficult to manage because of the scope of the particular project. For
instance, Jon Silver, producer of WATSONVILLE ON STRIKE, could not
have used a fully democratic approach within his documentary because of the
urgency to document the strike as it happened. Yet, because of his work in the
community prior to the 1985 strike, he possessed enough of the trust of the
largely Latino community to thoroughly document aspects of the personal
lives of workers during the strike. This project, while not completely democ-

ratic, nonetheless provided a forum during the strike for cannery workers to reflect upon their own situation.

Videography can be a powerful tool for representing workers' voices and worksites generally underrepresented in mainstream visual media. Visual representations of workers and the workplace are scarce on television, a central location in popular culture where dominant values and concerns in society are legitimated. Simply by watching the 11 o'clock news in the United States, we can obtain an understanding of what issues are prioritized in the mass media. The overwhelming focus of television news programs pertains to crime, mainstream politics, and entertainment. Rarely are there stories about workers. "What a society sees of itself on television may provide its mainstream with a kind of collective self-image" (Gaventa 1980:221). Nearly all television programs deal with occupations, yet most of the occupations represented do not reflect the experiences of the majority of working people in this country. "Television over-represents those in professional and other high-status occupational roles with men, especially white men, generally presented in more high status occupational roles than women and minorities" (Signorielli 1993:316). For some of the workers in the cafeteria, their identities as food service workers, as Mexican migrants, as women, or as Chicanos are underrepresented in U.S. television programming.

While the experiences of many working people in this country are not represented on television, television nonetheless relates many dominant (if misleading) notions about workers and work. "Television's occupational portrayals . . . do not typically revolve around specific work duties or capture the sense of the work-place" (Signorielli 1993:316–17). For instance, television programs pertaining to police work mostly focus on the action excitement of the job, rather than on the mundane paperwork that most police officers spend the majority of their work time performing. WE DO THE WORK, a series on PBS, has filled a void found in mainstream visual media by producing programs on workers that reveal the diversity of experiences among workers and the difficulty by which they struggle not only against management but also against the backdrop of larger societal issues.

In the making of the video A COLLEGE CAFETERIA, I imagined my immediate audience to be both the student customers of the dining hall as well as the majority of the participants in the video themselves, the workers. The perceptions students have of the dining hall revolve around the presence of the Bartlet Corporation, which operates food service on the campus, rather than the workers, because of the visibility by which Bartlet projects itself as the company that controls the entire operation of food services. For workers, their perception is also influenced by a powerful absentee corporation that officially dictates through on-site managers the ways in which production and reproduction of food services occurs.

In the opening montage of the video, the kitchen is presented as a mysterious place. The viewers only see images of vacated work spaces in the kitchen, yet they hear the sounds of knives chopping against the cutting board, dishes being stacked, and food simmering. By opening the video accordingly, I frame A COLLEGE CAFETERIA much in the same way that the title of the ethnographic film series DISAPPEARING WORLDS suggests the tenuous position of certain indigenous peoples around the world. My video begins in the world of work operated by invisible people about whom the audience knows nothing. Clearly, workers in a certain sense have been ignored in our society through both mainstream media representations and as a result of the decline in the labor movement and the changing nature of economies throughout the world. Visually, the video is contained within the cafeteria itself—the kitchen, the serving area, the dining area, and the back loading dock—which limits how viewers will understand the lives of these workers. However, the interviews and footage that follow the opening montage present these workers' labor in the hidden work spaces of the cafeteria, revealing their significance as a location of reproductive labor as well as political contestation.

My intention in the production of A COLLEGE CAFETERIA was to provide all the participants with a forum for expressing their own perspectives on working. However, I needed to ensure that in the crafting of the visual representation, these workers' identitities did not become naturalized as part of the expected social order. "The inherent problem in visual representation is precisely this: that it reifies and freezes cultural difference" (Hastrup 1992:19). With three Mexican migrant workers, two white women cooks, and two Chicano cooks providing the majority of the voices found in this video, I attempted to create ruptures within the video in critically represent their positions of power based on job task, citizenship, gender, and racial or ethnic difference.

Certain editing techniques such as the use of repetition, nonrealist representation, and self-reflexivity in documentary can potentially create ruptures in the viewers' expectations during the screening of a documentary, allowing them to more critically assess the subject matter. Moreover, ruptures within a film or video may provide the viewer with another perspective from which to view a politically oppressed group. The nonrealistic represention in the opening montage created such a rupture, functioning to unsettle the viewer about what A COLLEGE CAFETERIA might be about.

In order to avoid the presentation of a singular logic, the format of the video I made is multiperspectival; ten of the workers articulate their different perspectives. This format permits each participant to be seen as an individual expressing power based on their relationship to others in the cafeteria. I avoided using voice-over narration, a technique common to both ethnographic and documentary film and video. My intent in omitting a voice-over narration symbolically preserved the workers' power to represent the workplace themselves. I also decided not to use music other than the music that came organically while I was videotaping. And even though the sound at times is somewhat difficult to hear, it nonetheless depicts the noisy ambiance of a cafeteria.

I decided to place myself in the video as a student worker and as the videographer of A COLLEGE CAFETERIA because I realized that I could not step outside the positions of power that I wanted to critique in the production of the video. Here, I was following Nichols:

> It especially behooves the documentary film-maker to acknowledge what she/he is actually doing . . . to fashion documentaries that may more closely correspond to a contemporary understanding of our position within the world so that effective political formal strategies for describing and challenging that position can emerge. (Nichols 1983:18)

The self-reflexive aspect of the video imparts to viewers a sense of my relationship to the other participants in the documentary.

Over the five weeks of the project, I shot a total of twelve hours of footage and interviews. Upon the completion of the final edited piece of thirteen minutes, I was able to make an exchange with those who allowed me to videotape them by giving them each a copy of the video. A great feature of using video technology is that it is relatively inexpensive to distribute. Because the video was made with the intention of sharing it explicitly with the participants, I edited it with the awareness that both management and the workers would receive copies. The video symbolically provided a forum for the workers to communicate with one another concerning a variety of workplace issues that became politicized through the video itself. The reception of the documentary A COLLEGE CAFETERIA by the participants, including managers, was positive overall, in part because as a finished piece it less seriously challenged the normal power configurations in the cafeteria than the actual process of shooting the video. The political consequences, therefore, were beyond the scope of the camera, and were played out in participants' realizations about power relations during and after the filming.

The implications of this documentary video project for activists and academics indicate the significance of video technology as a way of representing workers and the labor they perform for wider audiences. The significance of a video representation may be in its revelations about spatial power relations, or in its reflection of language use. In this project, for example, my ability to speak Spanish enabled me to conduct interviews with the Spanish-speaking workers in Spanish as well as to present their perspectives in the video in Spanish. The use of video technology provided my study of power relations among customers, workers, and management in a college cafeteria with insight into the lack of awareness customers have about the workers who serve them.

Moreover, as I compiled footage and interviews throughout the project, the technology allowed the other workers and me to understand particular power relations—especially spatial ones—more concretely by having them visually recorded on tape. The camera, as a tool of power, can alter the normative power relations in the workplace and suggests possibilities for worker documentation in other service work settings.

REFERENCES CITED

Braverman, Harry
  1974 *Labor and Monopoly Capital: The Degradation of Labor in the Twentieth Century*. New York: Monthly Review Press.

Czepial, John, Michael Solomon, and Carol Surprenant
  1985 *The Service Encounter*. Lexington: Lexington Books.

Elder, Sarah
  1995 Collaborative filmmaking: An open space for making meaning, a moral ground for ethnographic film. *The Visual Anthropology Review* 11(2).

Foucault, Michel
  1979 *Discipline and Punish*. New York: Pantheon Books.

Freire, Paulo
  1989 *Education for Critical Consciousness*. New York: Continuum.
  1970 *Cultural Action for Freedom*. Cambridge: Harvard Educational Review.

Gaventa, John
  1980 *Power and Powerlessness: Quiescence and Rebellion in an Appalachian Valley*. Urbana: University of Illinois Press.

Giarini, Orio, and Walter Stahel
  1989 *The Limits to Certainty*. Boston: Kluwer Academic Publishers.

Gilpin, Toni, Gary Isaac, Dan Letwin, and Jack Mckivigan
  1995 *On Strike For Respect*. Urbana: University of Illinois Press.

Hastrup, Kirsten
  1992 Anthropological visions: Some notes on visual and textual authority. In *Film as Ethnography*. Peter Crawford and David Turton, eds. Pp. 8–25. Manchester: Manchester University Press.

Nakano-Glenn, Evelyn
  1992 From servitude to service work: Historical continuities in the racial division of paid reproductive labor. *Signs* 18:1–43.

Nichols, Bill
  1983 The voice of documentary. *Film Quarterly* 36(3):17–29.

Roediger, David
  1991 *The Wages of Whiteness*. London: Verso.

Scott, Allen, and Michael Storper
  1988 *Production, Work, Territory*. Boston: Allen and Unwin.

Signorielli, Nancy
  1993 Television and adolescents' perceptions about work. *Youth and Society* 24(3):314–41.

FILMS CITED

Cogan, Daniel
  1994 *A College Cafeteria*. University of California student production, undistributed.

Granada Television, producer
  1971– *Disappearing World* Series. Chicago: Films Incorporated, distributor.

O'Neil, Patrick, and Rhian Miller, producers
  1990– *We Do the Work* Series. Berkeley, CA: California Working Group.

Silver, Jon
  1989 *Watsonville on Strike*. Watsonville, CA: Migrant Media Productions.

Chapter 9

Participatory Economic Development: Activism, Education, and Earning an Income

Mary E. Hoyer

In the current economy, issues of power for workers and the under- and unemployed are played out both within and outside the workplace. Computerization and globalization of the economy mean that many people cannot find jobs and, in reality, may be only sporadically employed throughout their lives. This is particularly true in low-income communities of color where residents have been thoroughly marginalized in the economy. The inequities of emerging low-wage jobs, which are often acclaimed as legitimate replacements for historically unionized employment, must be addressed through workplace organizing. But organizing must reach beyond the workplace into communities if the overall dilemma of an economy that provides neither goods and services nor work and income for a significant segment of the citizenry is to be addressed.

Several methodologies are useful in this situation. They include nonformal, experiential, and cooperative education; action and participatory research; and alternative organizational development. Application of these methodologies to economic issues at the neighborhood level provides a starting point for bringing low-skilled workers and the unemployed into the economic arena through research, planning, job creation, employment, and ownership. These methodologies are being applied on projects in Hartford, Connecticut, Lawrence, Massachusetts, and New York City which will be discussed later in this chapter. Practitioners applying these methodologies are aware that racism in relation to national employment allocation convolutes the problem of classism and must be directly confronted. The strategies discussed here are particularly useful for racially or ethnically isolated communities where poverty is the norm.

THE CURRENT DILEMMA

Broadening the Civil Rights Agenda

In the United States, despite the fact that community demands in the 1960s and 70s resulted in significant advancement for middle-class African-Americans and Latinos, neither virulent racism nor poverty based on "race" have been eradicated. In the electoral arena, the number of officials of color has increased dramatically as a result of the Voting Rights Act of 1965, but still does not adequately reflect the proportion of U.S. citizens who are considered "minorities."[1] Electoral gains have been mitigated by public budget cuts initiated at all levels of government over the last twenty years. As a result, ascendant minority officials have been constrained in their initiatives for enabling poor constituents to escape the trap of poverty. Similarly, affirmative action efforts have been highly successful in placing people of color in positions of influence in many arenas, but have not significantly impacted the condition of poor people in urban ghettos. Rectification of poverty and social exclusion require that job creation, local control over economic development, and education toward that end augment the historical civil rights agenda.

The Changing Economy

At the end of the twentieth century, advanced capitalist economies are undergoing profound change. Industrial production is being replaced by service work and high technology production, with resulting net job loss. The creation of new jobs domestically is mainly in two areas: service and high technology manufacturing.[2] Nationally, over two-thirds of all workers are currently employed in service jobs, an arena expected to increase steadily as time passes (City of Hartford 1984:44).

Continued growth in the service sector and high tech sectors appears to be limited, however. In service industries, computerization of office tasks eliminates jobs, cutbacks in governmental spending eliminate both public and private sector employment, and limited discretionary income for citizens decreases the need for jobs in the retail sector. In the high tech sector, prospects for job creation are even more limited. This sector demonstrates high *rates* of growth (since such jobs did not previously exist) but low actual numbers of jobs.

Both net job loss and an increase in low-level jobs are evident (Mishel and Bernstein 1993; Rifkin 1996; Barnet 1993). Unemployment between 1967 and 1991 increased 76 percent (from 3.8 percent to 6.7 percent) while underemployment between 1973 and 1991 increased 46 percent—from 8.2 percent to 12 percent (Mishel and Bernstein 1993: 216). In 1992, fifteen percent of all Americans had incomes under the poverty line; in 1994, an individual working full-time at the minimum wage, even with income and transfer payments such as food stamps combined, earned below the poverty line for a family of three; in 1993, 27 percent of all workers earned less than the amount needed to keep a family of four above the poverty level (Albelda et al. 1996: 11, 66–67).

Connecticut may be cited as an instructive example. A small state where democratic strategies for economic inclusion are being researched and applied, Connecticut was hard hit by recent recessions and is afflicted with severe maldistribution of income. Here, only about a third of jobs lost have been replaced (State of Connecticut 1996:39). The service and high tech sectors are creating a situation in which workers are increasingly unable to provide for themselves and their dependents.

The persistence of unemployment for poor people of color is a devastating problem (Goldsmith and Blakely 1992; Tidwell 1994). Some authors speculate that poor African-Americans and Latinos in the U.S. have now been rendered expendable. In the words of Manning Marable:

> The benign but deadly elimination of the "parasitic" ghetto class that has ceased to be a necessary or productive element within modern capitalism. . . . The genocidal logic of the situation could demand, in the not too distant future, the rejection of the ghetto's right to survival in the capitalist order. Without gas chambers or pogroms, the dark ghetto's economic and social institutions might be destroyed, *and many of its residents would simply cease to exist.* (Marable 1983:253)

Recapitalization strategies tolerate a stable unemployment rate as high as six percent, but this figure insufficiently reflects the magnitude of the problem in the inner city. "Discouraged workers"—those who have given up looking for work and are therefore not counted in unemployment statistics—may be almost twice as numerous as those who are formally counted as unemployed (City of Hartford 1984:38). Young people of color between the ages of eighteen and twenty-one, whose inability to find jobs in the formal sector may set patterns for the remainder of their productive lives, are particularly hard hit. Innercity residents are to a great extent excluded from urban, service-sector jobs mainly in the area of finance. Most of these jobs are held by suburban residents who commute to work every day and who recirculate their earnings in their hometowns. In Hartford, 1980 data indicated that over 80 percent of jobs with major urban employers were held by suburbanites (City of Hartford 1984:33). Additionally, public transportation funds have been expended on highways that allow suburbanites who can afford cars access to city jobs, rather than on public transportation that would allow poor urban residents access to suburban jobs.

Education and Employment

The common wisdom that education is of critical importance for empowering poor, urban residents cannot be refuted. However, education alone is insufficient to address the pressing and intransigent problems of the inner city. Education does not necessarily result in employment. Many workforce trainers, "minority" workers, recent college graduates, and unemployed managers know that the natural consequence of additional education isn't *automatic* employment, increased earnings, or job complexity. Instead, the sequence is reversed: if workers are needed, education and training will be subsidized. That is, availability of employment encourages and legitimizes the educational project. Simply increasing or improving education without addressing job creation is futile (Levin 1983:237; Mishel and Bernstein 1993:359–78).

Furthermore, economic information needs to become an integral part of general education. Within the scope of human knowledge, economics is currently treated as protected, virtually religious, information. Economists, financiers, and business executives manipulate and guard this information, evoking the "natural" forces of the market on behalf of the wealthy ("God's chosen few," as some have put it). A majority of people are denied access to this information through lack of education and deliberate, "priestly" obfuscation. The democratic movement within society must claim and apply this body of knowledge, adding economic democracy to the civil rights agenda.

METHODOLOGICAL MODELS FOR DEMOCRATIC ECONOMIC ENGAGEMENT

The effort to democratically engage lay people in economic restructuring requires methodologies that tolerate a wide range of educational levels, including minimal ones. The methodologies must combine research, planning, activism, and practical application of information with the articulation of a larger vision of economic reality. Because the goal of the effort is economic participation and governance, albeit democratic rather than oligarchic, educational efforts should at least be as carefully and thoughtfully designed as traditional programs. Several methodologies are particularly useful in education for economic development. They are nonformal, informal, and cooperative education; action and participatory research; and alternative organizational development.

Formal education is the traditional teaching methodology with which most people are familiar. Within this methodology, programs are deliberately planned, operate according to a preset schedule established by an institution of learning, take place in an institutional setting, and often utilize lecture formats as well as much reading and writing. Students are perceived to be the receivers of knowledge and instructors the imparters of knowledge. While such a format is widely used to deliver information to learners, several other methodologies are less familiar and have demonstrated considerable efficacy for delivering complex information in relatively short amounts of time with most learners, but especially with those who may have limited educational backgrounds.

Nonformal, Informal, and Cooperative Education

Nonformal education is a teaching methodology that is deliberately planned but delivered in a relaxed atmosphere often in noninstitutional, community settings (Hoyer 1986a,1986b). Nonformal instruction begins with, and continuously refers back to, knowledge that students bring to a topic before new information is shared. Discussion and problem-solving techniques, with audiovisual aids that enhance reading and writing, are typically emphasized. Hands-on activities often follow delivery of new information.

Informal education refers to the casual absorption of information through daily activity. This is not really a methodology as such, because instruction is not deliberately planned, scheduled, or formatted. However, it is a powerful tool that all of us engage in regularly for both learning and teaching. In an informal fashion, we learn—and teach—a great deal simply by being in the company of others who are actively engaged in problem-solving. Learning through community involvement in issues such as voter registration, development of youth programs, and neighborhood planning are examples of informal education.

Cooperative education is a methodology currently in vogue in educational circles as an alternative to the factorystyle delivery of education that has produced workers who are unable to take initiative or solve problems independent of authority (Rose 1989; Cohen and Benton 1988). It involves working in small groups with each participant assuming responsibility for solving some aspect of a problem or assignment. This methodology encourages initiative, application of communication skills, mediation, prioritization, and achievement of consensus. It allows people to share knowledge and devise joint solutions that typically are richer conceptually and more effective when applied than solutions devised by individuals.

Action and Participatory Research

Action research as a method of inquiry emerged around 1950 and involves learning about social systems by trying to change them. Action research combines academic goals with practical problem solving, and stresses common values shared by researchers and clients (Brown and Tandon 1983). Action research attempts to integrate social concerns with the concerns of scientific inquiry in order to generate "usable knowledge." This method requires a broad-based and supportive client group, and an interactive process of data gathering, diagnosis, and revision.

Participatory research emerged in the 1960s from work with colonized peoples in the Third World on several continents independently. This type of research involves mutual definition of issues to be studied by community members and researchers together, engagement of community members in the entire research process, parity among researchers and community people as participants in inquiry together, enhancement of community members' abilities, and resulting militancy on behalf of social change rather than academic detachment.

Alternative Organizational Development

Because community activists need to understand how institutions originate, grow, and change in order for the economic democracy movement to thrive, an understanding of organizational development is useful. However, a distinction can be made between traditional organizational development, which focuses on top-down management and alternative organizational development, which focuses on democratic ownership and control (Holvino 1993).

Organizational development as a field emerged in the 1950s. The field represents an attempt to humanize rapid and regular organizational change while controlling it through planning. Change agents are perceived as professionals, and traditional organizational development strategies are management-driven and have the goal of enabling organizations to survive and adapt to changing social, economic, and environmental demands. By the 1960s, alternative paradigms characterizing organizational change had emerged. The new paradigm perceives organizational change as "organic" and democratic rather than mechanical and bureaucratic. Consensus decision-making replaces rule by benign authority or democratic majority.

ACTIVIST ECONOMIC STRATEGIES

The field of community economic development is a healthy and growing arena, although it remains relatively unknown to the general public due to lack of coverage in the established media. Within this arena, the case for localized, democratically controlled economic development is currently under construction as an alternative to typical remedies for economic depression and unequal distribution of wealth. Traditional development strategies emphasize individualistic, hierarchical, and welfare-oriented approaches rather than empowerment strategies. Alternatively, local development strategies aim at "taming the . . . poverty-reproducing character of capitalism" (Stanback 1984:64). Such strategies include social criteria such as equality, security, participation in decision-making, and a clean environment in the costs of production.

It may be argued that strategies involving locally controlled, collective, and egalitarian economic development, such as those discussed below that are currently being applied throughout New England, are especially useful in low-income urban settings. In poor communities, the influence of traditional institutions—family networks, welfare programs, churches, and labor unions, for example—have been severely weakened. In lieu of such structures, direct collective and cooperative approaches to economic development can provide support that is difficult for individuals to find elsewhere. In addition, local strategies that involve citizens in economic development address the crux of the problem, which is exclusion from a share in wealth and decision-making. Economic inclusion of poor citizens is not a primary concern of corporate owners and managers or of increasingly conservative politicians.

A number of activist strategies for engaging lay people in economic development currently exist and are being applied in a variety of settings with considerable success. The strategies discussed below make effective use of the educational and research methodologies reviewed above.

Peer Lending/Microenterprise Development

Peer lending is a strategy for microenterprise self-employment in low- and moderate-income communities (Asho 1995, ACCION International 1988; Clark et al. 1994). It derives from traditional community lending groups common in the West Indies and many African and Asian cultures. Within such groups, trusted members contribute regular donations to a collective fund that is then lent out to members on a rotating basis. An adapted form of this lending strategy has been used over the last two decades in developing countries and more recently in the U.S., in low-income urban and rural areas, with much success. The adapted strategy does not depend on donations from group members; instead, it relies on banks and other lenders for contributions of capital. The notion of a close-knit, local solidarity group based on mutual trust and support is retained, however, in this model.

Peer group participants are self-employed business owners or entrepreneurs who work from their homes or businesses on a part- or full-time basis. Participants meet regularly and support one another in business planning. Typically, they are not eligible for credit from traditional lending institutions because their funding needs fall below bank lending levels or because they have not established credit records. Participants apply directly to their group for loans in amounts well below levels offered by banks. Group members review applications and decide who will receive loans, a procedure that helps participants understand firsthand how credit allocation works. Additional group members cannot receive a loan unless all group members are up-to-date on loan payments, a procedure that ensures timely repayment. Because loan amounts start small and build gradually, group members acquire credit records that eventually allow them to access traditional lending institutions.

Peer lending groups function in the community rather than in formal institutions of higher education or finance. Loan applications are simplified and training is presented in a relaxed but organized fashion. The model addresses lack of capital in impacted areas and gives owners of small, local enterprises a chance to succeed and thrive. The model is designed to keep income generated by enterprises in the community, thus contributing to economic stability.

Worker Ownership and Management of Enterprise

Worker ownership is a concept that has been in existence for some two hundred years in Europe and more recently in Third World nations (Sethi et al. 1983; Horvat et al. 1975). Even fairly sizable businesses can be structured so that workers own and participate in the management of enterprises (Bryant 1994; Krimmerman and Lindenfeld 1992). This can be achieved through democratically structured Employee Stock Ownership Plans (ESOPs) or as directly controlled worker cooperatives. Several developments over the last twenty-five years are of interest for democratic economic development.

In the Basque region of northern Spain, a complex of industrial worker cooperatives and support structures—such as banking and education that sustain them—have been expanding steadily since the mid-1970s (Whyte and Whyte 1988). Known as the Mondragon cooperatives, they have managed to withstand the cyclical downturns that are so economically troublesome in Western capitalism. Initiated by Catholic priests and by citizens accustomed to resisting imposed authority, the Mondragon cooperatives represent a promising possibility for economic reorganization that is collective but not state-controlled.

A case for worker control and ownership of enterprise as a model for economic development in low-income, urban (or rural) communities can be made. The strategy increases productivity, making it possible for small enterprises to compete with large ones. Worker cooperatives are conducive to equitable distribution of wealth, allow workers to initiate economic activity, decrease layoffs during recessions, and allow for a collective response to poverty. Workers in such enterprises are empowered to understand their businesses and the economic reality in which they are ensconced, since direct benefits are reaped from this knowledge. Participants are in a position to design their own work experience, allowing them to challenge the perpetuation of racism and dead-end jobs.

There is evidence that the worker ownership and management strategy can be successfully applied in low-income communities (Hoyer 1992; Haynes 1993). Cooperative Home Care Associates in the Bronx, New York (discussed later in this chapter), and Valley Care Cooperative in Waterbury, Connecticut, are successful examples. The ICA Group in Boston, Massachusetts, runs a community jobs program that provides technical assistance to community worker-ownership projects throughout the nation.[3]

Several states have been encouraging worker ownership as an economic strategy (Ellerman and Pitegoff 1983; Sachs 1986). The state of Massachusetts passed legislation based on the Mondragon model that assists formation of worker-owned businesses, and initiated a Special Commission on Employee Involvement and Ownership that encouraged the state to focus effort on firms owned by low- and moderate-income groups, people of color, and women. New York State has established an employee ownership center that provides education, technical assistance, and business development to worker-owned firms.[4] New York City has passed what may be the first municipal program supporting worker ownership.

Asset-based Surveying

The notion of asset-based surveying was generated by John Kretzmann and John McKnight (1993) at Northwestern University. This strategy rejects the traditional approach to poor, troubled neighborhoods, which focuses on institutional and individual deficiencies and problems and their amelioration by external experts. Instead, the asset-based approach looks carefully at the strengths of local residents and institutions, identifying capacities, experience, and interests—building blocks that can provide a foundation for community development based on local problem-solving. Through this strategy, development funds are directed toward community problem-solving groups rather than toward service providers who offer maintenance of isolated, individual clients. Identifying the inherent strengths of communities is especially important in an era when support from both the public and private sectors has been severely curtailed. Involvement of neighborhood residents in surveying increases awareness of possibilities and commitment to solutions.

Community Development Credit Unions

Community development credit unions (CDCUs) are financial institutions created to serve low- to moderate-income communities often because traditional lenders have withdrawn due to low profit margins (Rosenthal and

Levy 1995; Tholin and Pogge 1991). In addition to making consumer and small business loans, CDCUs also provide typical banking services to members. CDCUs frequently offer financial education such as personal finance and credit repair to members as well.

Capitalization for CDCUs is achieved through member deposits as well as through nonmember deposits from organizations such as foundations, churches, and banks. CDCU membership must legally be made up largely of low-income people but, unlike a standard credit union, additional deposits may come from outside the field of membership as well. In this way, CDCUs provide an effective means for financial resources to be recirculated within local neighborhoods while creating nonprofit conduits for outside investment. Establishing and maintaining a CDCU requires collaboration between citizens, government, nonprofits, labor unions, businesses, and skilled volunteers. Depositors are considered members and are eligible to participate as directors of the board. CDCUs are structured as nonprofits, thus keeping costs low, and are regulated by state and federal agencies some of which insure deposits as well.

CDCUs function in poor communities in which disinvestment by traditional lenders has taken a severe toll. They have a long-term vision of the community in mind rather than short-term profit. They make an effort to adapt lending criteria to the needs of community members, accept unconventional collateral for loans, and provide training and support to borrowers.

Community Loan Funds

Community loan funds are structured as nonprofit organizations that operate at lower cost than for-profit institutions (U.S./HUD 1993; Shabecoff 1987). Funds lent out on a revolving basis are provided by religious investors, socially committed individual investors, philanthropic foundations, and banks interested in improving their national Community Reinvestment Act ratings. Monies are typically lent in restricted geographical areas to encourage local revitalization resulting in social returns, particularly to economically marginalized constituencies. Borrowers often have difficulty getting loans from traditional lenders because they are start-ups, their loan needs are quite low, or they are structured in nontraditional ways (for example, as cooperatives or collectives). Community loan funds typically provide technical assistance support beyond that provided by traditional lenders. The National Association of Community Development Loan Funds located in Philadelphia brings together community loan funds from around the nation.[5]

Jay Stone, in *Building a Movement for Economic Democracy* (1995:272–74), suggests that the socially responsible investment (SRI) arena must be a critical part of any larger movement. He cites the influential anti-apartheid movement for international divestment from South Africa as an example of how investment can be democratized. Democratic control of worker pension funds, which can free funds for community investment and provide a basis for a unified labor/community alliance, is another example of democratized investment. Stone argues that the SRI industry "has the potential to challenge the notion that investment decisions should be made exclusively on the basis of maximizing profit, without regard for broader social concerns."

Corporate Accountability Campaigns

Recently, a new wave of community and labor activism addressing the issue of corporate accountability has arisen.[6] Outrage at distorted executive salaries that rise as workers are dismissed as well as at increased corporate welfare such as tax breaks and environmental deregulation has helped fuel this activism. Initiatives in Massachusetts and Connecticut have focused on increasing the minimum wage so workers do not have to hold more than one job to meet expenses, improving workplace health and safety standards, and increasing job security. Legislation introduced in Massachusetts during the 1996 session included the Corporate Responsibility Act to eliminate "wealthfare," the Income Equity Act to curb executive take-home salaries and increase the minimum wage, and the Living Wage/Jobs for All Act. In Connecticut legislation to help fund microenterprise and peer lending projects was introduced. In addition to legislation and lobbying of elected officials, community/labor campaigns have involved informational leafleting at corporate headquarters where jobs are being eliminated and public hearings to air concerns and promote solutions to un- and underemployment.

Shorter Work Week Campaigns

Although U.S. labor has registered support for a shorter work week, the demand has not yet reached a wide audience, perhaps because so many workers currently must work more than forty hours a week to make ends meet. In the U.S., the AFL-CIO is attempting to force employers toward a shorter work week by requiring employers to pay workers twice their regular wages for overtime, compared with fifty percent now (Kilborn 1993; Moody and Sagovac 1995). In other highly industrialized nations, most notably in Europe, however, change toward a shorter work week has already begun to occur (Cohen 1993; Yalnizyan et al. 1994; Hinrichs et al. 1991). France and Italy have taken up the idea of a reduced work week, and the BMW and Volkswagen companies in Germany as well as Digital Equipment and Hewlett-Packard in France have adopted four-day schedules.

In *After the Waste Land: A Democratic Economics for the Year 2000*, Sam Bowles, Thomas Weisskopf, and David Gordon (1990:170–84) present an intriguing analysis of how U. S. resources could more efficiently be allocated in order to reduce and reallocate working time without commensurately reducing wages. They calculate that throughout the U.S., up to one and a half workdays per week could be eliminated without cutting pay if profits were maximized by (1) introducing worker participation in profit-sharing and decision-making; (2) eliminating excess supervisory staff employed to keep workers in line; (3) reducing welfare and unemployment costs through full employment; (4) directing public monies away from excessive military expenditure; (5) reducing business costs through nationalized health care; and (6) reducing energy waste through conservation.

GETTING THERE: THE ISSUE OF AGENCY

If progress on democratizing the economy is to be made, the fragility of the economic democracy movement must be acknowledged. To a great extent, democratic involvement with economic development has historically been characterized as "communist." In addition, to the extent that progressives are unfamiliar with the worker ownership model, the failure of state communism in the Soviet Union and eastern Europe has deprived activists of a clear alternative scenario for capitalism and has debilitated left activism in general.

Most people who support social and economic change, however well educated they may be on other topics, are not typically well educated in economics. As constituencies, union activists, human services personnel, educators, environmentalists, and cultural nationalists as well as welfare recipients, the disabled, and the homeless are not experts when it comes to the economy. Nevertheless, it is essential that we become so. Unless we wish to succumb to commercial exploitation, we must educate ourselves about economic development.

Constituencies and Coalitions

Natural constituency groups for the economic democracy movement include community economic development practitioners, communities of color, nonprofit agencies, labor unionists, welfare recipients, human services personnel, the religious community, the un- and underemployed, the disabled, and environmentalists. Participants adept at conceptualizing and executing alternative economic scenarios are needed as well as those with the more traditional skills of organizing rallies and civil disodedience.

Coalitions are essential (Anner 1996). None of the constituencies mentioned above is sufficiently numerous to promote a progressive agenda in isolation. Each constituency brings unique strengths to the conceptualization and implentation of projects. Whatever differences we may have with one another on a small scale must be tolerated in order to move an agenda of community-based, economic reorganization.

Acting Locally in a Global Economy

Local economic initiatives are often criticized as inadequate in an economy increasingly global in its structure and function. While this criticism must not be ignored, it is important to understand that both large- and small-scale efforts will be needed to rectify the current economic conundrum. The best established and funded developers typically play in arenas larger than neighborhoods. Many are not committed to democratic participation in decision-making and ownership. The crux of the problem in low-income, urban neighborhoods is not that there are no developers at all but that there is little or no democratic participation in economic decision-making and implementation.

Local economic initiatives have also been criticized as a capitulation to conservative political efforts that fragment and weaken large-scale, unified solutions to poverty and racism. Certainly neighborhood economic activists need to be cognizant of, and participants in, a national and international vision of economic development. The reality is that local initiatives can provide a foundation for increased understanding of and activism around larger issues.

A body of literature that addresses the issue of local development and its relation to the global economy is in formation. Jeremy Brecher and Tim Costello in *Global Village or Global Pillage* (1994) suggest that "globalization from below" should be a matter of primary—even desperate—concern among democratic forces throughout the world. Global plunder of the environment and the international workforce by corporations envisioning a never-ending consumerist frontier must be resisted vehemently. In fact, such resistance has begun. Multiple instances of international cooperation among workers, environmentalists, students, indigenous peoples, and farmers emerging naturally in response to global development and made possible by communication through computers may be cited (Brecher and Costello; Shuman 1994). Less prevalent but more relevant to the work discussed here are possible international linkages among local economic development initiatives. For example, arrangements similar to a Sister Cities project (Shuman 1994:61) but with the Mondragon or Italian cooperatives (Earle 1986) would be particularly instructive for U.S. worker-ownership initiatives.

CASE STUDIES:
PRACTICING ECONOMIC DEMOCRACY

Hartford Working Group on
Community Economic Development

In Hartford, Connecticut, a multiracial coalition of community activists, educators, and professionals with backgrounds in business development, law, social services, public education, the nonprofit sector, and traditional as well as third-party electoral work, came together in 1992 to form an unincorporated voluntary organization called the Hartford Working Group on Community Economic Development (HWGCED).[7] Concerned about increasing poverty and marginalization of the African-American and Latino communities in Hartford (which together constitute 60 percent of the population) and about the limitations of traditional strategies for addressing these problems, the group began to explore innovative, democratically-controlled economic strategies that had been applied successfully in other urban areas.

In order to acquaint the community with these novel strategies and why they were needed, two educational projects were organized. The first involved a series of evening workshops over several weeks in which participants under the leadership of HWGCED looked carefully at the changing employment situation nationally, regionally, and locally, analyzing recommendations for economic rejuvenation made by various task forces and agencies. Participants in the workshops included neighborhood residents and activists as well as policy setters. The second event was a one-day conference—the Grassroots/Neighborhood Economic Development Conference—planned and executed by representatives of a dozen community-based organizations. At the conference, local and national specialists and practitioners presented workshops on specific development strategies such as peer lending/microenterprise development, community development credit unions, asset-based surveying, church-based development, and worker ownership.

Following the second event, participants of HWGCED and the conference formed task forces to establish a peer-lending project and a community development credit union in Hartford. Both projects have moved ahead based largely on voluntary effort. Funding remaining from the conference has been used to pay for minimal expenses as the groups plan for implementation and seek financial support. Considerable expertise and staff time have been provided by the Citizens' Research Education Network (CREN), a well-established, city-based nonprofit.[8]

Hartford Community Development Credit Union and the Central Brooklyn Federal Credit Union

The Citizens' Research Education Network has provided significant ongoing support to the Hartford credit union project.[9] Before being taken up by the HWGCED Credit Union Task Force, CREN introduced the idea of a community development credit union to Hartford at an economic summit sponsored by the City of Hartford, an effort on the part of the City to identify new proposals worthy of attention. While the credit union proposal was not a finalist among those presented, it ranked suffciently high to attract the attention of community members and policy setters.

CREN has provided organizational and research support to the Hartford Community Development Credit Union (HCDCU), the Hartford Working Group on Community Economic Development has provided financial support, and the National Federation of Community Development Credit Unions[10] has provided technical assistance. Currently, HCDCU is planning its organizational structure and anticipated operations. A pledge drive aided by a recently hired Americorps staff person is underway, as is an effort to train neighborhood residents to disseminate information about the project and to solicit pledges. Elections for the first board of directors are scheduled for early 1997.

The Central Brooklyn Federal Credit Union (CBFCU) in New York City,[11] principals of which are providing moral support and technical advice to the Hartford project, is a functioning example of what activists are trying to achieve in Hartford (Valentine 1994; Lueck 1993; Sexton 1994). Founded in 1993 after several years of preparatory work, the institution offers the low- and moderate-income neighborhoods it serves a variety of services and products: savings, checking, direct deposit, check cashing, CDs, low-interest loans, money order services, peer lending opportunities, and financial education for adults and youth. Two of its principal founders, Mark Winston Griffith and Erroll Louis, describe the effort as a self-empowerment project that builds on the civil rights agenda. Depositors are members of the organization and, as such, can access institutional information and vote for representatives on the board of directors. In addition, members who need loans are evaluated in a much more flexible way than are loan applicants at traditional institutions. In early 1994, CBFCU controlled $1.5 million in assets and was growing at a rate of one hundred members per month.

Hartford Peer Lending Project and the Lawrence Working Capital Project

Like the Credit Union Task Force, the HWGCED Peer Lending Task Force began its in-depth pursuit of project implementation following the

Grassroots/Neighborhood Economic Development Conference. For a number of months, the group investigated various microenterprise models and technical assistance providers. A decision was made to engage Working Capital, a Cambridge, Massachusetts, nonprofit organization with a successful track record of advising peer lending projects in urban as well as rural areas both domestically and internationally.[12] The Peer Lending Task Force incorporated as the Hartford Peer Lending and Development Corporation (HPLDCo)[13] and is applying for 501(c)(3) nonprofit status. The acting board of directors—a small, multiracial, voluntary group of professionals and activists—is meeting with community residents and organizations as well as funders to generate interest and solicit funds for project start-up. Community response to the peer lending concept has been spontaneous and eager. Residents and community agencies are naturally attracted to the organizing (as opposed to academic or business) model on which the project is based.

One example of a successful, functioning, Working Capital-assisted program is the Lawrence Minority Business Council (LMBC) Working Capital Program in Lawrence, Massachusetts.[14] Lawrence is the largest town in its geographic region, has the highest poverty rate, and is experiencing an increasing and simultaneous decrease in its white, or Anglo, population and increase in its Latino population. LMBC was formed in 1989 to provide a vehicle for Latino community leaders to advise the mayor of Lawrence. Spanish-speaking business leaders were an integral part of the group, and LMBC over time began to offer business support and development services to the community. The Working Capital Program fit well with the mission of LMBC, and began operations in Lawrence in 1992. According to a 1994 evaluative report done by Mt. Auburn Associates, the Working Capital program has been utilized mostly by LMBC's smaller, less established clients:

> Many Hispanic residents of the area have sought to supplement their income from jobs or public assistance with part-time businesses, generally operated from the home. Many of them are recent immigrants from the Dominican Republic and Puerto Rico with limited financial resources, local roots, and English language skills. The business loan groups provide support from other entrepreneurs with similar cultural and linguistic backgrounds and help participants to gain knowledge about the local business environment and establish a credit record, along with developing general business skills. (Mt. Auburn Associates 1994:44)

During the two years prior to the report, the LMBC Working Capital Program established nineteen peer lending groups and had a waiting list of thirty individuals, making it one of Working Capital's most active projects. At least some participants had taken out first, second, and third loans with a loan write-off rate of only 2 percent. Ninety percent of participants were Spanish-speaking and the majority were women. The Mt. Auburn report concluded that:

- the loans provided by Working Capital enabled participants to make equipment investments or purchase inventory;
- the technical assistance provided by Working Capital helped participants to improve their business practices and become more knowledgeable about the lending criteria of private financial institutions;
- networking with other group members and members of other groups helped participants to identify new customers and suppliers; and
- group participation reduced isolation and provided valuable ideas, feedback, support, and peer pressure. (Mt. Auburn Associates 1994:45)

Although the businesses assisted remain small and mostly home-based, participants testify that involvement has empowered them to take greater responsibility for themselves, has familiarized them with local institutions and practices, and has increased their community involvement. In addition, LMBC as an organization has benefited as a result of increased visibility, influence, and programming.

Asset-based Surveying in Hartford

In Hartford, the Citizens' Research Education Network has employed asset-based surveying in its neighborhood planning work with the Coalition to Strengthen the Sheldon/Charter Oak Neighborhood (CSS/CON) (Vickers 1996). Surveys were administered by neighborhood residents with minimal training and supervisory oversight. Information gathered reveals institutional resources as well as individual residents' skills, experiences, and interests, all of which can be accessed for community improvement.

Although the Sheldon/Charter Oak neighborhood is a poor one, survey results indicate that there are many skilled members of the community. However, the skills people command do not necessarily translate into jobs for two reasons. First, there is an insufficient number of jobs for residents in the community and, second, residents' skills do not fit the job market that exists. The report on the survey recommends (1) increased and improved training and educational efforts for both youth and adults in the neighborhood; (2) training for residents in skills beyond low-level jobs in the service sector; and (3) concerted promotion by neighborhood organizations of existing and new local businesses. Interestingly, the CSS/CON survey, which appears to be one of only a few surveys of this type done throughout the country, reveals that a number of residents are interested in starting their own businesses. This information, along with more general information about residents' skills and interests, has the potential for significant job creation through self-employment in combination with the peer lending strategy.

Worker Ownership in the Bronx, New York

In the economically impacted neighborhood of the Bronx, New York, Cooperative Home Care Associates (CHCA) is having notable success applying worker ownership as a local development strategy. Initiated in 1985 with ten home health care workers, CHCA now employs some three hundred workers who are also managers and owners of the operation. Propitiously situated economically, the home health care industry is underwritten by a steady flow of insurance payments from a growing elderly and handicapped population. Worker-owners at CHCA command a stable, living wage and have access to a career path to nursing and administrative positions as well as to an upgraded, specialized home care aide position that is in the planning stages.

Not unlike the projects in Hartford described above, CHCA was initiated by professionals and activists who formed a community development group, the Center for Community Economic Development (CCED), within a well-established community support agency. As a result of a failed attempt to establish a low-income, worker-owned carpentry business, CCED members realized the critical importance of developing a solvent business before asking low-income workers, who have little expendable income for experimentation and investment, to share in enterprise ownership.

Implementation of CHCA was based on that premise. Workers there became owners and managers gradually, and in significant numbers only after two years of start-up operation. The strategy has been successful: about 78 percent of workers are owners. Payment of the worker-owner membership fee of one thousand dollars is made weekly over five years and is thus minimized. Each worker-owner wields one vote in deliberative sessions and in election of board members, and since 1991, CHCA home health aides have held a majority of board seats. CHCA workers earn more than their counterparts in other agencies and also enjoy health insurance, a certain number of discretionary days off each year, and an annual profit-sharing bonus—benefits that are rare or nonexistent elsewhere in the industry. CHCA home health aides indicate that involvement in worker-ownership has improved their job commitment and performance, and that they are more satisfied both at work and in their private lives. CHCA as an agency has received recognition for providing excellent service to customers.

The design employed by the projects described above combines four elements with critical relevance for educational efforts in low- and moderate-income neighborhoods: self-directed learning supported by experts, leadership development via organizational and business management, income generation, and a balance of individual and cooperative effort. Projects that combine these elements leverage enthusiasm, energy, commitment, and growth that have not been seen among economically marginalized constituencies since the civil rights movement.

CONCLUSION

We are currently in the midst of a prolonged era of conservative hegemony and economic oligarchy—a "collective dark night of the soul" (Stone 1995:265)—in which large numbers of people from varying walks of life find themselves unable to provide for themselves and their dependents. The post–World War II social contract that included at least some segments of the working class in the general economy is now in tatters (Bowles, Weisskopf, and Gordon 1990). The movement for civil and social justice is at a low ebb, exhausted from the conservative onslaught to turn public opinion from a liberal course, tarnishing and reversing the hard-won gains of the 1960s and 70s.

It is a propitious time to reactivate the civil rights movement as a broadened multiracial, multiethnic movement for economic democracy. At the time of his assassination, Dr. Martin Luther King, Jr., was reorienting his activism in this direction (Oates 1982:387–428). The decline of state-controlled economies in the Soviet Union and eastern Europe minimizes the communist threat in the American psyche. The alternative promise of privately but cooperatively controlled worker ownership and management of enterprise allows for articulation of a new progressive agenda. The widespread international movement for ecological balance is supported by the notion of sustainable, democratic economies. Members of the powerful "baby boom" generation, whose thinking was forged in the ideological struggle of the 1960s, are entering the most influential decades of their lives. Now is the time to bring Dr. King's democratic economic agenda to fruition.

NOTES

1. In her 1988 essay in *New Black Politics*, Linda Williams indicates that, for example, a mere 1.2% of all elected officials were African-American although the percentage of African-Americans in the total population was 12%. Even if elected according to their percentage of the population, African-American officials would need to compromise with other constituencies to effect a majority or a significant plurality. While necessary, this becomes complicated because elections are often unduly influenced by the white power structure through money, connections, expertise, and sheer numbers.

2. For the purposes of this essay, the service sector includes retail and food service, health care, finance and real estate, education, law, government, etc.—sectors of the economy that do not involve agricultural or industrial production.

3. ICA Group, 20 Park Plaza, Suite 1127, Boston, Massachusetts 02116.

4. New York Center for Employee Ownership and Participation, 1515 Broadway, New York, New York 10036.

5. National Association of Community Development Loan Funds, 924 Cherry Street, Philadelphia, Pennsylvania 19107.

6. Groups that have been working on this issue in New England include the Committee on Economic Insecurity in Boston, Massachusetts (617–923–8418); Citizens for Economic Opportunity c/o United Auto Workers in Farmington, Connecticut (860–674–0760); and the Connecticut Jobs Task Force c/o Northeast Citizen Action Resource Center in Hartford, Connecticut (860–231–2410).

7. Hartford Working Group on Community Economic Development, P. O. Box 2494, Hartford, CT 06146.

8. Citizens' Research Education Network, 32 Elm Street, Hartford, CT 06106.

9. The Hartford Community Development Credit Union can be reached through the Citizens' Research Education Network cited in note 4, above.

10. National Federation of Community Development Credit Unions, 120 Wall Street, New York, New York 10005.

11. Central Brooklyn Federal Credit Union, 1205 Fulton Street, Brooklyn, New York 11216.

12. Working Capital, Inc., 99 Bishop Allen Drive, Cambridge, Massachusetts 02139.

13. The Hartford Peer Lending and Development Corporation can be reached through the Hartford Working Group on Community Economic Development cited in note 3, above.

14. Lawrence Minority Business Council, 203 Essex Street, Lawrence, Massachusetts 01840

REFERENCES CITED

ACCION International
   1988 *An Operational Guide for Micro-Enterprise Projects.* Toronto, Ontario: Calmeadow Foundation.

Albelda, Randy, and Nancy Folbre
   1996 *The War on the Poor: A Defense Manual.* New York: New Press.

Anner, John, ed.
  1996 *Beyond Identity Politics: Emerging Social Justice Movements in Communities of Color.* Boston: South End Press.

Ashe, Jeff
  1995 *Working Capital Overview: Basic Information for Potential Replication Sites.* Cambridge, MA: Working Capital, Inc.

Barnet, Richard
  1993 The end of jobs. *Harper's.* September:47–52.

Bowles, Sam, Thomas Weisskopf, and David Gordon
  1990 *After the Wasteland: A Democratic Economics for the Year 2000.* Armonk, NY: M. E. Sharpe.

Brecher, Jeremy, and Tim Costello
  1994 *Global Village or Global Pillage.* Boston: South End Press.

Brown, David, and Rajesh Tandon
  1983 Ideology and political economy in inquiry: Action research and participatory research. *Journal of Applied Behavioral Science* 19(2):277–94.

Bryant, Adam
  1994 After seven years, employees win United Airlines *New York Times.* July 13th:A-1,D-13.

Clark, Margaret, Tracy Huston, and Barbara Meister
  1994 *1994 Directory of U.S. Microenterprise Programs.* Washington, D.C.: Aspen Institute.

Cohen, Elizabeth, and Joan Benton
  1988 Making groupwork work. *American Educator.* Fall: 10–17,45–46.

Cohen, Roger
  1993 Europeans consider shortening workweek to relieve joblessness. *New York Times.* November 22nd:A1,A6.

Connecticut, State of
  1996 *Report on the State of Democracy in Connecticut.* Office of the Secretary of State.

Earle, John
  1986 *The Italian Cooperative Movement.* Boston: Allen and Unwin.

Ellerman, David, and Peter Pitegoff
  1983 The democratic corporation: The new worker cooperative statute in Massachusetts. *New York University Review of Law and Social Change* 11(2):441–72.

Goldsmith, William, and Edward Blakely
  1992 *Separate Societies.* Philadelphia: Temple University Press.

Hartford, City of
1984 *Comprehensive Plan of Development: Economics and Employment Component.* Hartford, Connecticut.

Haynes, Curtis
1993 An Essay in the Art of Economic Cooperation: Cooperative Enterprise and
Economic Development in Black America. Dissertation. University of
Massachusetts at Amherst, Department of Economics.

Hinrichs, Karl, William Roche, and Carmen Sirianni
1991 *Working Time in Transition.* Philadelphia: Temple University Press.

Holvino, Evangelina
1993 Organization Development from the Margins: Reading Class, Race and Gender in O. D. Texts. Dissertation. University of Massachusetts at Amherst,
School of Education.

Horvat, Branko, Mihailo Markovic, and Rudi Rupek, eds.
1975 *Self-Governing Socialism* (volume 1). White Plains, NY: International Arts
and Sciences Press.

Hoyer, Mary
1986a Nonformal education: Benefits and limitations. University of Massachusetts
at Amherst, School of Education (unpublished).
1986b Issues of leadership in participatory education. University of Massachusetts
at Amherst, School of Education (unpublished).
1992 *Education for Worker Management and Ownership of an Inner-City Enterprise.* Dissertation. University of Massachusetts at Amherst, School of Education.

Kilborn, Peter
1993 U.S. unions back shorter week, but employers seem reluctant. *New York
Times.* November 20th.

Kretzmann, John, and John McKnight
1993 *Building Communities from the Inside Out.* Evanston, IL: Center for Urban
Affairs and Policy Research/Neighborhood Innovations Network, Northwestern University.

Krimmerman, Len, and Frank Lindenfeld
1992 *When Workers Decide: Workplace Democracy Takes Root in North America.*
Philadelphia: New Society Publishers.

Levin, Henry
1983 Education and organizational democracy. *International Yearbook of Organizational Democracy* (volume 1):227–48. New York: John Wiley and Sons.

Lueck, Thomas
1993 Into the world of banking comes a hip-hop credit union. *New York Times.*
April 25th.

Marable, Manning
    1983 *How Capitalism Underdeveloped Black America*. Boston: South End Press.

Mishel, Lawrence, and Jared Bernstein
    1993 *The State of Working America 1992–1993*. New York: Economic Policy Institute.

Moody, Kim, and Simone Sagovac
    1995 *Time Out! The Case for a Shorter Work Week*. Detroit: Labor Notes.

Mt. Auburn Associates
    1994 *An Evaluation of the Working Capital Micro-Enterprise Lending Program*; volume II: Case Studies. Somerville, Massachusetts.

Oates, Steven
    1982 *Let the Trumpets Sound: The Life of Martin Luther King, Jr.* New York: Harper and Row.

Rifkin, Jeremy
    1996 Civil society in the information age: Workerless factories and virtual companies. *The Nation*. February 26th:11–16.

Rose, Mike
    1989 What the airlines can teach us about cooperative learning. *American Teacher* 74(2):8–9.

Rosenthal, Cliff, and Levy, L.
    1995 *Organizing Credit Unions: A Manual*. New York: National Federation of Commuity Development Credit Unions.

Sachs, Steven
    1986 Along comes the state. *Workplace Democracy* 53:16–17.

Sethi, Krishan, Stanislav Grozdanic, Jacob Mankidy, and Vladimir Stambuk, eds.
    1983 *Workers' Self-Management and Participation in Developing Countries*. Ljubljana, Yugoslavia: International Center for Public Enterprises in Developing Countries.

Sexton, Joe
    1994 The piggy bank in the real world. *New York Times* February 10th.

Shabecoff, Alice
    1987 *Alternative Investing in Community Development*. Washington, D.C.: Community Information Exchange.

Shuman, Michael
    1994 *Towards a Global Village*. Boulder, Colorado: Pluto Press.

Stanback, Howard
    1984 Attacking poverty with economic policy. In *Beyond Reagan: Alternatives for the '80's*. A. Gartner, C. Greer, and F. Reissman, eds. Pp. 57–73. New York: W. W. Norton and Company.

Stone, Jay
    1995 Building a movement for economic democracy. *Socialist Review* 24(1&2):272.

Tholin, Kathryn, and J. Pogge
    1991 *Banking Services for the Poor: Community Development Credit Unions.* Chicago: Woodstock Institute.

Tidwell, Billy, ed.
    1994 *The State of Black America 1994.* New York: National Urban League, Inc.

U.S. Department of Housing and Urban Development
    1993 *Profiles of Community Development Lending Institutions.* Washington, D.C.: Office of Economic Development/Community Planning and Development.

Valentine, Victoria
    1994 Credit union banks on its community. *Emerge* 5(5):13–14.

Vickers, Greg
    1996 *Uncovering Community Treasures: An Asset Survey of Sheldon/Charter Oak.* Hartford, CT: Citizens' Research Education Network.

Whyte, William Foote, and Kathleen King Whyte
    1988 *Making Mondragon.* Ithaca, NY: ILR Press, Cornell University.

Williams, Linda
    1987 *Black political progress in the 1980s. New Black Politics.* Michael B. Preston, Lenneal J. Henderson, Jr., and Paul L. Puryear, eds. pp. 97–135. New York: Longman.

Yalnizyan, Armine, T. Ran Ide, and Arthur Cordell
    1994 *Shifting Time: Social Policy and the Future of Work.* Toronto: Between the Lines Press.

About the Authors

Mary K. Anglin is Assistant Professor of Anthropology at the University of Kentucky, where she holds a joint appointment in the Department of Behavioral Science in the College of Medicine.

Tressa L. Berman is Assistant Professor of Anthropology at Arizona State University West.

Daniel Cogan graduated recently with a B.A. in Anthropology from a northern California university and is now working as a bilingual teacher in the Oakland public school system.

Mary E. Hoyer received her Ed.D. from the University of Massachusetts, Amherst, and is a public schools educator and community activist in participatory economic development in Hartford, Connecticut.

María de la Luz Ibarra is a doctoral student in Anthropology at the University of California–Santa Barbara.

Ann E. Kingsolver is Assistant Professor of Anthropology at the University of South Carolina, and was Assistant Professor of Anthropology at the University of California–Santa Cruz during most of the preparation of this manuscript.

Anita Puckett is Assistant Professor of Appalachian Studies in the Center for Interdisciplinary Studies, Virginia Tech University.

Monica Schoch-Spana is a doctoral student in Anthropology at Johns Hopkins University.

Suzanne E. Tallichet is Assistant Professor of Sociology at Morehead State University.

Index

Banks, Alan, 101
Barber, Bob, 155, 167
Barnet, Richard, 187
Baron, Ava, 56, 64
Batteau, Allen, 102
Bauman, Richard, and Joel Sherzer, 97
Behar, Ruth, 56, 65
Benería, Lourdes, and Catherine
    Stimpson, 75
Benson, Susan Porter, 55, 64
Benton, Joan. *See* Cohen, Elizabeth
Berk, Sarah Fenstermaker, 151
Berman, Tressa, 14, 151
Beynon, H. and R. M. Blackburn, 2
BIA. *See* Bureau of Indian Affairs
black women, as workers, 151
Blackburn, R.M. *See* Beynon, H.
Blakely, Edward. *See* Goldsmith,
    William
Blau, Francine D., and Marianne A.
    Ferber, 124
Blewett, Mary, 56, 64
Blim, Michael L., 5. *See also* Rothstein,
    Frances Abrahamer
Bloch, Maurice, 97
Bluestone, Barry, and Bennett Harrison,
    150
bodies, 143
Dolu, Hlcls, 21, 48
Bookman, Ann, and Sandra Morgen,
    76
border crossing, 156
Bose, Christine, Roslyn Feldberg, and
    Natalie Sokoloff, 75
Bourdieu, Pierre, 6–7, 24, 73, 89, 96–97,
    114
Bowers, Alfred, 79, 80, 82, 83
Bowles, Sam, Thomas Weisskopf, and
    David Gordon, 197, 204
Braverman, Harry, 175
Brecher, Jeremy, and Tim Costello, 198
Brenneis, Donald, and Fred Myers, 97
Bruner, Edward, 82
Bryant, Adam, 193
Bureau of Indian Affairs (BIA), 75, 77
Butler, Judith, 63, 66

C

Calagione, John, 75; and Daniel Nugent,
    74; and Doris Francis and Daniel
    Nugent, 9
California, 3, 148–185
Camarillo, Albert, 149
cancer, 60–61
capitalist, economies, 187; ideologies, 4;
    influence on traditional modes of
    production, 86–89
Case, Harold and Eva, 80, 81
case studies in economic democracy,
    199–204
Caulfield, Mina, 74
CDCUs. *See* community development
    credit unions
ceremonial, relations of production, 74,
    76–78, 86–89; objects, 78, 80–81.
    See also quilling; quilting; traditional
    motifs
Chapa, Jorge. *See* Hayes-Bautista, David
Chicana, defined, 166. *See also*
    Mexicanas
Chicano workers, 182
Child Protective Services, 157
childcare providers, 150–152, 155–158
Civil Rights Movement, 107
Clark, Margaret, Tracy Huston, and
    Barbara Meister, 192
class, construction, 6; structuration, 4;
    studies, 3–5
Clifford, James, and George Marcus, 56,
    65
Coal Employment Project, 126
coal mining industry, 99, 124–147
Coe, Ralph T., 85–86
Cogan, Daniel, 9, 14
Cohen, Elizabeth, and Joan Benton, 190
Cohen, Roger, 196
Cohn, Carol, 22
Cold War, 21, 25
Colen, Shellee, 151. *See also* Sanjek,
    Roger
Collendar, Charles, and Lee Kochems,
    81, 89